Danger and Risk as Challenges for HRM

Questions related to managing people in hostile environments have become more central on the agenda of business leaders and HR professionals in multinational corporations (MNCs). This is due to developments such as the increase of terrorism or the political instability in many regions. In consequence, research on the role of HR in hostile environments has increased, though it can still be considered in its early stages.

Danger and Risk as Challenges for HRM: Managing People in Hostile Environments adds to this emerging field of research by investigating the management of people in hostile environments from conceptual as well as empirical perspectives. It delivers an essential and comprehensive overview and gives deep insight into this highly relevant topic from leading authors in the field.

This book will be of great value to scholars and researchers interested in the role of human resource management (HRM) in hostile environments, people management in companies in conflict-affected areas and to those interested in new grounds in HR research.

The chapters in this book were originally published as a special issue of *The International Journal of Human Resource Management.*

Benjamin Bader is Deputy Head of the Leadership, Work and Organisation Subject Group, and Senior Lecturer (Associate Professor) in International Human Resource Management at Newcastle University Business School, UK, and Associate Editor of *The International Journal of Human Resource Management*. Benjamin's research focuses on international human resource management, particularly expatriation in dynamic environments, global leadership, the impact of digitalisation on managing people and topics related to the future of work.

Tassilo Schuster is Senior Lecturer at the Friedrich-Alexander University Erlangen–Nürnberg, Germany. His main research interests are in the areas of international management, international human resource management and digitalisation of international companies. He is particularly interested in business strategies focusing on expatriate management, psychological contracts and the future of work.

Michael Dickmann is Full Professor of International Human Resource Management at Cranfield University, School of Management, UK, and the Senior Editor-in-Chief of *The International Journal of Human Resource Management*. Michael's research focuses on human resource strategies, structures and processes of multinational organisations, cross-cultural management, international mobility and global careers. He is the lead author/editor of several books on international HRM and global careers.

Danger and Risk as Challenges for HRM

Managing People in Hostile Environments

Edited by

Benjamin Bader, Tassilo Schuster and Michael Dickmann

LONDON AND NEW YORK

First published 2021
by Routledge
2 Park Square, Milton Park, Abingdon, Oxon OX14 4RN

and by Routledge
52 Vanderbilt Avenue, New York, NY 10017

Routledge is an imprint of the Taylor & Francis Group, an informa business

British Library Cataloguing in Publication Data
A catalogue record for this book is available from the British Library

ISBN 13: 978-0-367-62864-2

Typeset in MinionPro
by Newgen Publishing UK

Publisher's Note
The publisher accepts responsibility for any inconsistencies that may have arisen during the conversion of this book from journal articles to book chapters, namely the inclusion of journal terminology.

Disclaimer
Every effort has been made to contact copyright holders for their permission to reprint material in this book. The publishers would be grateful to hear from any copyright holder who is not here acknowledged and will undertake to rectify any errors or omissions in future editions of this book.

Contents

Citation Information

The following chapters, except Chapter 1, were originally published in *The International Journal of Human Resource Management*, volume 30, issue 11 (2019). Chapter 1 was originally published in volume 30, issue 20 (2019) of the same journal. When citing this material, please use the original page numbering for each article, as follows:

Chapter 1

Managing people in hostile environments: lessons learned and new grounds in HR research
Benjamin Bader, Tassilo Schuster and Michael Dickmann
The International Journal of Human Resource Management, volume 30, issue 20 (2019), pp. 2809–2830

Chapter 2

Engaging in duty of care: towards a terrorism preparedness plan
Michael Harvey, Marina Dabic, Tim Kiessling, Jane Maley and Miriam Moeller
The International Journal of Human Resource Management, volume 30, issue 11 (2019), pp. 1683–1708

Chapter 3

Protecting expatriates in hostile environments: institutional forces influencing the safety and security practices of internationally active organisations
Anthony Fee, Susan McGrath-Champ and Marco Berti
The International Journal of Human Resource Management, volume 30, issue 11 (2019), pp. 1709–1736

Chapter 4

In the line of fire: managing expatriates in hostile environments
Judie Gannon and Alexandros Paraskevas
The International Journal of Human Resource Management, volume 30, issue 11 (2019), pp. 1737–1768

Chapter 5

Terrorism and expatriate withdrawal cognitions: the differential role of perceived work and non-work constraints
Anna Katharina Bader, Carol Reade and Fabian Jintae Froese
The International Journal of Human Resource Management, volume 30, issue 11 (2019), pp. 1769–1793

Chapter 6

Mind the gap: the role of HRM in creating, capturing and leveraging rare knowledge in hostile environments
Gabriele Suder, Carol Reade, Monica Riviere, Andreas Birnik and Niklas Nielsen
The International Journal of Human Resource Management, volume 30, issue 11 (2019), pp. 1794–1821

Chapter 7

A risk management model for research on expatriates in hostile work environments
Richard A. Posthuma, Jase R. Ramsey, Gabriela L. Flores, Carl Maertz and Rawia O. Ahmed
The International Journal of Human Resource Management, volume 30, issue 11 (2019), pp. 1822–1838

Chapter 8

Localization of staff in a hostile context: an exploratory investigation in Afghanistan
Michael Dickmann, Emma Parry and Nadia Keshavjee
The International Journal of Human Resource Management, volume 30, issue 11 (2019), pp. 1839–1867

Notes on Contributors

Rawia O. Ahmed, College of Business Administration, University of Texas at El Paso, El Paso, TX, USA.

Anna Katharina Bader, Associate Professor, Northumbria University, Newcastle upon Tyne, UK.

Benjamin Bader, Leadership, Work and Organisation, Newcastle University Business School, Newcastle upon Tyne, UK.

Marco Berti, UTS Business School, University of Technology Sydney, Ultimo, Australia.

Andreas Birnik, CreoPop, Singapore.

Marina Dabic, Faculty of Economics and Business, University of Zagreb, Zagreb, Croatia; Nottingham Business School, Nottingham Trent University, Nottingham, UK.

John D. Daniels, Samuel N. Friedland Chair Emeritus, University of Miami, FL, USA.

Michael Dickmann, International Human Resource Management, Cranfield School of Management, Cranfield University, UK.

Anthony Fee, UTS Business School, University of Technology Sydney, Ultimo, Australia.

Gabriela L. Flores, College of Business Administration, University of Texas at El Paso, El Paso, TX, USA.

Fabian Jintae Froese, Chair of HRM and Asian Business, Georg-August-University Goettingen, Goettingen, Germany.

Judie Gannon, International Centre for Coaching and Mentoring Studies, Department of Business and Management, Business School, Oxford Brookes University, Oxford, UK.

Michael Harvey, Cox School of Business, Southern Methodist University, Dallas, TX, USA; Price College of Business, University of Oklahoma, Norman, OK, USA; Business School, Bond University, Robina, Queensland, Australia; Business School, University of Mississippi,

Oxford, MS, USA; Eller College of Management, University of Arizona, Tucson, AZ, USA.

Nadia Keshavjee, BSR (Business for Social Responsibility), San Francisco, CA, USA.

Tim Kiessling, Faculty of Business Administration, Global Business Strategy in Management and Marketing, Bilkent University, Ankara, Turkey.

Carl Maertz, John Cook School of Business, Saint Louis University, St. Louis, MO, USA.

Jane Maley, School of Management and Marketing, Charles Sturt University, Bathurst, Australia.

Susan McGrath-Champ, Business School, University of Sydney, Darlington, Australia.

Miriam Moeller, School of Business, Economics and Law, The University of Queensland, Brisbane, Australia.

Niklas Nielsen, Mecom Holding W.L.L., Juffair, Bahrain.

Alexandros Paraskevas, London Geller College of Hospitality and Tourism, University of West London, London, UK.

Emma Parry, School of Management, Cranfield University, Cranfield, UK.

Richard A. Posthuma, College of Business Administration, University of Texas at El Paso, El Paso, TX, USA.

Jase R. Ramsey, John Cook School of Business, Saint Louis University, St. Louis, MO, USA.

Carol Reade, School of Global Innovation and Leadership, Lucas College and Graduate School of Business, San José State University, San José, CA, USA; College of Business, San José State University, San José, CA, USA.

Monica Riviere, Institut Supérieur du Commerce (ISC), Paris Business School, Paris, France.

Tassilo Schuster, Faculty of Business Administration, Ludwig-Maximilians-Universitat Munchen, Munich, Germany.

Gabriele Suder, Melbourne Business School, Carlton, Australia.

Foreword

I felt trepidation about writing this foreword because I am retired, not a specialist on expatriate policies, and without any publications on the subject since 2007. However, on further examination of my experience, I feel sufficiently qualified to make some limited comments about this compendium.

Once I dusted off my résumé, I saw that starting in 1973 I authored occasional articles about expatriates (expats) that covered such themes as multinational corporations' (MNCs) preference for home country nationals over foreign nationals, the classification of issues and types of international mobility, a disagreement with the long-held assumption of high expat turnover, and the relationship between foreign transfers and international strategies. However, none of these dealt specifically with the issue of terrorism. Nevertheless, I have used macro risk indicators (including terrorism) in several studies focusing on direct investors' location decisions and have incorporated sections on companies' transfer of personnel to risky locations within my long-running *International Business* textbook.

My interest and experience about expatriates within so-called high-risk environments actually comes mainly from (a) my own work as an expat within several of these areas and (b) my coverage of the subject within some university courses I have taught. (I have never written these up.) First, I worked as an expat for about six years in these environments. My first-hand experience included armored fighting in front of my residence, a tear-gassed apartment, frequent robberies, electrical outages because of power plant sabotage, an armed attack of a restaurant I frequented (but not that evening), a detonated bomb in my office building, the garrisoning of my young son's school, and an extended hospital stay because of dengue fever. Second, I taught a university course for several years on expat adjustment and protection. I managed (because of a security company's security lapse) to surreptitiously obtain training materials prepared for ten MNCs on dangers and security measures abroad. I depended highly on these materials along with the experiences of the many expats I had known abroad. An unexpected and unwanted outcome from these seminars was that one of my students became a terrorist.

Given that most of my research has been in global strategy and structure, I admit being somewhat biased toward publications dealing with MNCs' overall performance. In this respect, I find the book important for the performance of organizations engaged in or contemplating international business, especially those more dependent on foreign operations. Despite some detours, such as because of Covid-19, this dependence has been growing and is expected to become even more important in the future. Human resources are, of course, a major component in both the cost and explanation of performance. Further, expats continue to be a vital element within organizations' human resources abroad. Expatriates' adaptation and success versus failure have long been a subject in international resource studies, but their relationship to terrorism is a much newer area of interest.

While terrorism has long existed – especially as a method to affect political, religious, or ideological change – its use for self-publicity is a much newer phenomenon. Yet we have seen widespread incidents, such as the shooting of schoolchildren, driving into crowds of pedestrians, and gassing people on public transport. As both terrorism and its attendant publicity have grown, many individuals have become more concerned about uncertainties outside their home countries, especially about those in so-called hostile areas. Thus, terrorism adds a dimension to the array of human and naturally induced hardships in which MNCs have long dealt when sending employees to work abroad. This book emphasizes the additional perspective to human resource management abroad.

I believe that almost any academic treatise should raise nearly as many questions as it answers. Fortunately, this compendium includes an extensive section on suggestions for further research, and I support all of them. In addition, I have two suggestions for follow-up work to amplify the focus of this study. The first is to deal with the total spectrum of international human resources, thus including host country nationals (HCNs) along with expatriates in future studies. The second is to aggregate, disaggregate, and compare different types of hardships in foreign locations.

First, why do I think HCNs should be included? The first thing that comes to my mind is that the terrorism of 9/11 is often cited as the inception of heightened concern about the relationship between expats and terrorism. Yet, about 90 percent of fatalities in 9/11 were of HCNs. Further, with few exceptions, expats comprise a small (albeit important and expensive) portion of organizations' human resources abroad. Thus, there are a number of intriguing questions. For instance, is there is a difference in danger from terrorism and anxiety between expatriates and HCNs working for foreign-owned companies? For instance, the danger of being kidnapped has been higher for expatriates, but terrorism has largely targeted facilities, including those owned by MNCs. Thus, both expats and HCNs are at risk when facilities are attacked. Additionally, many (most?) MNCs offer safety programs for expats. But, to what extent do they include HCNs within these? If HCNs are less included, is this an ethical omission that could affect an MNC's reputation negatively?

Second, terrorism is sometimes included within the overall context of political risk and sometimes within the overall context of hostile environmental risk that includes natural disasters and disease as well. It is also sometimes treated separately as if it has nothing to do with the abovementioned risks.

For clarity in future studies and MNC practices, knowing the relationship of the different components, say between levels of crime and terrorism, could be useful. As an analogy, political scientists built models with a fair amount of success several decades ago by relating different macro conditions to property expropriation. Further, this type of data mining might gain insights as to the relative importance of different components to potential expats. It may also reveal more about how countries differ among the types of risks.

In conclusion, I have been absent from academic inquiry and teaching about expatriates for about a decade and a half. I am particularly impressed with the depth, breadth, and quality of more recent research that is encompassed in this compendium. I am also pleased that the authors treat the expatriate subject from macro, meso, and micro levels. In addition, all the individual papers are presented in a style that can serve not only specialists in the field, but also generalists and practitioners. They also rely on appropriate methodologies that cement their validity and can serve as good backgrounds for further inquiries. I am confident that all readers will gain from each of the chapters.

Professor John D. Daniels

Samuel N. Friedland Chair Emeritus, University of Miami

Managing people in hostile environments: lessons learned and new grounds in HR research

Benjamin Bader, Tassilo Schuster and Michael Dickmann

ABSTRACT

Questions related to managing people in hostile environments have become more central on the agenda of business leaders and HR professionals in MNCs. This is due to developments such as the increase of terrorism or the political instability in many regions. In consequence, research on the role of HR in hostile environments has increased as well, though it can still be considered in its early stages. We would like to review the current state of research on managing people in hostile environment. In particular, with this article we contribute to the literature by developing a conceptual framework that distinguishes between micro-, meso- and marco-level research and charts progress, mechanisms and results. We call this the Situation – Response – Outcome (SRO) Framework of HRM in hostile environments. Depending on the level of analysis, the framework further differentiates between a pre-crises, acute-crisis, and post-crises phases of HRM in hostile environments. As a result, it serves as the basis to cluster existing literature around it and to show avenues for future research.

Introduction

With the terrorist attacks in New York and Washington on September 11, 2001 (hereafter 9/11), terrorism was catapulted to the top of governmental agendas around the world. We can certainly say that this event has been a tipping point at least in how terrorism is perceived in the wider society (Woods, Eyck, Kaplowitz, & Shlapentokh, 2008). But not only governments started to change their perception on terrorism. Terrorism suddenly became highly relevant in the business context as well (Suder, 2004). Terrorist groups seek to destabilize the economy as a whole by attacking business premises or specific companies to advance their political or ideological agendas (Alexander, 2004). Despite a slight drop of terrorism-related incidents between 2001 and 2004, the number of attacks has tremendously grown year by year with a peak of 16,860 incidents in 2014 (Global Terrorism Database, 2017). A significant terrorist threat comes from international terrorism, which generally targets Western businesses and people located outside or inside their home country, with the ambition to mount high impact attacks designed to result in mass casualties in order to receive a broad media attention. Therefore, it is not surprising to see that the number of terrorism-related incidents in OECD countries has also dramatically increased in recent years, largely due to ISIS/ISIL inspired attacks. In fact, according to the Institute for Economics and Peace, we witnessed a 67 percent increase in attacks and a nearly 600 percent increase in deaths from terrorism between 2014 and 2016. A significant portion of the fatalities was caused by a few high-impact attacks. For example, the Paris attacks in November 2015 resulted in 137 deaths; the Nice truck attack in July 2016 caused 87 deaths; and the Orlando nightclub shooting in June 2016 resulted in 50 deaths (Institute for Economics and Peace, 2017).

In the literature on terrorism, there is a consensus that a main goal of the perpetrators of terrorist attacks is to disrupt society by evoking a culture of fear, anxiety and panic. This is achieved by transmuting a specific terrorist incident beyond its localized setting and thereby creating a perception that every resident and company is vulnerable to terrorism (Cronin, 2003; Victoroff, 2005). Repeated and large-scale terrorist attacks targeting the business sector and its employees caused that Multinational Companies (MNCs) from any part of the world are affected, especially if they operate in and send employees to high-risk countries where terrorism and other disturbances are a commonplace occurrence. This does not necessarily mean that MNCs face direct consequences of terrorism such as human costs (loss of life, physical injury) or the destruction of buildings and equipment. In fact, only few MNCs experience these direct effects. Instead terrorism's indirect effects tend to be widely felt (Czinkota, Knight, Liesch, & Steen, 2010). Indirect effects include declines in foreign direct investments, disruptions in the international supply chains of MNCs, new governmental regulations and immigration laws and negative reactions of employees towards their employers (Czinkota, Knight, Liesch, & Steen, 2005; Frey, Luechinger, & Stutzer, 2007). In particular, employees that are exposed to terrorism-related threats often suffer from post-traumatic stress, anxiety, feelings of insecurity, decreased self-efficacy, and a decrease in subjectively rated health (Peus, 2011).

However, terrorism is not the only form of violent risk and danger to which MNCs and its employees are exposed. Apart from terrorism, there are other leading causes of violence and instability around the world such as ethnopolitical conflicts, civil unrest, civil war, and drug-related crime, which show tremendous effects on the business activities of MNCs, especially for subsidiaries of foreign MNCs (Oh & Oetzel, 2011; Ramirez, Madero, & Muñiz, 2016).

Therefore, it can be considered as a natural response that questions related to managing people in those hostile environments[1] have nowadays become commonplace on the agenda of business leaders and HR professionals in MNCs (Dickmann, 2017), especially since the expatriate population who is sent to a broad set of countries continues to grow (Brookfield Global Relocation Services, 2016). When comparing the agendas of human resource management (HRM) in hostile environments with those in normal settings, we see that HRM is confronted with additional challenges, which do not occur in such intensity in normal settings. This starts with finding employees who are willing to work in hostile environments, executing safety and security policies, providing safety trainings, developing internal intelligence and communication strategies of potential hazards and risks, developing emergency and recovery plans, adapting compensation schemes by adding appropriate hardship allowances, and offering post-trauma support when employees are involved in a terrorist incident. Also for individual expatriates who live and work in high-risk countries, those hostile environments cause additional challenges beyond those of a common international assignment as they cannot move freely throughout the country, have to live in closed and secured compounds, often require bodyguards for being chauffeured to their work location, and need to handle an increased vulnerability and stress levels.

To better understand the unique setting of hostile environments for managing people, an increasing number of scholars, academics, and specialized business consultants started to address those topics from an HR perspective. In this regard, we contribute to this research by developing a framework that distinguishes between a pre-crises, acute-crisis, and postcrises phases (i.e. has a process perspective). We then cluster existing literature around it and show starting points for future research.

People management in hostile environments: lessons learned

Despite a very early, ground-breaking study of Michael Harvey (1993) and frequent calls for more research with some initial studies on the topic in the first years after 9/11 (e.g. Czinkota et al., 2005; Howie, 2007), research on managing people in hostile environments still has not made its way into mainstream IHRM literature. In fact, even though we witnessed a significant increase of research on hostile environments in the IHRM literature over the last decade, the research stream is still in its infancy and scattered. We do not intend to present a comprehensive literature review here but rather like to outline the current state of knowledge in the field and systemize previous studies regarding people management in hostile environments. This does not only help us to better understand different streams of research on hostile environments but also enables us to better categorize the articles in this Special Issue and to provide recommendation on how research on hostile environments can break new grounds. As outlined above, Harvey (1993) was among the very first scholars to explore the impact of terrorism on business in general and on HRM in particular. In this seminal study, it becomes apparent that research on terrorism simultaneously takes place on different levels of analysis. Based on this observation, we create an overarching framework for managing people in hostile environments by distinguishing between three perspectives: macro, meso, and micro.

On the macro level, the role of national governments has played a vital role for managing people in hostile environments. Already in 1993, Harvey pointed out that national governments do not provide adequate assistance when companies were attacked by terrorists. Sandler and Enders (2005), who studied the economic consequences of terrorism in developed and developing countries, showed that governments of developed markets may be better to support the business sector after a terrorist attack. It is outlined that governments in developed markets are better equipped with monetary or fiscal stimuli following terrorist attacks and have more sophisticated defensive measures such as anti-terrorism laws, immigration policies, or public security means (law enforcement, intelligence and information services, emergency management) that enable the state to restore confidence in society after terrorist attacks. It is clear that the security apparatus of the state – military, intelligence, and police forces – have a key role in identifying and dealing with terrorist threats and atrocities. Moreover, there is evidence that terrorism can have severe consequences for the business sector by reducing per-capita income growth (Blomberg, Hess, & Orphanides, 2004), shrinking GDP, investments and exports (Eckstein & Tsiddon, 2004), decreasing firms' international competitiveness (Spich & Grosse, 2005), or lowering bilateral trade when a country that experienced a terrorist incident is a trading partner (Nitsch & Schumacher, 2004). Another important issue at the macro-level is to differentiate between types of hostile environments (terrorism, crime, civil unrest, etc.) in order to show the unique impact on MNCs and their employees. In this matter, there is already initial evidence in the literature that the feeling of vulnerability and anxiety after terrorist incidents is more pervasive and persistent with greater mental health consequences than effects from other types of hostile environment and disasters (Holloway & Fullerton, 1994; Jacobs & Kulkarni, 1999; James, 2011b; Ryan, West, & Carr, 2003). In contrast, a recent study by Faeth and Kittler (2017) showed that expatriates in a more terrorism-exposed context perceive fear less strongly than expatriates in environments with high degrees of conventional crime. A reason for this could be that becoming victim in a crime is regarded as more likely than becoming victim in a terrorist attack, even though the consequences may be less severe.

At the meso-level, the focus has been on how MNCs and their HR departments can manage people in hostile environments. The topics here have been widely connected to corporate strategies, HR policies, and HR practices in the context of hostile environments. The global mobility literature takes a process perspective that distinguishes between pre-, during- and post-assignment phases (Harris, Brewster and Sparrow, 2003). To analyze HR strategies, policies, and practices for global workers in hostile environments, it seems reasonable to develop a framework that follows a process-related perspective and distinguishes between a pre-crises,, acute-crisis, and postcrises phase (Devlin, 2006; Fee, McGrath-Champ, & Liu, 2013). These three process categories were already underlying the work of Harvey (1993). Concerning the pre-crises phase he revealed – based on the survey results of 79 US Fortune 500 companies – that more than half of those companies had absolutely no formal programs to deal with the impact of potential terrorist attacks. Those that had a program in place prioritized to spend money on security equipment instead of training executives, expatriates, and accompanying family members. Based on his findings, he recommended that in a precrisis phase, companies need to gather information about potential terrorist threats, provide training to executives and their families, and to form a crisis management team that will be prepared for the possibility of a terrorist attack. More recent research outlines various instruments on how MNCs can increase the safety and security of expatriates in hostile environments. For instance, it is argued that MNCs can better guide expatriates during terrorist-related incidents when they have developed formal HR policies related to employees safety and security and created evacuation plans prior to an actual incident (Devlin, 2006; Fee & McGrath-Champ, 2017; Sánchez & Goldberg, 2003).

Moreover, MNCs should gather intelligence on potential hazards and risks by collecting and analyzing information on possible crisis triggers (Kalbassi, 2016). In addition, Fowler, Kling and Larson (2007) investigate whether different organizations vary in their corporate strategies toward organizational preparedness for coping with hostile environments and provide initial evidence that for-profit organizations have a lower organizational preparedness than public organizations. They also conclude that decision-makers in for-profit companies may be less willing to spend money on these types of plans than those in public organizations. Finally, it is argued that MNCs can offer trainings and briefings to increase expatriates' awareness of potential risks and to provide them with instruments on how to reacted when they face a potential crisis (Darby & Williamson, 2012).

In the acute-crisis phase, it is of utmost importance to have a crisis management team at hand that ensures the implementation of safety and security plans on site and that guides and supports expatriates during incidents (James, 2011a). A study amongst global mobility professional has shown that many MNCs cooperate with government and private security forces in terms of working on crisis reaction plans and provisions (Dickmann, 2015). It is interesting to note, that some companies seem to treat their expatriates differently from local partners and family. Unfortunately, a large number of MNCs do not have any elaborated crisis reaction approach which indicates that much of the host country risk is borne by assignees themselves. Many authors have observed a substantial increase into the exploration of self-initiated expatriates (Andresen; Al Ariss & Walter, 2012; Vaiman & Haslberger, 2013). Little is known about these SIEs living in hostile environments and their reaction to, say, terrorist incidents.

Finally, in the post-crisis phase, MNCs need to support expatriates to deal with psychological trauma and ensure an efficient readjustment of the expatriate in the work and social environment (Hirshon, Eng, Brunkow, & Hartzell, 1997). In this matter, Waldman, Carmeli and Halevi (2011) revealed that organizations are ineffective in simultaneously responding to both material and psychological needs of individuals in the aftermath of a terrorist event. A second important instrument in the post-crisis phase is that MNCs reflect on the effectiveness of their crisis management and critically evaluate where improvements can be implemented (Wang, 2008). Other studies showed how firms respond to major disasters (Oh & Oetzel, 2011) and violent conflicts (Oetzel & Getz, 2011), revealing that firms reduce the number of their foreign subsidiaries in response to terrorism but not natural disasters.

Up to now, micro-level research has concentrated predominantly on acute- and post-crisis analysis. However, there is some general expatriation research that allows some speculation on probably important elements in the pre-crisis phase. Many studies in the general expatriation literature explore the importance of influencing factors on the decision to live and work abroad (Doherty, Dickmann, & Mills, 2011), which show that the attitudes and personality of expatriates, their career and development plans, financial circumstances, their family situation, general living conditions, and support structures have a strong impact on the decision to work abroad. Where a host environment was seen as insecure and risky, this factor became more prominent and important for the expatriation decision. In addition, research indicates that the impression that individuals have about a specific location and the host national's attitudes as well as behaviors shapes their willingness to move there (Dickmann & Mills, 2009). This is likely to be reflected with respect to hostile environments where there are regions that are more risky compared to other regions in most states that experience hostile and terrorist activities.

Regarding the acute- and post-crisis phase, most studies have focused on the HR side of terrorism and investigated attitudes and behaviors of expatriates in hostile environments. For instance, previous research showed that employees respond to terrorism with lower work motivation and involvement (Bader & Berg, 2013; Reade, 2009), lack of concentration at work (Mainiero & Gibson, 2003), higher absenteeism (Byron & Peterson, 2002), worse work attitudes (Bader, 2015), and lower job satisfaction or commitment (Reade & Lee, 2012; Vinokur, Pierce, Lewandowski-Romps, Hobfoll, & Galea, 2011).

New scales, for instance to measure sensitivity to terrorism, were introduced (Reade, 2009), fear and coping strategies were studied (Beutell, O'Hare, Schneer, & Alstete, 2017), and also the role of the expatriates' families was analyzed (Bader, Berg, & Holtbrügge, 2015). Research showed that terrorism negatively affects expatriates' organizational networking (Kastenmüller et al., 2011) and that working in a hostile environment per se does not decline expatriates' psychological well-being, yet it amplifies the impact of social network characteristics (Bader & Schuster, 2015). Just recently, Pinto, Bader, & Schuster (2017) compiled a Special Issue that exclusively focuses on risky international assignments, presenting new insights into those topics.

We have argued that research on managing people in hostile environments can be done on three different levels. Above, we have outlined a range of relevant factors on the macro, meso, and micro levels and we have depicted some of the mechanism and outcomes for expatriates (and their families) living in hostile environments in Figure 1. It can be readily seen how a government's approach to dealing with a hostile environment may engage mechanisms such as (anti-terrorism) laws and (immigration) regulations which in turn impacts economic outcomes and the reputation and confidence of citizens and foreigners in the

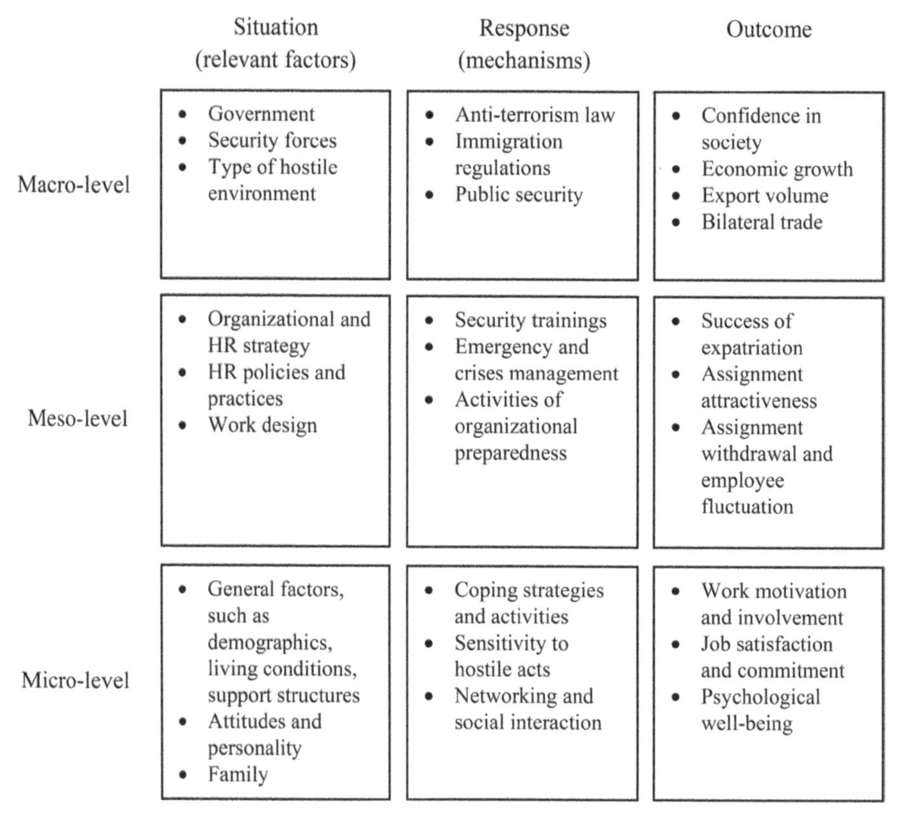

Figure 1. Situation – Response – Outcome (SRO) Framework of HRM in hostile environments.

country. On the meso, level, it is reasonable to argue that organizational and HR strategies, policies, and practices will be reflected in security trainings, efforts to prepare organizations and crisis reaction approaches. These will have a range of outcomes linked to the attractiveness to go into high-risk locations or premature assignment return in case of hostile acts. Lastly, on the micro-level, there are a range of factors that determine the willingness to go to hostile environments and the ability to successfully cope with the hardship this often involves. Our framework outlines a variety of personal drivers and personality factors that are reflected in the sensitivity of individuals to terrorism and other hostile acts, their coping strategies and activities while they are embedded in their own host country social networks. We call this the Situation – Response – Outcome (SRO) Framework of HRM in Hostile Environments.

With this Special Issue and our introductory article, we hope to make an important step to further establishing research related to people management in hostile environments in the IHRM literature. By contributing to the current knowledge on this topic, we hope that it will foster even more research in the future. When we first discussed proposing this

Special Issue during the 2014 Annual Meeting of the Academy of Management in Philadelphia, we were already looking back at a tremendous increase of terrorist attacks worldwide. At that time, we realized that, given the practical relevance of the topic, there is a dire need for more research on managing people in hostile environments and we were projecting that terrorism and violent conflict will increase in magnitude and, therefore, affect more and more businesses. In response to our Call for Papers (Bader, Schuster, & Dickmann, 2015), we received a great number of manuscripts, of which twelve were sent out to external reviewers. Overall, these manuscripts covered a variety of research questions on the micro-, meso-, and macro-level and we welcomed the diversity and the quality of the studies. After almost two years of revisions and improvements of the manuscripts done by the authors, we are happy to include seven of them in this Special Issue. They all make a great contribution to this small, yet emerging field of research and we are convinced that besides their individual contribution, they are also a great starting point for further research on this important topic. On a personal note, when we first received a submission lead by Michael Harvey, we were very excited, since he can be considered the forerunner of terrorism research in the business context. During the revisions there was a very interesting E-mail conversation on where the field may be moving, that was suddenly stopped by the sad news that Mike had passed away in July 2016. It has been an honor to exchange thoughts with him and to be able to include his last article, which has been further revised and finalized by his co-authors, in our Special Issue.

Topics in the articles of the Special Issue range from exploring expatriate safety and security practices (Fee, Mcgrath-Champ, & Berti, 2018), withdrawal cognitions (Bader, Reade, & Froese, 2018), to employee protection (Gannon & Paraskevas, 2018) or staff localization (Dickmann, Parry, & Keshavjee, 2018). Other articles focused on the role of knowledge (Suder, Reade, Riviere, & Birnik, 2018) and adjustment, psychological contracts, and risk management (Posthuma, Ramsey, Flores, Maertz, & Ahmed, 2018) in hostile environments. Finally, Harvey, Dabic, Kiessling, Maley, & Moeller (2018) propose a terrorism preparedness plan for companies, pointing out the employer's Duty of Care. Overall, we believe they are a great mix of different approaches (methodologically and theoretically) to answer questions in this important research field.

Our Special Issues opens with Harvey et al. (2018), whose study is located at the meso-level. In this study, the authors look at the increasing impact of global terrorism on multinational organizations and its significance for strategic global human resource management. They claim that it is the responsibility of corporations doing business in hostile environments to protect their human capital from external terrorism by being proactive about its effects and specifically outline that this is a part of the employer's Duty of Care. In addition, they discuss the need to keep international assignees safe as working outside one's home country is an exceptional challenge that could worsen by disaster-related situations that might occur from the effects of terrorism. The article provides an overview about the current literature dealing with terrorism's effects on business as well as a 'terrorism preparedness plan' that aims to inform international assignees about 'what if' situations in a country before moving there. Its major contribution can be seen in the fact that it enables assignees to handle possible threats of terrorism in a better way and that it helps companies to decrease a possible lack of legitimacy, which in turn prevent companies to face a reduced talent pool.

The second article, authored by Fee et al. (2018), looks at managing people in hostile environments from both a macro-level and a meso-level perspective by investigating institutional forces that can impact the security and safety of international organizations operating in a hostile location, e.g. countries with a difficult political situation, terrorism, or natural disasters. The study provides an insight into the security practices of 28 global companies from three industries that operate in such locations. Drawing on institutional theory, Fee et al. (2018) classify the observed security practices into three approaches: 'regulatory,' 'informal mentoring,' and 'empowering'. By identifying between- and within-sector patterns of safety and security practices that are shaped by institutional pressures, the authors develop a platform for initial theory building in relation to the elements of organizations' safety and security practices which are influenced by institutional factors. In addition, the authors reveal that there is more than one institutional force driving a company's operations in foreign countries, as the analyzed practices were shaped by the home country and the organization's internal culture as well as the relationship to the host country and the specific industry they are operating in. Overall, this study provides answers on how the HR practices are influenced by different institutional forces and what options a company has for supporting expatriate safety and security in hostile locations – thus contributing to a better comprehension of HR choices in these locations.

The third article, authored by Gannon and Paraskevas (2018), is located at the meso-level and examines best practices for preparing and protecting employees of multinational organizations in hostile environments. By conducting interviews with corporate executives, insurers, and relocation specialists who have a strong professional expertise on the topic, the authors deliver insight into the development and utilization of support and protection practices as well as the risks to which managers are exposed in hostile locations. Choosing the international hotel industry and its role in high-risk countries as the setting for the study, the results highlight the challenges that internationally active organizations face when protecting their expatriates and emphasizes the importance of expertise from specialists and management dealing with risk, security, and insurance. Accounting for the managers' point of view, the article focuses on an investigation of organizational challenges rather than the challenges that might occur for individuals. At the end, the authors offer a set of meaningful propositions for human resource management in hostile locations by systematically considering ethical and strategic challenges that might arise in a multinational company.

The fourth study evolves around the issue of withdrawal cognitions of expatriates in terrorism-endangered countries (Bader et al., 2018) and is consequently located at the micro-level. The study builds on stress theory and takes influences of perceived threats and constraints into account. More precisely, the authors differentiate between the perception of work (related to the new job requirements in the host country and thus the work domain), interaction (related to social interactions with host country nationals in the work and non-work domains), and general constraints (related to the general living conditions particularly in the nonwork domain). They therefore make a contribution to the literature on expatriates in terrorism-endangered countries by specifically linking terrorism to stressors that influence withdrawal cognitions. Empirical results from a survey among 160 expatriates working in hostile environments show a relation between the level of terrorism and the perceived threat, furthermore identifying a much stronger effect of this perceived threat in the non-work constraints. While work-related constraints have a direct effect on job turnover intentions, non-work constraints have a direct effect on country leave intentions. By also looking at spillover effects from the non-work to the work domain, the authors could further identify an indirect effect from perceived nonwork constraints to job turnover intentions through intentions to leave the country. Based on these results, the study develops suggestions on how multinational organizations can best support their employees in the expatriation process.

This is followed by a qualitative study by Suder et al. (2018), which is once again located at the meso-level. The study looks into the human resource management of a European telecommunications joint venture in Afghanistan. It especially highlights the managerial learning and knowledge acquisition in hostile and often unknown environments by investigating how knowledge gaps can be addressed and how rare knowledge can be captured and leveraged by HR practices. This is important as organizations operating in developed countries often need to adapt to dangerous and 'extreme' contexts and moreover fill institutional voids by creating supplies that would usually be offered by the government. Their study examines how the telecommunications company is dealing with the issue of learning in a hostile environment while also trying to leverage the acquired knowledge to other hostile locations. The authors state that human resource management as well as the willingness of the expatriate to learn and share knowledge play a critical role in the knowledge acquisition process, because assignees can act as knowledge carriers between the head office and the subsidiary. Specialized consultants can further support the learning process. It is proposed that by using the right HR practices to support the acquisition of rare knowledge in hostile locations, organizational learning will be enhanced, hence creating competitive advantages for internationally operating corporations and benefiting such organizations in their operations. On top of that, the study includes theory development in terms of a mechanism for capturing and leveraging the rare knowledge gained in one extreme location to other hostile environments, based on experiential learning used by the military. The findings contribute to the international human resource management, organizational learning, and international business literatures by offering implications for both international human resource management and building organizational resilience through acquisition and exploitation of knowledge.

In the sixth article, Posthuma et al. (2018) offer a model of guidance for management practices to reduce environmental stress and its negative effects on expatriate adjustment. As a result, the article combines a meso-level and a micro-level perspective. The authors state that as expatriates move to hostile locations because of their work, there is a perceived need for the employer to not only fulfill core work-related obligations but to also get proactive in non-work issues. The authors argue that the psychological contract between the employer and the employee working in a hostile environment needs to be expanded by protecting expatriates from the direct and indirect effects of the risks they are exposed to. The developed risk management framework is based on the idea of a psychological contract and proposes ways how HRM practices can contribute to expatriates' adjustment. Its foundation is built upon literature streams on expatriate adjustment, psychological contract, and risk management. In particular, the article examines the effect of expatriate adjustment on role performance, proposing expatriate psychological resilience as a moderator. Posthuma et al. (2018) conclude with a discussion about the role of expatriate risk management by the organization. They argue that the approach of psychological contracts to understand the negative effects of hostile environment can lead to the reduction of environment-related stress on the individual level.

Finally, the last article in this Special Issue is an exploratory investigation located at the meso-level by Dickmann et al. (2018), dealing with the localization of staff in Afghanistan. Localization is considered important to manage risks and gain resources needed for competitive advantage. Dickmann et al. (2018) expand the existing literature by illustrating a set of relevant drivers and constraints that influence the decision to localize staff in hostile environments. It further explores resource-based and institutional influences, using the resource-based view and institutional theory as a theoretical background. Their goal is to help multinational companies to make better decisions in localizing professional staff in hostile environments. Notably, the article offers a practical guide to assist companies thinking about localizing staff in Afghanistan or similar hostile environments. The results identify new influences on localization, like ongoing security issues, corruption, impartiality, and the need for outside experiences among others. The authors additionally emphasize the importance of not just picking appropriate local human resources but also using the right internal capabilities to develop and deploy them for a sustainable competitive advantage and therefore connect theory and practical usability.

People management in hostile environments: new grounds

While the articles enrich our thinking and understanding on managing people in hostile environments, they also raise new questions and show avenues for future research. As argued above, given its increased practical relevance for MNCs, we are only at the beginning and believe that this important stream of research will further make its way into mainstream literature. To break new grounds, we apply the newly developed SRO Framework of HRM in Hostile Environments and outline several research avenues that have the potential to strongly contribute to our current understanding in the filed of managing people in hostile environments.[2]

On the macro-level, research needs to better tie the relevant factors to the outcomes. For instance, how does the type of hostile environment actually affect economic growth and the creation of jobs? What can the government do in order to (re)build confidence in society? And, maybe in a more fundamental way, what is the 'economic cost' of terrorism for business in a given country? In addition, a more nuanced understanding of hostile environment may be highly useful. Distinguishing between human-induced terrorism or natural disasters will have an impact on state, organizational and individual activities and concerns. Developing a classification of degrees of different hostility in certain countries or specific intra-country locations would advance our knowledge. In fact, previous research often relies on either sensitivity and perception of terrorism risk by individuals, external data on country level, such as from the Global Terrorism data base, or a combination of both. However, neither approach is superior per se. For instance, relying on the perception by individuals may be adequate when the outcome variables are exclusively on individual level. However, using individual perceptions may cause potential issues of common method variance (CMV) when all data are obtained by a single informant. Using external data may overcome problems with CMV, yet if it does not account for the very specific location, it may be flawed. In many countries that suffer from terrorism, there are certain regions that are severely affected, while others are much better off. Using a country-average may cause the problem that it over- or underestimates the true threat level. Macro-level research can add great value in explaining the context of meso- and micro-level research. It sets the scene and we know very little about the respective influence macro-level factors have on people management in hostile environments.

On the meso-level, we need to extend our knowledge on HR policies and practices. In other words, what are companies doing in order to protect their staff abroad, what is their role in terms of Duty of Care, and how does this shape the companies' strategies? We have argued above that intra-country location has a bearing on whether individuals want to go to a specific city or rural area (Dickmann, 2013). Internationally operating organizations often have a good feeling for the relative attractiveness of their diverse locations and could start to 'manage' the foreign experiences and associated (including monetary) outcomes that assignees experience. We know that going to hardship locations within a UN organization was associated with different career outcomes than going to non-hardship duty stations (Dickman & Cerdin, 2016). Much more research is needed to understand the range of company activities to attract and manage assignees and their families going to hostile environments and to explore individual and organizational outcomes.

Following our call among the authors of the articles in this Special Issue, one of them raised the question of how to deal with increased real and perceived inequality between expatriates and the local population in various countries. They shared a story of an incident, where an expatriate got violently robbed on their way to the airport while getting stuck in traffic and under the (correct) assumption of the assailant that the person in the car is (relatively) rich. It is quite common for expatriates at a certain hierarchical level to have a chauffeur and be driven around in the back seat of a nice car. Had the company adviced to travel 'low profile', for instance using a regular taxi or inconspicuous car, the risk level would have been different. Yet, by showcasing their status, the company presented an opportunity for the attacker. The robbery could also have resulted in kidnapping. In this case, the expatriate was not harmed physically but suffered from this traumatic event by having developed a travel anxiety and not being able to continue the assignment. Hence, future research should dig much deeper in corporate HR practices in hostile environments, investigating unconventional tatics and practices and their efficiency in order to protect their staff abroad and find the right balance between pleasing their expatriates with amenities and at the same time increasing their safety. Especially, in poor countries, the income of expatriates allows them to have a lifestyle that is well beyond the typical lifestyle in the host country. This inequality awakens desires among elements of the local population and, consequentially, might cause some individuals to take criminal action.

Another interesting avenue for meso-level research is managing perceived fear of individuals. Basically, fear on the individual level may aggregate up to the team, subsidiary, and firm level. Media reports and contagion effects in social networks (Bader & Schuster, 2015) may even fuel this fountain effect. However, research has yet to answer what mechanisms are underlying this multi-level aggregation and which theories can be applied to understand the effects of higher level HRM practices on lower level relationships and vice versa.

On the interface between the meso- (HR policies) and micro-level, the role of expatriates' families regarding assignments in hostile environments needs more research. Despite a first approach by Bader et al. (2015), given the long-acknowledged importance of the expatriate's family (Caligiuri, Hyland, & Joshi, 1998), we know very little about the consequences of making the choice between leaving the family in the home country and opt for a temporal separation and bringing the family along and also expose them to danger. This is pretty much a choice to be between a rock and a hard place. However, with regard to our initial definition of 'hostile environments' and the increasing number of assignments in all regions of this world, questions regarding the families of expatriates in hostile environments increase in relevance as well.

Finally, even though a big part of research on managing people in hostile environments is actually dealing with the micro-level, we are still far from understanding the whole phenomenon. Again, taking a process perspective might be useful. For instance regarding pre-crisis exposure, it might be fruitful to explore the reasons to go to hostile environments in depth. Findings on the reasons would not only be useful for individuals, but also for organizations and even government actors. Indeed, a more profound understanding of the social and host country (support) networks is likely to be important for potential expatriates and for those global mobility professionals who look to increase the attractiveness of their locations in hostile environments. During assignees' stay in hostile locations, it would be intriguing to explore their personal risk management strategies and gain more insights into their (and their families') coping strategies regarding the increased insecurity and stress. This might be enlightening especially with a view to a more nuanced understanding of degrees and forms of hostility. In addition, a better understanding of what working under hardship may mean for the career journey of individuals and their organization's career, knowledge and talent management approaches could be very valuable to global talent management professionals and career scholars. In terms of understanding post-crisis effects, further studies exploring family effects and long-term influences on children and partners would be welcome. There are some indications that some organizations have a substantial percentage of staff who have a preference to go from one hardship location to another (Dickmann & Cerdin, 2016; Dickmann & Watson, 2017). It might be possible to learn from their attitudes and coping behaviours so as to prepare those individuals who are embarking for their first sojourn into a hostile environment. In addition, we would welcome research that explores the potential positive effects of working in a high-risk context as this may increase the self-esteem or the self-efficacy of individuals. Overall, the field of working in hostile environments is only at its beginning and there are a wide array of future possible research avenues to pursue.

In addition, we would like to argue that one of the next steps needs to be more rigorous study designs, on all levels of analysis, macro, meso, and micro. Despite the value and the understandable concerns and hesitations of respondents regarding the collection of longitudinal data, we need to overcome cross-sectional designs in order to understand the dynamic processes of managing people in hostile environments. Collecting data from a single informant at multiple points in time, as well as adding additional data sources in a study to overcome issues related to common method variance (Podsakoff, MacKenzie, Lee, & Podsakoff, 2003) is necessary to base research questions and respective hypothesis testing on a solid empirical fundament.

While these are mere methodological issues, there is need for future research from a theoretical point of view as well. To begin with, despite the notion that working in hostile environments potentially has negative consequences for expatriates, we need to better understand how these negative consequences can be mitigated. For instance, coping strategies might be a useful mechanism to deal with stress. However, which coping strategies in particular should be applied in a certain situation and how successful one may be over another, is still unclear. Regarding the post-assignment phase, research needs to focus on repatriation from hostile environments. While repatriation is a difficult issue in general and the success widely varies (Breitenmoser & Bader, 2016, Breitenmoser, Bader, & Berg, 2018; Doherty & Dickmann, 2012), it is reasonable to assume that repatriating from a hostile environment comes along with additional challenges. While repatriation research has included various outcome variables, such as job satisfaction, employee turnover, and psychological well-being (Knocke & Schuster, 2017), it remains silent yet concerning long-term effects that occur only years after repatriation, for instance, when having experienced a traumatizing events during international assignments. Thus, it would be worthwhile to follow up on this and investigate if former expatriates in hostile environments do experience forms of posttraumatic stress disorder or how such experience affects their lifestyle in general.

Conclusion

The content of this Special Issue clearly reflects the growing research attention for managing people in hostile environments. We therefore reviewed the literature with regard to lessons learned already and developed the SRO Framework identifying relevant elements of research on people management in hostile environments. After having introduced the articles included in this Special Issue, we proposed new grounds for future research, again clustered along our framework. By doing so, we aim to contribute to further setting and refining the research agenda in this important and emerging field.

Notes

1. We define 'hostile environment' as a country, region, or specified location, which is subject to war, terrorism, insurgency, civil unrest, or extreme levels of crime, banditry, lawlessness, or public disorder.
2. When working on this part of the introductory article, we felt that some of the best experts are, in fact the authors contributing to this Special Issue. Thus, besides summarizing what they wrote in their respective articles, we approached them via E-mail and asked them to share their thoughts with us. We gladly incorporated their valuable feedback when drafting the section on new grounds in research on people management in hostile environments.

References

Andresen, M., Ariss, A.A., & Walther, M. (2012). *Self-initiated expatriation: Individual, organizational, and national perspectives*. London, UK: Routledge.

Alexander, D. C. (2004). *Business confronts terrorism: risks and responses*. Madison, WI: The University of Wisconsin Press.

Bader, A. K., Reade, C., & Froese, F. J. (2018). Terrorism and expatriate withdrawal cognitions: the differential role of perceived work and non-work constraints. *International Journal of Human Resource Management, (Part of Special Issue)*, doi: 10.1080/09585192.2016.1233448

Bader, B. (2015). The power of support in high-risk countries: compensation and social support as antecedents of expatriate work attitudes. *International Journal of Human Resource Management, 26*, 1712–1736. doi:10.1080/09585192.2014.962071

Bader, B., & Berg, N. (2013). An empirical investigation of terrorism-induced stress on expatriate attitudes and performance. *Journal of International Management, 19*, 163–175. doi:10.1016/j.intman.2013.01.003

Bader, B., & Berg, N. (2014). The influence of terrorism on expatriate performance: a conceptual approach. *International Journal of Human Resource Management, 25*, 539–557. doi:10.1080/09585192.2013.814702

Bader, B., Berg, N., & Holtbrügge, D. (2015). Expatriate performance in terrorism-endangered countries: The role of family and organizational support. *International Business Review, 24*, 849–860. doi:10.1016/j.ibusrev.2015.03.005

Bader, B., & Schuster, T. (2015). Expatriate social networks in terrorism-endangered countries: an empirical analysis in Afghanistan, India, Pakistan, and Saudi Arabia. *Journal of International Management, 21*, 63–77. doi: doi:10.1016/j.intman.2014.09.004

Bader, B., Schuster, T., & Dickmann, M. (2015). Call for papers - danger and risk as challenges for HRM: how to manage people in hostile environments. *International Journal of Human Resource Management, 26*, 1517–1519. doi:10.1080/09585192.2015.1019256

Beutell, N. J., O'Hare, M. M., Schneer, J. A., & Alstete, J. W. (2017). Coping with fear of and exposure to terrorism among expatriates. *International Journal of Environmental Research and Public Health, 14*(7), 1–13. doi:10.3390/ijerph14070808

Blomberg, S. B., Hess, G. D., & Orphanides, A. (2004). The macroeconomic consequences of terrorism. *Journal of Monetary Economics, 51*, 1007–1032. doi:10.1016/j.jmoneco.2004.04.001

Breitenmoser, A., & Bader, B. (2016). Repatriation outcomes affecting corporate ROI: a critical review and future agenda. *Management Review Quarterly, 66*, 195–234. doi: 10.1007/s11301-016-0119-6

Breitenmoser, A., Bader, B., & Berg, N. (2018). Why does repatriate career success vary? An empirical investigation from both traditional and protean career perspectives. *Human Resource Management, 57*, 1049–1063. doi:10.1002/hrm.21888

Brookfield Global Relocation Services (2016). *Global relocation trends 2016 survey report*. Woodridge, IL: Brookfield Asset Management.

Byron, K., & Peterson, S. (2002). The impact of a large-scale traumatic event on individual and organizational outcomes: Exploring employee and company reactions to September 11, 2001. *Journal of Organizational Behavior, 23*, 895–910. doi:10.1002/job.176

Caligiuri, P. M., Hyland, M. M., & Joshi, A. (1998). Families in Global Assignments: Applying Work Family Theories Abroad. In M. A. Rahim & R. T. Golembiewski (Eds.), *Current Topics in Management* (Vol. 3, pp. 313–328). Greenwich, CT: JAI Press.

Cronin, A. K. (2003). Behind the curve: Globalization and international terrorism. *International Security, 27*, 30–58. doi:10.1162/01622880260553624

Czinkota, M. R., Knight, G. A., Liesch, P. W., & Steen, J. (2005). Positioning terrorism in management and marketing: Research propositions. *Journal of International Management, 11*, 581–604. doi:10.1016/j.intman.2005.09.011

Czinkota, M. R., Knight, G., Liesch, P. W., & Steen, J. (2010). Terrorism and international business: A research agenda. *Journal of International Business Studies, 41*, 826–843. doi:10.1057/jibs.2010.12

Darby, R., & Williamson, C. (2012). Challenges to international human resource management: the management of employee risk in the humanitarian aid and security sectors. *International Journal of Human Resources Development and Management, 12*, 159–186. doi:10.1504/IJHRDM.2012.048658

Devlin, E. S. (2006). *Crisis management planning and execution.* Boca Raton and New York: Auerbach Publications.

Dickmann, M. (2017). *The RES Forum Annual Report 2017: The New Normal of Global Mobility.* London: The RES Forum.

Dickmann, M. (2015). The RES Forum Annual Report: Global Mobility and the Global Talent Management Conundrum, RES Forum, UniGroup Relocation Network and Equus Software, 108 pages, London.

Dickmann, M. (2012). Why do they come to London? Exploring the motivations of expatriates to work in the British capital. *Journal of Management Development, 31*, 783–800. doi:10.1108/02621711211253240

Dickmann, M., & Cerdin, J.-L. (2016). Exploring the development and transfer of career capital in an international governmental organization. *The International Journal of Human Resource Management, 27*, 2253–2283. doi:10.1080/09585192.2016.1239217

Dickmann, M., & Mills, T. (2009). "The importance of intelligent career and location considerations: exploring the decision to go to London". *Personnel Review, 39*, 116–134. doi:10.1108/00483481011007896

Dickmann, M., Parry, E., & Keshavjee, N. (2018). Localization of staff in a hostile context: an exploratory investigation in Afghanistan. *International Journal of Human Resource Management, (Part of Special Issue)*, doi:10.1080/09585192.2017.1291531

Dickmann, M., & Watson, A. H. (2017). "I might be shot at!" Exploring the drivers to work in hostile environments using an intelligent careers perspective. *Journal of Global Mobility: The Home of Expatriate Management Research, 5*, 348–373. doi: 10.1108/JGM-12-2016-0066

Doherty, N., & Dickmann, M. (2012). Measuring the return on investment in international assignments: an action research approach. *The International Journal of Human Resource Management, 23*, 3434–3454. doi:10.1080/09585192.2011.637062

Doherty, N., Dickmann, M., & Mills, T. (2011). Exploring the motives of company-backed and self-initiated expatriates. *The International Journal of Human Resource Management, 22*, 595–611. doi:10.1080/09585192.2011.543637

Eckstein, Z., & Tsiddon, D. (2004). Macroeconomic consequences of terror: theory and the case of Israel. *Journal of Monetary Economics, 51*, 971–1002. doi:10.1016/j.jmoneco.2004.05.001

Fee, A., & McGrath-Champ, S. (2017). The role of human resources in protecting expatriates: Insights from the international aid and development sector. *The International Journal of Human Resource Management, 28*, 1960–1985. doi:10.1080/09585192.2015.1137617

Fee, A., Mcgrath-Champ, S., & Berti, M. (2018). Protecting expatriates in hostile environments: institutional forces influencing the safety and security practices of internationally active organisations. *International Journal of Human Resource Management, (Part of Special Issue)*, doi:10.1080/09585192.2017.1322121

Fee, A., McGrath-Champ, S., & Liu, H. (2013). Human resources and expatriate evacuation: A conceptual model. *Journal of Global Mobility: The Home of Expatriate Management Research, 1*, 246–263. doi:10.1108/JGM-01-2013-0007

Fowler, K. L., Kling, N. D., & Larson, M. D. (2007). Organizational preparedness for coping with a major crisis or disaster. *Business & Society, 46*, 88–103. doi:10.1177/0007650306293390

Frey, B. S., Luechinger, S., & Stutzer, A. (2007). Calculating tragedy: Assessing the costs of terrorism. *Journal of Economic Surveys, 21*, 1–24. doi:10.1111/j.1467-6419.2007.00505.x

Gannon, J., & Paraskevas, A. (2018). In the line of fire: managing expatriates in hostile environments. *International Journal of Human Resource Management, (Part of Special Issue)*, doi:10.1080/09585192.2017.1322122

Global Terrorism Database (2017). National Consortium for the Study of Terrorism and Responses to Terrorism (START).

Harris, H., Brewster, C., & Sparrow, P. (2003). *International Human Resource Management*, London, UK: CIPD Publishing.

Harvey, M. G. (1993). A survey of corporate programs for managing terrorist threats. *Journal of International Business Studies, 24*, 465–478. doi:10.1057/palgrave.jibs.8490241

Harvey, M. G., Dabic, M., Kiessling, T., Maley, J., & Moeller, M. (2018). Engaging in duty of care: towards a terrorism preparedness plan. *International Journal of Human Resource Management, (Part of Special Issue)*, doi:10.1080/09585192.2017.1298651

Hirshon, J. M., Eng, T. R., Brunkow, K. A., & Hartzell, N. (1997). Psychological and readjustment problems associated with emergency evacuation of Peace Corps volunteers. *Journal of Travel Medicine, 4*, 128–131. doi:10.1111/j.1708-8305.1997.tb00799.x

Holloway, H. C., & Fullerton, C. S. (1994). *The psychology of terror and its aftermath. Individual and Community Responses to Trauma and Disaster: The Structure of Human Chaos*, New York: Cambridge University Press 31–45.

Howie, L. (2007). The terrorism threat and managing workplaces. *Disaster Prevention and Management: An International Journal, 16*, 70–78. doi:10.1108/09653560710729820

Institute for Economics and Peace (2017). Global Terrorism Index 2017. Retrieved from http://visionofhumanity.org/app/uploads/2017/11/Global-Terrorism-Index-2017.pdf

Jacobs, G. A., & Kulkarni, N. (1999). Mental health responses to terrorism. *Psychiatric Annals, 29*, 376–380. doi:10.3928/0048-5713-19990601-12

James, K. (2011). Introduction to the special issue: Terrorism, disaster, and organizational science. *Journal of Organizational Behavior, 32*, 933–937. https://doi.org/10.1002/job doi:10.1002/job.758

James, K. (2011). The organizational science of disaster/terrorism prevention and response: Theory-building toward the future of the field. *Journal of Organizational Behavior, 32*, 1013–1032. https://doi.org/10.1002/job doi:10.1002/job.782

Kalbassi, C. (2016). identifying crisis threats: a partial synthesis of the literature on crisis threat assessment with relevance to public administrations. *Journal of Risk Analysis and Crisis Response, 6*, 110–121. doi:10.2991/jrarc.2016.6.3.1

Kastenmüller, A., Greitemeyer, T., Aydin, N., Tattersall, A. J., Peus, C., Bussmann, P., … Fischer, P. (2011). Terrorism threat and networking: Evidence that terrorism salience decreases occupational networking. *Journal of Organizational Behavior, 32*, 961–977. doi:10.1002/job.745

Knocke, J., & Schuster, T. (2017). Repatriation of international assignees: Where are we and where do we go from here? A systematic literature review. *Journal of Global Mobility: The Home of Expatriate Management Research, 5*, 275–303. doi:10.1108/JGM-01-2017-0001

Mainiero, L. A., & Gibson, D. E. (2003). Managing employee trauma: Dealing with the emotional fallout from 9-11. *Academy of Management Perspectives, 17*, 130–143. doi:10.5465/ame.2003.10954782

Nitsch, V., & Schumacher, D. (2004). Terrorism and international trade: an empirical investigation. *European Journal of Political Economy, 20*, 423–433. doi:10.1016/j.ejpoleco.2003.12.009

Oetzel, J., & Getz, K. (2012). Why and how might firms respond strategically to violent conflict?. *Journal of International Business Studies, 43*, 166–186. https://doi.org/10.1057/jibs.2011.50 doi:10.1057/jibs.2011.50

Oh, C. H., & Oetzel, J. (2011). Multinationals' response to major disasters: How does subsidiary investment vary in response to the type of disaster and the quality of country governance?. *Strategic Management Journal, 32*, 658–681. doi:10.1002/smj.904

Peus, C. (2011). Money over man versus caring and compassion? Challenges for today's organizations and their leaders. *Journal of Organizational Behavior, 32*, 955–960.

Pinto, L. H. F., Bader, B., & Schuster, T. (2017). Dangerous settings and risky international assignments. *Journal of Global Mobility: The Home of Expatriate Management Research, 5*, 342–347. doi:10.1108/JGM-10-2017-0042

Podsakoff, P. M., MacKenzie, S. B., Lee, J. Y., & Podsakoff, N. P. (2003). Common Method Biases in Behavioral Research: A Critical Review of the Literature and Recommended Remedies. *Journal of Applied Psychology, 88*, 879–903. doi:10.1037/0021-9010.88.5.879

Posthuma, R. A., Ramsey, J. R., Flores, G. L., Maertz, C., & Ahmed, R. O. (2018). A risk management model for research on expatriates in hostile work environments. *International Journal of Human Resource Management, (Part of Special Issue)*, doi:10.1080/09585192.2017.1376222

Ramirez, J., Madero, S., & Muñiz, C. (2016). The impact of narcoterrorism on HRM systems. *The International Journal of Human Resource Management, 27*, 2202–2232. doi:10.1080/09585192.2015.1091371

Reade, C. (2009). Human resource management implications of terrorist threats to firms in the supply chain. *International Journal of Physical Distribution & Logistics Management, 39*, 469–485. doi:10.1108/09600030910985820

Reade, C., & Lee, H.-J. (2012). Organizational commitment in time of war: assessing the impact and attenuation of employee sensitivity to ethnopolitical conflict. *Journal of International Management, 18*, 85–101. https://doi.org/10.1016/j.intman.2011.09.002 doi:10.1016/j.intman.2011.09.002

Ryan, A. M., West, B. J., & Carr, J. Z. (2003). Effects of the terrorist attacks of 9/11/01 on employee attitudes. *Journal of Applied Psychology, 88*, 647–659. https://doi.org/10.1037/0021-9010.88.4.647 doi:10.1037/0021-9010.88.4.647

Sánchez, C., & Goldberg, S. R. (2003). How to handle the threat of catastrophe. *Journal of Corporate Accounting & Finance, 14*, 35–40. doi:10.1002/jcaf.10196

Sandler, T., & Enders, W. (2005). Economic consequences of terrorism in developed and developing countries. In P. Keefer & N. Loayza (Eds.), *Terrorism, economic development, and political openness* (pp. 17–47). Cambridge, MA: Cambridge University Press.

Spich, R., & Grosse, R. (2005). How does homeland security affect U.S. firms' international competitiveness?. *Journal of International Management, 11*, 457–478. doi: 10.1016/j.intman.2005.09.005

Suder, G. S. (Ed.) (2004). *Terrorism and the international business environment: The security-business nexus.*Northampton, MA: Edward Elgar Publishing Ltd.

Suder, G. S., Reade, C., Riviere, M., & Birnik, A. (2018). Mind the gap: the role of HRM in creating, capturing and leveraging rare knowledge in hostile environments. *International Journal of Human Resource Management, (Part of Special Issue),*

Vaiman, V., & Haslberger, A. (2013). *Talent management of self-initiated expatriates: A neglected source of global talent.* Hamburg: Springer.

Victoroff, J. (2005). The mind of the terrorist: A review and critique. *Of Psychological Approaches. Journal of Conflict Resolution, 49*, 3–42. doi:10.1177/0022002704272040

Vinokur, A. D., Pierce, P. F., Lewandowski-Romps, L., Hobfoll, S. E., & Galea, S. (2011). Effects of war exposure on air force personnel's mental health, job burnout and other organizational related outcomes. *Journal of Occupational Health Psychology, 16*, 3. doi: 10.1037/a0021617

Waldman, D. A., Carmeli, A., & Halevi, M. Y. (2011). Beyond the red tape: How victims of terrorism perceive and react to organizational responses to their suffering. *Journal of Organizational Behavior, 32*, 938–954. doi:10.1002/job.710

Wang, J. (2008). Developing organizational learning capacity in crisis management. *Advances in Developing Human Resources, 10*, 425–445. doi:10.1177/1523422308316464

Woods, J., Eyck, T. A. T., Kaplowitz, S. A., & Shlapentokh, V. (2008). Terrorism risk perceptions and proximity to primary terrorist targets: how close is too close? *Human Ecology Review, 15*, 63–70. www.jstor.org/stable/24707484

Engaging in duty of care: towards a terrorism preparedness plan

Michael Harvey, Marina Dabic, Tim Kiessling, Jane Maley and Miriam Moeller

ABSTRACT
A minor digression, if you will: it has been over 30 years since I (referring to lead author) first wrote on the topic of terrorism and its potential impact on conducting business in a global context. The most vivid memory I have relative to that initial foray into this new topic was making a presentation at the annual summer American Marketing Association (AMA) conference in Chicago. I got halfway through the paper and I started to hear jeering noises emanating from the audience. As I remember (it is not a pleasant memory), the audience thought that I had lost my mind and that the reviewers of the paper allowed this rubbish into the AMA meeting (the implication was that they must have been drinking at the time). This is a true account of the presentation and when I left the session, I would be dishonest if I didn't tell you that I had made a terrible error and there would be significant ramifications to my young academic career. Yet, no country is untouched by global terrorism today, and the ramifications for global organizations are escalating year by year.

One man's terrorism is another man's freedom fighter (Arafat, 1974)

Introduction

Strategic global human resource management (SGHRM) is a highly dynamic field, with new themes and challenges constantly emerging (Stahl & Björkman, 2006). One undeniable feature that is of current significance for SGHRM is the prevalence of terrorism in a global context (Czinkota, Knight, Liesch, & Steen,

2010; Harvey, 1983; Harvey, 1993; Scullion, Colling, & Gunnigle, 2007). While there is a wide range of influences that one could discuss in relation to terrorism, this paper focuses on the increasing challenges relative to multinational corporations (MNCs) in managing and safeguarding global human resources in relation to external terrorism events.

With this paper, we aim to add to the scarce Duty of Care (Claus, 2009, 2011) literature on this topic and to engage academics and practitioners alike in a discussion concerning suitable mechanisms for MNCs, and SGHRM departments specifically, to engage in and be proactive about terrorism effects on global human resource talent. Duty of Care is the obligation of MNCs to protect their international assignees (IAs) from often unfamiliar and virtually unforeseeable threats to physical safety and security (Claus, 2009, 2011). There is an increasing amount of terrorism globally that is seemingly random (Fox & Gilbert, 2016; German Press Agency, 2016), and MNCs must engage in the safekeeping of IAs and their accompanying family members on the myriad of assignment types (Harvey, Mayerhofer, Hartmann, & Moeller, 2010) in existence today. IAs typically have difficulty in adapting to new situations outside their home country (Maley, Moeller, & Harvey, 2015); a scenario that is likely to be exacerbated in disaster-related settings such as those that evolve out of terrorism.

The impact of terrorism is poorly understood by MNCs, despite its notoriety and threat for internationally operating organizations (Harvey, 1985; Perry & Mankin, 2005; Scullion et al., 2007). The impact can be explained from a direct and indirect perspective (Spich & Grosse, 2005). While the direct impact effects of terrorism, such as damaged buildings or ransom paid for kidnapped employees only affect a limited number of MNCs; indirect effects of terrorism are far-reaching, and are thus an important topic for SGHRM (Fee, McGrath-Champ, & Liu, 2013). For instance, companies that assign staff in an endangered area incur significant costs for armored vehicles, bodyguards and other security measures. While these expenses are pre-emptive and directly classifiable, the costs of failed international assignments due to premature return or lower employee performance are harder to foresee.

This paper focuses on moderating potential IA failure by arguing for the necessity of a 'terrorism preparedness plan' that accompanies the information available to assignees and their families in light of making a decision to move abroad for a short and/or extended period of time (Moeller & Reiche, in press). Having a preparedness plan has the potential to put IAs at ease to take the assignment without anxiety or the question of 'what should I do if a terror attack were to happen'. Without coming forth with such a plan, the MNC runs the risk of limiting its legitimacy in the eyes of global talent pool. Legitimacy is manifested and expressed in the MNCs' global duty of care programs. A lack of legitimacy through duty of care initiatives can lead individuals to: completely refuse global assignments; uneasiness on the assignment; constant worry about 'what if' situations; and concerns for family members in 'what if' situations and/or a premature return.

A terrorism preparedness plan is vital for two critical reasons: first, global terrorism has increased in recent years and occurs in unexpected places, at unexpected times, with unexpected casualties. Second, the repercussions of not being prepared are too high. For example, Harzing (1995) would suggest that 'a high failure rate is likely to discourage potential candidates, shrinking the pool even further' (p. 458). In the realm of global talent management, shrinking the talent pool should be avoided at all cost to circumvent increasingly what appears to be a great talent shortage gap (Cappelli, 2008; Farndale, Scullion, & Sparrow, 2010; Moeller, Maley, Harvey, & Kiessling, 2016). This paper makes the point that a lack of organizational legitimacy regarding terrorism management increases the risk of IA failure as defined by the situation.

Clearly, IAs require SGHRM policies that help inform and enable them to manage and survive the threat of terror. Thus, it seems crucial to consider how SGHRM policies should be shaped or modified to address the dynamic nature and constant peril of global terror. Based on this rationale, this paper has several key objectives: we attempt to pinpoint the types of terrorist activities that can impact MNCs and to map SGHRM processes that will help MNCs to prevent future or to mitigate present terrorism influences, thereby engaging in duty of care for its IAs. The research question accompanying these objectives is as follows: to help retain organizational legitimacy and manage talent shortage challenges effectively, How can MNCs mitigate by means of their global mobility programs the ramifications of external terrorist threats and activities?

The subsequent sections of this paper progress as follows: we first offer a detailed review of literature on 'terrorism and business' related to the individual-, organizational- and country-level contexts. By observing cross-level outcomes of terrorism displays, we are able to propose a more informed and comprehensive anti-terrorism legitimacy perspective adopted by MNCs that incorporates existing perspectives of the influence of terrorism on business as it is represented in extant literature. In essence, we develop a MNC terrorism preparedness plan that can be implemented in order to attract and retain IAs; the plan is conscious of the individual- and organizational-level influences of terrorism activities. Finally, we offer some preliminary conclusions on the topic and suggest areas for impactful future research (FR) activities. We are optimistic that this paper will be the catalyst for ongoing research on the increasingly important issue of global terrorism and that it delivers ways to mitigate its negative albeit indirect effects on MNCs operating globally.

Literature review

Terrorism has increased, will continue to increase, and IAs and their families must be given duty of care that is not only an ethical approach by MNCs, but will persuade IAs to take an overseas position. For example, in the period from 2003 to 2013, according to the global terrorism database, terrorist groups or individuals have executed more than 330 different attacks. Although the data is not completed for 2014 and 2015, it appears that terrorist groups have killed more people than ever before. We therewith highlight that terrorism is unpredictable, potentially deadly, and will directly affect international personnel and their families. No one is excluded from its threat and danger, whether directly through personal injury, or indirectly, through the fear and stress imposed. Terrorism has not abated, but contrarily continues to rise (Czinkota & Ronkainen, 2009) due to the number of terrorist groups and the funding they are receiving. Certain geographical areas are more prone to terrorism, but it can occur anywhere due to globalization and radicalization of individuals (lone wolves) over the Internet. MNCs need to have a terrorism preparedness plan to address these potential issues for the IAs.

Although prevalent in the global marketplace, very little research has been published on terrorism in business; hence there is a dearth of theoretical foundations (Frey, 2009; Steen, Liesch, Knight, & Czinkota, 2006). No specific theories appear to have been developed for terrorism in SGHRM and management of IAs; not surprisingly then, very little research has focused on the impact of terrorism on personnel, much less the global personnel that are affected (Frey, 2009). In this vein, it is important to recognize that terrorism does certainly not operate in a vacuum, and that the literature would benefit from a comprehensive, multi-level, multi-faceted understanding of factors that play into MNCs' ability to react to threats of terrorism.

A synopsis of key studies on 'terrorism and business' can be found in Table 1 and are further elaborated on in subsequent paragraphs. We begin by describing the country-level terrorism phenomenon and its economic and financial business linkages to the national level. Next, we describe the influence of terrorism on organization-level aspects such as supply chain interruptions, sales fluctuations, elevated security and banking costs, before articulating the resulting implications on various stakeholders including management and other stakeholders at the individual-level of analysis. The third and final level addresses the influence of terrorism on perspectives of work safety, increased stress level, declining commitment, unknown psychological well-being, network engagement, workplace support, leading to compromises in workplace safety, declining work attitudes that potentially lead to assignment failure.

Country-level perspective

Country-level research includes whether country stability and economic growth exert a dampening effect on terrorism (Choi, 2015) and whether terrorism reduces foreign direct investment as a consequence of damage to MNCs' buildings, stock, potential death of employees and ever-increasing insurance premiums (Powers & Choi, 2012). Terrorism is frequently perceived as a type of political risk (Saha & Yap, 2014) and therefore may deter foreign investors by creating awareness of an unsafe investment environment. In a recent study, Lee (2016) found that terrorism reduces foreign direct investment inflows and contends that foreign investors adjust their information by observing whether the host country has

Table 1. Terrorism in the business literature.[a]

	Authors	Title	Journal	Key Results	Perspectives and Theories	Level of Analysis
1	Abadie and Gardeazabal (2008)	Terrorism and the world economy	*European Economic Review*	Mobility of productive capital in an open economy may account for much of the difference between the direct and the equilibrium impact of terrorism on business	The paper uses a simple economic model to show that terrorism may have a large impact on the allocation of productive capital across countries. The model emphasizes that, in addition to increasing uncertainty, terrorism reduces the expected return to investment.	Country
2	Choi (2015)	Economic growth and terrorism: domestic, international, and suicide	*Oxford Economic Papers*	The paper shows evidence that when countries enjoy high levels of industrial growth, they are less disposed to domestic and international terrorist events, but are more likely to experience suicide attacks	The paper offers a modified theory of hard targets, where richer industrial, but not richer agricultural, countries are more likely to attract suicide attacks. It contains a cross-national, time-series data analysis of 127 countries for 1970–2007	Country
3	Lee (2016)	Terrorism, counterterrorism aid, and foreign direct investment	*Foreign Policy Analysis*	While terrorism can be an obstacle to FDI inflows, countries that receive more counterterrorism aid are less vulnerable to this adverse effect	The paper uses two commonly used terrorism data-sets and draws upon a time-series cross-sectional data analysis	Country
4	Powers and Choi (2012)	Does transnational terrorism reduce FDI? Business-related versus non-business-related terrorism	*Journal of Peace Research*	The paper deals with the possible differences in the effects of business-related and non-business-related terrorism FDI investments. The study reveals that transnational terrorism harms MNCs and contributes to a decrease in FDI, but transnational terrorism that afflicts non-business-related targets is statistically irrelevant	The key independent variable, terrorism, is the number of terrorist attacks that occurred in one country-year. The authors used data from the ITERATE data-set, which contains only transnational terrorist events	Country
5	Saha and Yap (2014)	The moderation effects of political instability and terrorism on tourism development	*Journal of Travel Research*	Using cross-sectional data over a hundred countries for the period 1999–2009, this study measures the extent to which a country's political conflicts and terrorism can negatively impact its tourism industry. In addition, the paper highlights that political volatility and terrorism together can cause serious damage to the tourism industry	This article analyses the impact of political instability and terrorism on tourism demand using the moderation effect (interaction effect) technique – widely used in economics literature to determine the joint effect of political instability and terrorism on industry	Country

(*Continued*)

Table 1. *(Continued)*

	Authors	Title	Journal	Key Results	Perspectives and Theories	Level of Analysis
6	Barth et al. (2006)	Economic impacts of global terrorism: From Munich to Bali	*Milken Institute*	The research documents the changing pattern and intensity of terrorist attacks from governmental to civilian targets that have spiked since 1998. Authors conclude that targeting civilian populations to attain political aims has become more ubiquitous and effective in economic terms	Milken Institute researchers examine the economic impacts of terrorism from 1970 to 2004. They studied attacks in 149 countries and compared them with various financial market measurements, such as economic growth, capital formation and stock market capitalization	Organization
7	Czinkota et al. (2010)	Terrorism and international business: A research agenda	*Journal of International Business Studies*	The paper highlights that terrorism is becoming a fundamental variable of study. It highlights the importance of organizational preparedness, company strategy and HR issues in terrorism	The paper presents a comprehensive review of extant, relevant literature to provide background for scholarship on the relationship between terrorism and IB	Organization
8	Czinkota and Ronkainen (2009)	Trends and indications in international business	*Management International Review*	The paper reports results of study conducted with a panel of 34 international business experts. The outcomes evidence a rise of terrorism and corruption as relevant topics for international business in the next decades	This article involves a Delphi study which features three rounds of interchanges between experts on possible changes in international business practice to guide decisions into investing in new technologies and markets in the threat of terror	Organization
9	Dunn (2000)	A desire to leave?: Foreign policy radicalism and opposition to Atlanticism at century's end	*Studies in Conflict & Terrorism*	The author suggests that waters we are now entering are unchartered and perhaps treacherous, and we are not likely to steer safely through them unless we have the courage to question the old assumptions which once seemed eternal and have now become so threadbare	The author debates the need to challenge existing assumptions across economic imperatives, policy, leadership and followership, all of which are applicable to chartering the organizational context	Organization
10	Frey et al. (2007)	Calculating tragedy: Assessing the costs of terrorism	*Journal of Economic Surveys*	The paper suggests that people's utility losses may far exceed the purely economic consequences which feed into decision-making by organizations to operate in certain country locations	As economic consequences are only a part of the overall costs of terrorism, possible approaches for estimating the utility losses of the people affected are discussed. To do so, the paper uses the life satisfaction approach in which individual utility is approximated by self-reported subjective well-being	Organization

11	Jain & Grosse (2009)	Impact of terrorism and security measures on global business transaction: Some international guidelines	*Journal of Transnational Management*	This paper outlines different streams of research relative to terrorism, related security measures for MNCs. Suggestions are made regarding the unique role that MNCs can play in abating terrorism, for example, by taking steps to reduce global poverty and hatred, directly negotiating with terrorists, and developing new technology to counter terrorism	Systems theory is used as a frame to in the context of a broader environment or system. In light of terrorism threat, systems theory indicates that adjustments are needed. For example, businesses must examine which aspects of the system should be altered and what effect, if any, terrorism may have on the social role of the firm or its definition of stakeholders	Organization
12	Spich and Grosse (2005)	How does homeland security affect US firms' international competitiveness?	*Journal of International Management*	This paper looked at the impact of security-related regulations and risks on international competitiveness. Authors recommend some policy dimensions for both MNCs and the U.S. Government toward mitigating the negative impacts of the homeland security problem	The paper illustrates the value of using theory from various disciplines for analyzing a multi-dimensional problem. Systems theory refers to the overview of a phenomenon in the context of a broader environment or system. The paper concludes that a systems approach is an especially useful in its relation to business	Organization
13	Steen et al. (2006)	The contagion of international terrorism and its effects on the firm in an interconnected world	*Public Money and Management*	The paper reviews the networks of inter-dependencies in the IB economy and the impact that a terrorist attack has in disrupting networks	The authors draw on the new science of complex networks to explain organizational and economic phenomena related to terror	Organization
14	Bader and Berg (2013)	An empirical investigation of terrorism-induced stress on expatriate attitudes and performance	*Journal of International Management*	The paper shows that several terrorism-related stressors create a significant stress level for the expatriate managers. It concludes that stress from terrorism has a negative impact on the expatriate's performance. The study suggests shorter assignments and improving fringe benefits, in order to foster a better acceptance of the living conditions	The paper applies partial least squares (PLS) structural equation modeling (SEM) to analyze the entire impact path and found intra-family conflicts due to terrorism have the most extreme impact	Individual
15	Bader et al. (2015)	Global assignee performance in terrorism-endangered countries: The role of family and organizational support	*International Business Review*	This study focuses on the role of expatriates' families on assignments in terrorism-endangered countries. The study reviewed the experiences of 121 expatriate managers assigned to a terrorism-endangered country and found that the safety-related intra-family tension significantly impedes expatriates' work performance	The paper utilizes a perceived organizational support (POS) framework to help diminish the safety-related intra-family tension	Individual

(Continued)

Table 1. (*Continued*)

	Authors	Title	Journal	Key Results	Perspectives and Theories	Level of Analysis
16	Bader and Schuster (2015)	Expatriate social networks in terrorism-endangered countries: An empirical analysis in Afghanistan, India, Pakistan, and Saudi Arabia	*Journal of International Management*	The study investigates the impact of expatriate social network characteristics on psychological well-being in the terrorism-endangered environment of Afghanistan, India, and Pakistan. The study suggests social networks are more beneficial on expatriates' psychological well-being in countries which suffer from terrorism	The study considers the relationship between network characteristics, social support, and psychological well-being as a black-box, which tests the impact of certain inputs (characteristics of a social network) on a certain output (psychological well-being), while the underlying processes (social support) are used to theoretically explain why characteristics of social networks affect psychological well-being	Individual
17	Claus (2009)	Duty of care of employers for protecting international assignees, their dependents, and international business travelers	*International SOS White Paper*	This is first of two white papers. The author's main recommendation is for companies to develop an integrated risk management strategy to assume their Duty of Care obligations. Threats and risks faced by international business travelers, expatriates, and their dependents traveling abroad are elucidated	The paper uses many empirical case examples to stress the importance of duty of care	Individual
18	Claus (2011)	Duty of care and travel risk management: Global benchmarking study	*International SOS Foundation*	This white paper reports on a global benchmarking study to compare MNC's 'Duty of Care' policies and develop best practices to protect and support the global mobility of their employees and dependents	The author refers to duty of care and duty of loyalty. Taken together, these refer to a broad culture in which employers care about the health, safety, security and well-being of their traveling employees (and their dependents), and develop and deploy appropriate travel risk management approaches to protect them from possible harm	Individual
19	Fee and McGrath-Champ (2016)	The role of human resources in protecting expatriates: Insights from the international aid and development sector	*International Journal of Human Resource Management*	The paper unearths four areas where these organizations seek to build in-house competence, centered on culture building, and supported by a suite of human resource practices relating to people services, information services and communication services	This paper reports an empirical study exploring the ways in which 10 international non-government organizations from 5 nations (USA, UK, Germany, Switzerland, Australia), all with substantial experience operating in high-risk contexts, manage the safety and security of their expatriate staff	Individual

20	Fee et al. (2013)	Human resources and expatriate evacuation: A conceptual model	*Journal of Global Mobility*	The paper critically reviews research in crisis and evacuation management in IHRM. The paper articulates a framework that delineates what role HR managers should, play during crisis preparation and response	The paper uses a conceptual model that integrates multi-disciplinary research in relation to crisis management, and to consider its application for IHRM in managing the evacuation of expatriate staff during crises	Individual
21	James (2011)	The organizational science of disaster/terrorism prevention and response: Theory-building toward the future of the field	*Journal of Organizational Behavior*	In this study two models are proposed for future management of disaster and terrorism. Proposed linkages among constructs are offered to produce nomological networks for the organizational science of disaster/terrorism	The models developed in this study span multiple levels and use system, network, and identity theories to tie together key constructs	Individual
22	Knastenmüller et al. (2011)	Terrorism threat and networking: evidence that terrorism salience decreases occupational networking	*Journal of Organizational Behavior*	As terrorism threat appears to decrease the intent to engage in occupational networking, this study tested to what extent employees focus on their personal social networks in the threat of terrorist attacks. The findings suggest that the threat of terrorism appears to decrease the intent to engage in networking	The study draws on 'Terror Management Theory' (TMT) and 'affects event theory' (AET) as theoretical settings	Individual
23	Reade (2009)	HRM implications of terrorist threats to firms in the supply chain	*International Journal of Physical Distribution & Logistics Management*	The paper analyses the relationship between employee sensitivity to terrorism and employee attitudes in supply chain firms located in Sri Lanka. The paper suggests that perceived support from supervisors and peers can enhance psychological contract	The scholarship relies on trust and psychological contract literature to emphasize the importance to HRM in supply chains when there is a threat of terror	Individual
24	Victoroff (2005)	The mind of the terrorist: A review and critique of psychological approaches	*Journal of Conflict Resolution*	Modifiable social and psychological factors contribute to the genesis of the terrorist mind-set	The paper offers a multi-faceted review of theories across fields as a step to overcome what appear to be practical, conceptual and psychological barriers to understanding this important field	Individual

[a]Papers are listed by level of analysis first and alphabetical order second.

the capability to deal with terrorism. Abadie and Gardeazabal (2008) develop an endogenous growth model showing that the risk of terrorism significantly lowers expected returns to investments.

Organization-level perspective

From an organization perspective, network theory addresses terrorism in light of indirect effects of terrorism (Spich & Grosse, 2005) as firms are increasingly interconnected globally and terrorism can affect sales declines, increase costs due to government regulations or security measures, and supply chain interruptions (Barth, Li, McCarthy, Phumiwasana, & Yago, 2006; Steen et al., 2006). Although the direct effects of terrorism are estimable to an extent though unpredictable, the indirect effects are more difficult to ascertain. Sales may decrease in a particular area due to consumer fear (e.g. the shopping malls/restaurants were empty after the attacks in Turkey/France), increased transaction costs (e.g. traveling due to security concerns has increased time for global business, bank costs have gone up considerably due to concerns of tracking the funding of terrorist groups), supply chain interruptions, and FDI can decline due to MNCs' fear of setting up operations in dangerous locations (Czinkota et al., 2010; Frey, Luechinger, & Stutzer, 2007).

Transaction cost economics (TCE) focuses on uncertainty and the increase in transaction costs of doing business globally (Williamson, 1981). Due to bounded rationality, the unpredictability of terrorism (no one predicted the 9/11 terrorism in New York), a complete decision tree cannot be developed and managerial risk cannot be calculated (Steen et al., 2006). Albeit terrorism being an important topic for international business (Czinkota & Ronkainen, 2009), past occurrences and experiences cannot be relied on due to global terrorism and the costs cannot be estimated in strategic planning (Dunn, 2000).

Systems theory has been used as a frame to in the context of a broader environment or system in light of terrorism threat (Jain & Grosse, 2009). Systems theory indicates that adjustments are needed. For example, firms must examine which aspects of the system should be altered and what effect, if any, terrorism may have on the social role of the firm or its definition of stakeholders.

Individual-level perspective

Research on terrorism and the effect on the individual have used the resource-based view (RBV) of the firm, stress, network theory and social exchange theory (SET). The RBV suggests that the human resources of a firm can be a rare, inimitable, and valuable resource that must be protected and engendered globally for the firm to be successful (Colbert, 2004). The principles of RBV indicate that that the actions of the MNC towards IAs will result in organizational commitment and further development of the psychological contract between the IA and the

MNC through fulfillment of its legal and moral responsibility (McNulty & Inkson, 2013). Perceived support from supervisors and peers has been found to enhance employee identification with, or psychological attachment to, the organization in an environment of terror (Reade, 2009). Thus, through meaningful policies and procedures, focusing on employees subject to possible global and local terrorism, stakeholder theory suggests that investors, bondholders and others will be more apt to support the organization (Claus, 2011).

Bader and Schuster (2015) investigated the impact of IAs social network characteristics on psychological well-being in the terrorism-endangered environment of Afghanistan, India, and Pakistan. The authors found that social networks are more beneficial on IAs' psychological well-being in countries which suffer from terrorism. Findings suggest that the threat of terrorism appears to decrease employee intent to engage in networking (Knastenmüller et al., 2011). Little research has focused on the individual and terrorism (Fee & McGrath-Champ, 2016). Research into stress and terrorism has ensued as stress is suggested to be the main cause of IA failure (Wang & Kanungo, 2004). Several terrorism-related stressors have been found to cause negative work attitudes and attitudes towards host country nationals and impact negatively on the IA's performance (Bader & Berg, 2013). An increased stress level significantly compromises positive work attitudes and eventually leads to the expatriate performing worse on the job. The goal of terrorism by focusing on soft targets is to spread fear (Victoroff, 2005) and the effect to IAs is considered one of the top concerns of MNCs (Bader & Berg, 2013). Terrorism causes high stress to IAs and their family (Bader, Berg, & Holtbrügge, 2015), and research suggests that this will have a detrimental effect on the IAs' mood and perceived well-being with resulting negative attitudes towards their environment (Hang-yue, Foley, & Loi, 2005). This high stress level, unless organizations intercede, will result in poorer performance and IA failure (Knastenmüller et al., 2011; Levitt & Lamba-Nieves, 2011).

SET suggests that the interactions between individuals develop socio-emotional and economic value, are interdependent and can generate high-quality relationships (Cropanzano & Mitchell, 2005; Emerson, 1976). Perceived organizational support can be established through SET and has been a foundational theory for IA research in the past (Shore & Coyle-Shapiro, 2003; Takeuchi, Wang, Marinova, & Yao, 2009). For example, lucrative compensation packages for high risk areas of a firm is perceived as organizational support as it indicates the organization's appreciation of the IA accepting the assignment resulting with reciprocal positive attitudes (Chenevert & Tremblay, 2009). However, in times of terrorism, the development of social networks from the organization, IA, and IA family will moderate the stress and concern of the IA (Peng, Wang, & Jiang, 2008). The larger and higher the quality of the social network will directly affect the reactions of the IA and their family when terrorism occurs (James, 2011).

Organizational legitimacy theory and the development of a terrorism preparedness program

This paper makes an attempt to integrate the two proposed perspectives – the individual- and organizational-level perspectives – by developing a terrorism preparedness plan. Integrating knowledge on these perspectives will provide impressions that can ultimately enable MNCs to benefit in two ways: (1) MNCs will be able to safeguard themselves and their IAs from unexpected terrorism events; and (2) MNCs will be more likely to retain current and attract viable IA candidates (see Hearit, 1995; Neu, Warsame, & Pedwell, 1998) and conceivably leave a positive impression on departing employees. We assert that a country-level understanding of the effect of terrorism on business is important, yet it relates only *indirectly* to the conception of a terrorism preparedness plan. Plainly put, the unique scale and scope of a MNC's terrorism preparedness plan is at the mercy of terrorist activities and the impression it brands on country-stability, foreign direction investment risk, and thus prospective economic growth (note our forthcoming discussion on page 29, hurdle 3).

Returning to the benefits of a terrorism preparedness plan, a lens through which the moderation of IA failure risk can then be viewed is that of organizational legitimacy (Kaplan & Ruland, 1991; Mathews, 1993; Suchman, 1995). To help explain such a mechanism, this section proceeds by utilizing organizational legitimacy theory (OLT) to portray the influential role of MNCs or SGHRM departments in managing perceptions about exposure to terrorism threat to reduce failure (Harzing, 1995; Kraimer, Bolino, & Mead, 2016). Specifically, we propose that the key to lowering IA failure risk and thus retention is to focus on how the MNC can exercise legitimacy in the eyes of IAs. MNCs cannot take away the threat of terrorism, but they can work on how to manage threats and how threats are perceived by IAs.

As per Ashforth and Gibbs (1990), the concept of legitimacy is socially construed by stakeholders. Stakeholders, such as IAs in MNCs, evaluate an organization and make inferences based on their evaluation about the appropriateness, acceptability, reasonableness (meaning legitimacy) of MNC programs, processes, and actions/reactions. It would appear to be in the interest of IAs to hold their employers accountable to a terrorism preparedness plan in the (unlikely) event of being involved in such circumstances. The importance is hinged on having a plan in place for so-called dangerous assignment locations like Brazil, Colombia, India, Indonesia, Mexico, Nigeria, UAE, Russia among others, which are – interestingly – some of the more common and prevalent current assignment destinations (Brookfield, 2015, 2016).

According to Kaplan and Ruland (1991), organizational legitimacy is 'a process, by which an organization seeks approval (or avoidance of sanction) from groups in society' (p. 370), whereby legitimacy can also be defined in terms of acceptability or acceptance, taken-for-grandness, reasonableness, appropriateness, and congruence (Suchman, 1995). OLT as such accounts for the strategic actions of the MNC which are in line with IA approval or avoidance of disapproval of such safekeeping actions extended by the MNC. Furthermore, organizational support in terms of terrorism must inherently extend well beyond the more traditional pre-, during, and post-assignment training models organizations feel comfortable to practice. Accordingly, a lack of communication between the MNC and the IA relative to terrorism-related concerns can lead to increased IA failure risk (e.g. under/inefficient performance on assignment and/or early repatriation) (Harvey, 1982).

A lack of legitimacy may also lead to the potential IAs turning down the assignments in the first place. For that reason, reputation and legitimacy play a major role in managing the threat of terrorism in organizations as it is perceived by global personnel. Working towards legitimacy helps MNCs to increase the level of trust extended by IAs (as well as all employees) to the MNC and to get a 'buy-in' to the duty of care provided. Howie (2009), for example, found that when terrorism emerges, managers need to have a role of counter-terrors in creating trust between all stakeholders and the MNC. However, building organizational legitimacy in the eyes of global personnel is made more complex and challenging due to the unknowns of whether, when, where and who may undertake terrorist-related actions.

The level and type of organizational support needed would subsequently vary according to the context of terrorism. As a response to these kinds of unknowns, this paper proposes that the endeavor of building organizational legitimacy needs to be applied in a holistic way, by assessing and preempting/responding to potential terrorist threats external to the organization, on a continuous basis. The foundation for this research continues these streams of research as MNCs can engage in the following to develop organizational legitimacy: (1) acknowledging that terrorism is/can be a real threat to MNCs and their host/home country environments; (2) extending an open line of communication with IAs and families about all external terrorism concerns; (3) generating and managing a terrorism preparedness plan for IAs and their respective families. In this vein, OLT strengthens our theoretical contribution as it integrates the individual and organizational perspectives and supports the development of a terrorism preparedness program that spans across a process rather than any particular point in time. Much like Lee (2016) recognized in her country-level study, we suggest that IAs (compared to foreign investors) make decisions by observing whether the MNC (compared to the host country) has the capability to deal with terrorism. These impressions and more are now presented and discussed in the following section.

Towards a terrorism preparedness program

In principle, an organizationally-embedded terrorism preparedness program supports the MNC's ability to take ownership of a problem that can potentially negatively affect the existence of its global talent pool. Terrorism, as alluded to in this paper, is a series of continuous shocks to entire continents, individual nations, cities big and small, institutions/organizations inclusive of its staff, and individual civilians worldwide. No country, organization or individual is immune to the threat of terrorism. One way MNCs can safeguard themselves against imminent threats of global terrorism is to commit to the duty of care (Fee & McGrath-Champ, 2016; McPhail & McNulty, 2015) of its international employment base worldwide, and its IAs in particular. In this paper, duty of care refers to protecting the safety, security and general health and well-being of short-/long-term IAs and their dependents. By nature, legitimacy is manifested in MNCs' global duty of care programs.

Recent works by Claus (2009, 2011) suggest that the majority of MNCs are becoming increasingly aware about their duty of care responsibilities, although progress on taking action has been remarkably miniscule. It is suggested that the lack of planning and implementation of appropriate practices around the duty of care relative to safety and security or terrorism is wide-spread in MNCs, further highlighting the unknowns surrounding IA perceptions of MNC actions or inactions for that matter. Global mobility programs lack the urgency and may be overwhelmed by the complexity of generating a terrorism threat/activity support system worldwide. Although the statistics show that the chance of being attacked by a terrorist is significantly lower compared to, for instance, dying in a car crash (Shaver, 2015), it is also worthwhile to know that since the year 2000, the number of deaths due to terrorist activities has increased fivefold, leading to nearly 18,000 people in total in 2013 (Institute of Economics and Peace, 2014). These statistics show that although low in numbers, the reality is that terrorism threats and events are increasing at a rapid rate. IAs and frequent business travelers are exposed to this type of danger, making MNCs vulnerable to the expectations and inferences of IAs on this issue.

Although it used to be that the deployment to dangerous locations got the spotlight, the malice with regard to terrorism would appear to have a much greater wingspan now than ever before, covering the entire globe. We allude to the need for individual organizations for prevention against terrorism. This means that MNCs are challenged by balancing the requirement to incorporate preventative as well as reactive measures to terrorism that leads to duty of care measures extended to its IAs. MNCs must demonstrate their competence to manage global threats to terrorism in order to establish and maintain legitimacy in the eyes of its present and future talent pool.

A preparedness program has a better chance of working if embedded in a strong organizational culture (Harvey, 1982), which signals to employees that they are valued and that they matter. Moreover, global human resources as a strategic function has a social responsibility to ensure the MNC is sensitive and equipped to deal with global challenges – of which terrorism is one. Corporate human resource is the guardian of culture (Brewster, Sparrow, & Harris, 2005), and has a responsibility to implement global values (such as the war against terrorism) and accompanying systems to 'fight for the cause' which would boost the employer brand across the organization and instill and perpetuate a culture of trust, collectivism, and ownership of communal/global issues. We assert that the duty of care extended by MNCs is a vital element not only for IA well-being, but also to ensure the legitimacy of the MNC as an employer of choice for global assignments.

Research has illustrated that the organizational environment such as is exemplified by corporate culture can be conducive to individuals' actions and that the corporation should expend much energy and resources to assure a positive corporate, ethical, and supportive corporate culture (Heames & Harvey, 2006; Jacobs & Scott, 2011). It is through the acknowledgment and collective support of new programs, policies and procedures that a terrorism preparedness plan can reach its potential. Doing so signals to present and potential future talent pool members that the organization acknowledges the threat of terrorism as real; it also shows that the organization is forward-thinking and proactive. As ample research has concluded, effective management such as is seen in proactive measures again terrorism would reduce assignment failure rates of IAs.

This paper does not promote a standard of global duty of care towards terrorism threats, but rather provides a set of guidelines that MNCs may wish to follow and modify to fit their global mobility program reach and structure. The preparedness program can help shed light on a convoluted issue. It can present an invaluable component to the well-being of IAs, which permeates into the well-being of operation, and MNC in whole. For those organizations contemplating the cost–benefit ration/analysis, these organizations should contemplate what it would be like to lose its top talent.

Based on the information presented in this paper, a terrorism preparedness plan would emphasize the relevance of the following: (1) to assess past and present situations of terrorism threats and the likelihood of threats occurring in the MNC's country operating locations, (2) to contemplate the level of global organizational preparedness or 'readiness' to respond to any threat or act of terrorism in these operating locations, (3) to manage global mobility programs according to data interpretation/analysis and readiness assessment, and finally (4) to track, analyze and modify global mobility practices longitudinally to reflect the status quo of terrorism threats and activities globally. Figure 1 explicates the four identified hurdles towards conceptualizing and eventually implementing a terrorism preparedness program. We specifically speak to hurdles rather than phases in this program due to the formative nature of each element.

Hurdle 1: external terrorism threat assessment

In line with Drucker's (1995) notion that one is not truly able to manage without adequate measurement of the problem, we propose that it is necessary to align the organization's mission to engage in and manage the war against terrorism with

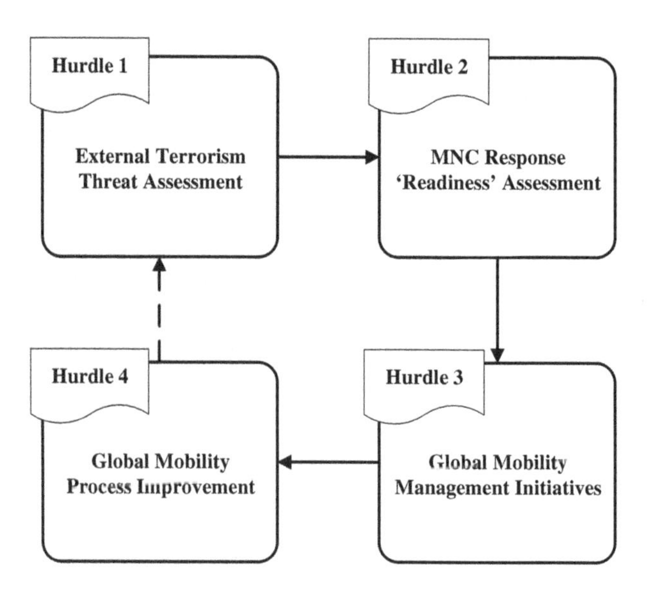

Figure 1. External terrorism preparedness program framework.

their ability to seek adequate information. In this vein, the first hurdle MNCs must 'jump' is that of scanning and identifying environmental, political and social changes that are likely going to have an impact on MNC performance. We make a case for identifying and evaluating external terrorism threats, and the potential these have on global talent management efforts. Making educated decisions on this front requires MNCs to obtain access to most adequate data to properly evaluate external threats and their potential to harm IAs, global assignment outcomes and global business operations in general.

Pertinent to this hurdle is the ability of MNCs to assess past as well as present situations of terrorism threats and evaluating the likelihood of threats occurring in the MNC's country operating locations in the future. Given the complexity of articulating terrorism threats, data has to be relevant and be retrieved from reliable source or sources. Continuity of data access is absolutely crucial. A triangulation of data taken from sources such as individuals (through their experiences), national efforts and what we propose herein, creative MNC methods, ought to generate a more objectively-subjectively balanced and informed assessment of terrorism threat. MNC decisions made with access to a continuous and reliable set of data can in effect increase the level of trust and acceptance extended by IAs towards the MNC.

International SOS, the world's leading medical and travel security service organization, has nearly two-thirds of Fortune Global 500 companies as clients, and has identified 141 countries (that is, 73% of countries in the world) as dangerous countries in which they presently operate (International SOS, 2016). Mexico, Nigeria, Afghanistan, India and Pakistan represent the five most dangerous countries. We observe parallel to this statistic that the most recent Brookfield Global Relocation

Trends Surveys (2015, 2016) observe Mexico, Nigeria, and India (three out of the five) as not only top of emerging assignment destination countries, but those with the greatest challenges for assignees (pointing out safety and security concerns).

According to International SOS (2016), threats include terrorism and other forms of violence and crime such as kidnapping, hijacking, piracy, lawlessness, violent crime, opportunistic crime, and organized crime. Terrorism ranks as a medium threat, whereas road accidents or infectious diseases rank as high, while hotel fires or insurgency rank as low. Risk perception of terrorism is high in the construction and real estate, agriculture and agribusiness and aerospace and defense industry sector. All industries found the threat of terrorism to be at least ranked medium, including manufacturing, energy and natural resources, automotive, and logistics and distribution. Geographically, threats appear to be more likely in Europe, Middle-East/North Africa, and North America, although no countries in the world is presently excluded, as is visible by the media coverage of terrorism activities around the world.

The approaches to conquering this hurdle of data access and evaluation will differ across MNCs. It will differ due to financial, time and other resource constraints, subjectivity on the phenomenon and its relevance to global operations, as well as the leadership team. Whichever scenario it might be, we assert that the 'best' approach will be one which depends on the most creative processes that can result in legitimacy creation. In the book *Wise Beyond Your Field*, Napier et al. (2015) advise leaders/managers to be open-minded about learning from different fields to boost organizational performance. Performance in this paper is the ability to manage external terrorism threats in MNCs to which IAs hold the MNC accountable. Napier et al. (2015) suggests that stepping away from an entrenched routine to problem-solve can help MNCs realize the overlap in concerns and challenges faced by leaders from wildly diverse areas. Terrorism is a globally-perplexing conundrum and it would foolish not to explore approaches countering such a threat that go beyond common organizational knowledge.

Those MNCs which tackle this threat with urgency, discipline and endurance will be most successful at conquering this hurdle prior to proceeding with a rational and strategic plan. It is the duty of the employer to identify risks and threats in operating locations through a reliable set of sources. The process of accumulating this type of data is problematic at best, and therefore creativity is sought. Contingent upon an accurate threat assessment, the second hurdle is to assess organizational readiness relative to the identified level of threat exposure.

Hurdle 2: MNC response 'readiness' assessment

The second hurdle speaks to the MNC's ability to assess its level of preparedness provided an accurate understanding of perceived threats. It is possible that the threat, at the point of investigating hurdle 1, may seem so remote that MNCs find it too premature or even unnecessary to engage in a resource-intensive task such as creating and implementing a terrorism preparedness plan. Weighing the options, it is feasible for the MNC to put such a program on hold, if it is prepared to answer IA concerns otherwise. In lieu of a preparedness plan, hardship premiums may be continued, although it is questionable that those alone with suffice given the increase in international assignment destination belonging to so-called dangerous assignment locations. Having said that presently classified non-dangerous assignment locations are seemingly at risk as well (i.e. no one could have predicted the tragedy on Bastille Day in France where 85 innocent people lost their lives, among those 12 foreigners).

Without a plan, IAs are not safeguarded and exposed to heightened risk either in preventing, during or after a terrorism event occurs. Because organizational legitimacy is socially construed MNCs should promptly contemplate the level of global organizational preparedness or 'readiness' to respond to threats or actual terrorism activities in/around their operating locations. Some of the questions MNCs may ask is: How prepared is the organization to understand, evaluate and respond to identified and presently unidentified terrorism threats and terrorism activity? What is the protocol or common practice? How accepting is the organization of flexibility in their responses as the threat may evolve into something we can't possibly conceptualize today? The old adage 'one size does not fit all' applies here; over time, different terrorism threats require different responses. In the (unlikely) event, is the organization able to track IAs and their families? How? Likewise, is transparency in approaches desired and for whom? Who is leading these initiatives and does it makes sense from a resource commitment standpoint? What form do terrorism threat responses take? Are these culturally-driven, regionally influenced, or does the organization opt for one common overarching approach? What fits best? Why? The level of confidence in any of these questions and subsequent actions will determine the extent to which global mobility programs (or likewise HR systems) will enact and manage the perceived threats and thus the organizational legitimacy as perceived by IAs. Hurdle 3 speaks to the management of initiatives in global mobility programs and how these might deviate from those organizations not concerned with external terrorism threats.

Hurdle 3: global mobility management initiatives

Following the organizational readiness assessment, hurdle 3 speaks to the MNC's implementation of global mobility program initiatives that can help to physically and emotionally protect IAs and their dependents. With information from hurdles 1 and 2 at hand, global mobility programs are likely to see changes in implementation and management, and, although there is perhaps little direct/obvious economic value added, the idea is to create legitimacy in the eyes of the talent pool to undermine the need to leave (referring to turnover and turnover intentions) due to the perceived lack of expertise of the organization to protect the workforce from external terrorism threats.

It seems that IAs already get much of the spotlight due to the involvedness of an international assignment; however, if there is an element important enough to be added to pre-departure assignment training it is that of safety and security briefings. As part of the pre-departure preparation component, we suggest MNCs to focus their attention on: building a platform for collective awareness and responsibility for the management of terrorism by engaging imminent IAs in a realistic preview of assignment location and potential hostilities, including any previous perceived or true experiences of threats that the organization has been exposed to. We are advocating transparency in process, which has shown to build corporate culture, trust and thus can be linked to organizational legitimacy development. Pre-departure preparation and training may also include expert presentations on the topic (listening and visualizing real and hypothetical situations), getting IAs involved in articulating hypothetical scenarios and possible contingency plans (i.e. How might communication channels be reestablished in case of Internet/phone lines going down in an entire country?), and thereby create a more vigilant, knowledgeable and astute talent pool and organization's culture.

Much like the organizationally-orientated preparedness plan, at the individual level IA's pre-departure 'readiness' assessment consists of targeted one-on-one discussions with IAs, addressing their concerns in terms of potential hostilities on assignment location. The time investment is accordingly gigantic, but a sensible approach to further anchor organizational legitimacy development. An online training module may not be out of the norm and could be extended to accompanying family members, as would be country-specific threat briefings. On-assignment assistance consists of real-time ongoing support, fostering an open communication policy about real (or perceived to be real) terrorism threats, as well as regular mandatory evacuation reminders and drills which MNCs may opt to pursue. Returning IA's, although knowingly plagued with typical repatriation challenges (Harvey, 1982) carry a responsibility to provide feedback on country-level terrorism concerns such that it can help inform the next cohort of IAs. These steps for all intents and purposes contribute to building ownership in duty of care across both the organization and individual persons, making it a multi-level effort much to the benefit of the organization. In sum, MNC actions arising in hurdle 3 is an illustration of their unique, context-specific interpretation of hurdle 1 and 2 threat and response readiness assessments, respectively. As a final point, hurdle 4 imposes a need to continuously improve responses.

Hurdle 4: global mobility process improvement

The approach to dealing with external threats of terrorism appears to be a most confronting for MNCs. For SGHRM policy makers, this represents challenges in not only defining terrorism, but in charting who is at risk and when and where they may be at risk, and what form the 'attack' might take. External threats of terrorism are hence fundamentally more risky due to greater proliferation of unknowns as firms are exposed to new dynamics due to being a small component of a significantly larger environment.

Global terrorism is no longer a phenomenon or something unusual. It is quite the opposite. By engaging in ongoing awareness building (exercised in ways described in hurdle 3), we are building interdependence among individual, groups/functions/departments, and subsidiaries. The greater the awareness and interdependence across the MNC, the greater is the chance for achieving collective power to counteract external terrorism threats. As a result, organizational legitimacy is actively built and can be maintained if subsequent exposures to threat are managed accordingly. It is through interdependence that we collectively understand the strengths of each other and each unit, and how we may combine these strengths to fight global terrorism threats, again highlighting how organizational legitimacy is socially construed.

We are advocating a sensible approach, not an approach that gives terrorism more attention than it already has. The caveat to having any type of terrorism preparedness plan in place is that activities of terrorism are by and large relatively unpredictable, despite tracking systems and vigilant lists. Building collective ownership of this issue is a good way to counter any uncertainty. And, the process of developing collective ownership requires a Kaizen approach: continuous improvements sought as the face of terrorism is unremittingly changing. As MNCs continue to compete for the best global talent (whether it'd be attracting or retaining it), an honorable terrorism preparedness plan is one way to differentiate one employer from the next; but only if it is done effectively. Although this line of preparedness might in this day and age still seem preposterous, we draw on Harvey (1993) to suggest that although some efforts have been extended by MNCs to counteract terrorism threats, much works remains to be done to match the smarts and pace of external terrorism threats. The best way to conquer uncertainty and risk is to be prepared for nearly anything, anytime.

Summary and conclusion

We highlight the fact that SGHRM departments lack in the preparation of their personnel whom they send overseas to understand and work with people in these often considered 'risky' locations. Exposure to terrorism threat and actual attacks among other factors heightens stress levels in IAs and can influence their work attitude and performance (Bader & Berg, 2014). Terrorism-related stress and strain can be moderated by perceived organizational support given and training provided, which means that IAs' well-being and performance will be directly affected by their perception of exposure to terrorist threats and activities. How they make sense of it all they will, in part, lie in the hands of the MNC. The paper suggests that organizational support can stem from a series of implemented proactive and reactive maneuvers taken to influence the overall well-being of IAs while abroad, meanwhile creating organizational legitimacy in the eyes of IAs.

Research on terrorism has used theoretical foundations such as, for example: about growth and investment from a country perspective on terrorism, from a MNC perspective on terrorism, TCE, social network theory and contingency theory; from a SGHRM or individual perspective, RBV of the firm, stress, SET and psychological contracts; and our research suggests that OLT should also be explored in regard to this phenomenon. OLT illustrates the importance of duty of care for current employees and well as attraction of new employees. A developed terrorism preparedness plan signals duty of care and engenders trust from stakeholders, and most importantly IAs (Ramirez, Madero, & Muñiz, 2015).

The types of terrorism vary significantly, the participants are always changing, and the places and times vary. For example, ISIS had been thought to be trying to incite individuals to stage small-scale attacks, possibly using knives or vehicles. It had been hoped that tougher laws had made the planning and execution of larger-scale 'spectaculars' next to impossible. However, after the 2016 Paris and Nice attacks and alleged plotting in Europe, counter-terrorism chiefs fear that ISIS has the capability and intent to stage a mass-casualty attack in the west (*The Guardian*, 2016). Moreover, Al-Qaeda released an audio speech calling on Muslims to reclaim their lost glory and dignity by attacking both MNCs and Western capitals (Jihadist News, 2015). Hence this terrorism preparedness program is hampered by so many contingencies.

Despite these knowns, we are confident that the program used by MNCs will prepare them to counteract a terrorist act and perhaps prevent it. The four proposed hurdles attempt to set guidelines for managers of MNCs to assess their preparedness for terrorism. A threat assessment needs to first prevail as there are different threat levels per country per region. Although terrorism does occur in other regions (i.e. France, USA, and Germany most recently), there are certain areas more prone for terrorism to occur. Secondly, the management must look internally to see if the firm, local managers, and IAs have been prepared and are able to respond. Thirdly, the global mobility program needs to include training and have identified the appropriate individuals living and working in a hostile environment. Finally, our program suggests a continuous improvement policy as new information is revealed and relayed to the program manager from IAs or from other external information. The program can then be appropriately adjusted per person and per location.

In summary, this paper illustrates a severe lack of both research and theoretical development in regard to SGHRM in the context of terrorism. There are many issues that have to be explored for successful programs to be developed, which must entail relevance and endurance due to the new harsh reality of terrorism and its effects on IAs. Similar to early research in regard to expatriation that explored how failure of an assignment created poor firm performance, but later trended to the value of IAs globally, terrorism research has not evolved into a theoretically well-founded research stream. Much work exists for this stream to develop in regard to terrorism and preventive programs, individual characteristics, family characteristics, among other elements.

For now, we have made an attempt to first of all provide an in-depth overview of the works related to terrorism in the international business domain. As such, our contribution rests on assessing the current body of research, develop an approach for MNCs, and to assist researchers in developing a stream whereby this phenomenon can be explored. Although our MNC preparedness program is broad, it encompasses all the key foci in regard to terrorism in international business as best as one can, since terrorism is random, unexpected, and individuals are prone to react differently. In closing, we present the reader with a selective set of FR ideas imminently important to extending our understanding the individual- and organizational-level prior to or immediately after a terrorist event in which the MNC or its IAs are involved.

Pre-terrorism attack

FR_1: Development of a terrorist training programs for global managers/family on how to survive a terrorist activity (i.e. kidnapping, bombing, etc.).

FR_2: Development of a corporate level antiterrorist team (e.g., a 'Delta Force') to serve as a public relation deterrent for terrorist attacks and at the same time be ready to travel to assuage damage.

Post-terrorism attack

FR_3: Development of physiological/medical programs to address the stress that can/will occur for global managers *after* a terrorist attack.

FR_4: Development of a public relations team to debrief the public and organization in the aftermath, and deal with any negative publicity that could/will occur during/after the terrorist attack.

While this is not an exhaustive set of FR ideas that could be taken in regard to global terrorism and IAs, the organization and manager could through these measures become better prepared than their domestic counterpoints. Terrorism threats are going to continue to occur and grow in severity to the point that terrorism programs and training will become normative behavior rather than the exception. The present lack of research may be because until recently, terrorism has occurred, but not at level of extremity. Researchers need to be focused on this topic, as it is predicted that this is the new norm of global business, provided that terrorists continue to easily access mass methods at relatively low costs (i.e. car bombs, weapons, suicide vests, and others). This topic, though underexplored in the past, requires a wealth of new research and theoretical development.

Disclosure statement

No potential conflict of interest was reported by the authors.

References

Abadie, A., & Gardeazabal, J. (2008). Terrorism and the world economy. *European Economic Review, 52*(1), 1–27.

Ashforth, B. E., & Gibbs, B. W. (1990). The double-edge of organizational legitimation. *Organization Science, 1*, 177–194.

Bader, B., & Berg, N. (2013). An empirical investigation of terrorism-induced stress on expatriate attitudes and performance. *Journal of International Management, 19*, 163–175.

Bader, B., & Berg, N. (2014). The influence of terrorism on expatriate performance: A conceptual approach. *The International Journal of Human Resource Management, 25*, 539–557.

Bader, B., Berg, N., & Holtbrügge, D. (2015). Expatriate performance in terrorism-endangered countries: The role of family and organizational support. *International Business Review, 24*, 849–860.

Bader, B., & Schuster, T. (2015). Expatriate social networks in terrorism-endangered countries: An empirical analysis in Afghanistan, India, Pakistan, and Saudi Arabia. *Journal of International Management, 21*, 63–77.

Barth, J. R., Li, T., McCarthy, D., Phumiwasana, T., & Yago, G. (2006). *Economic impacts of global terrorism: From Munich to Bali.* Hyderabad : Icfai Books, The Icfair University Press. doi: 10.2139/ssrn.892033

Brewster, C., Sparrow, P. R., & Harris, H. (2005). Towards a new model of globalizing human resource management. *International Journal of Human Resource Management, 16*, 953–974.

Brookfield. (2015). 2015 global mobility trends survey. Retrieved from http://globalmobilitytrends.brookfieldgrs.com/

Brookfield. (2016). 2016 global mobility trends survey. Retrieved from http://globalmobilitytrends.brookfieldgrs.com/

Cappelli, P. (2008). *Talent on demand: Managing talent in an age of uncertainty.* Boston, MA: Harvard Business Press

Chenevert, D., & Tremblay, M. (2009). Fits in strategic human resource management and methodological challenge: Empirical evidence of influence of empowerment and compensation practices on human resource performance in Canadian firms. *The International Journal of Human Resource Management, 20*, 738–770.

Choi, S. W. (2015). Economic growth and terrorism: Domestic, international, and suicide. *Oxford Economic Papers, 67*, 157–181.

Claus, L. (2009). *Duty of care of employers for protecting international assignees, their dependents, and international business travellers.* International SOS White Paper Series. Salem, OR: AEA International Holdings Pte. Ltd..

Claus, L. (2011). *Duty of care and travel risk management: Global Benchmarking Study.* Salem, OR: International SOS Foundation.

Colbert, B. A. (2004). The complex resource-based view: Implications for theory and practice in strategic human resource management. *Academy of Management Review, 29*, 341–358.

Cropanzano, R., & Mitchell, M. S. (2005). Social exchange theory: An interdisciplinary review. *Journal of Management, 31*, 874–900.

Czinkota, M. R., Knight, G. A., Liesch, P. W., & Steen, J. (2010). Terrorism and international business: A research agenda. *Journal of International Business Studies, 41*, 826–843.

Czinkota, M. R., & Ronkainen, I. A. (2009). Trends and Indications in International Business. *Management International Review, 49*, 249–265.

Drucker, P. F. (1995). *People and performance: The best of Peter Drucker on management*. Abingdon: Routledge.

Dunn, D. (2000). A desire to leave?: Foreign policy radicalism and opposition to Atlanticism at century's end. *Studies in Conflict & Terrorism, 23*, 37–59.

Emerson, R. M. (1976). Social exchange theory. *Annual Review of Sociology, 2*, 335–362.

Farndale, E., Scullion, H., & Sparrow, P. (2010). The role of the corporate HR function in global talent management. *Journal of World Business, 45*, 161–168.

Fee, A., & McGrath-Champ, S. (2016). The role of human resources in protecting expatriates: Insights from the international aid and development sector. *The International Journal of Human Resource Management, 27*, 1–26.

Fee, A., McGrath-Champ, S., & Liu, H. (2013). Human resources and expatriate evacuation: A conceptual model. *Journal of Global Mobility, 1*, 246–263.

Fox, K., & Gilbert, D. (2016, November 16). Terror attacks in developed world surge 650% in one year. *CNN*. Retrieved from http://edition.cnn.com/2016/11/16/world/global-terrorism-report/

Frey, B. S. (2009). How can business cope with terrorism? *Journal of Policy Modeling, 31*, 779–787.

Frey, B., Luechinger, S., & Stutzer, A. (2007). Calculating tragedy: Assessing the costs of terrorism. *Journal of Economic Surveys, 21*(1), 1–24.

German Press Agency. (2016, November 16). Rate of terror-linked deaths in OECD countries increase sevenfold. *DailySabah*. Retrieved from http://www.dailysabah.com/world/2016/11/16/rate-of-terror-linked-deaths-in-oecd-countries-increase-sevenfold

Hang-yue, N., Foley, S., & Loi, R. (2005). Work role stressors and turnover intentions: A study of professional clergy in Hong Kong. *The International Journal of Human Resource Management, 16*, 2133–2146.

Harvey, M. (1982). The other side of foreign assignments: Dealing with the repatriation dilemma. *Columbia Journal of World Business, 17*, 53–59.

Harvey, M. (1983). Multinational corporations mass media strategy when dealing with terrorists. *Managing the International Marketing Function: Creating Challenges for the Eighties Proceedings. World Marketing Congress*. Canada: Halifax.

Harvey, M. (1985). A new corporate weapon against terrorism. *Business Horizons, 28*, 42–47.

Harvey, M. (1993). A survey of corporate programs for managing terrorist threats. *Journal of International Business Studies, 24*, 465–478.

Harvey, M., Mayerhofer, H., Hartmann, L., & Moeller, M. (2010). Corralling the "horses" to staff the global organization of 21st century. *Organizational Dynamics, 39*, 258–268.

Harzing, A. W. K. (1995). The persistent myth of high expatriate failure rates. *The International Journal of Human Resource Management, 6*, 457–474.

Heames, J., & Harvey, M. (2006). Workplace bullying: A cross-level assessment. *Management Decision, 44*, 1214–1230.

Hearit, K. M. (1995). "Mistakes were made": Organizations, apologia, and crises of social legitimacy. *Communication Studies, 46*, 1–17.

Howie, L. (2009). A role for business in the War on Terror. *Disaster Prevention and Management: An International Journal, 18*, 100–107.

Institute of Economics and Peace. (2014). *Global terrorism index 2014*. Retrieved from http://economicsandpeace.org/wp-content/uploads/2015/06/2014-Global-Peace-Index-REPORT_0-1.pdf

International SOS. (2016). Retrieved from Database: https://www.internationalsos.com/

ISIS planning 'enormous and spectacular attacks', anti-terror chief warns. (2016, March 8). *The Guardian*. Retrieved from https://www.theguardian.com/uk-news/2016/mar/07/isis-planning-enormous-and-spectacular-attacks-uk-counter-terrorism-chief-warns

Jacobs, J. L., & Scott, C. L. (2011). Hate crimes as one aspect of workplace violence: Recommendations for HRD. *Advances in Developing Human Resources, 13*, 85–98.

Jain, S. C., & Grosse, R. (2009). Impact of terrorism and security measures on global business transactions: Some international business guidelines. *Journal of Transnational Management, 14*, 42–73.

James, K. (2011). The organizational science of disaster/terrorism prevention and response: Theory-building toward the future of the field. *Journal of Organizational Behavior, 32*, 1013–1032.

Jihadist News. (2015, September 29). AQIM official calls to attack multinational corporations, western capitals. *Jihadist News*. Retrieved from https://news.siteintelgroup.com/Jihadist-News/aqim-official-calls-to-attack-multinational-corporations-western-capitals.html

Kaplan, S. E., & Ruland, R. G. (1991). Positive theory, rationality and accounting regulation. *Critical Perspectives on Accounting, 2*, 361–374.

Knastenmüller, A., Greitemeyer, T., Aydin, N., Tattersall, A. J., Peus, C., Bussmann, P., … Fischer, P. (2011). Terrorism threat and networking: Evidence that terrorism salience decreases occupational networking. *Journal of Organizational Behavior, 32*, 961–977.

Kraimer, M., Bolino, M., & Mead, B. (2016). Themes in global assignees and repatriate research over four decades: What do we know and what do we still need to learn? *Annual Review of Organizational Psychology and Organizational Behavior, 3*(1), 1–17.

Lee, C. Y. (2016). Terrorism, counterterrorism aid, and foreign direct investment. *Foreign Policy Analysis*, fpa-12087, *13*, 168–187.

Levitt, P., & Lamba-Nieves, D. (2011). Social remittances revisited. *Journal of Ethnic and Migration Studies, 37*(1), 1–22.

Maley, J., Moeller, M., & Harvey, M. (2015). Strategic inpatriate acculturation: A stress perspective. *International Journal of Intercultural Relations, 49*, 308–321.

Mathews, M. R. (1993). *Socially responsible accounting*. London: Chapman and Hall.

McNulty, Y., & Inkson, K. (2013). *Managing expatriates: A return on investment approach*. New York, NY: Business Expert Press.

McPhail, R., & McNulty, Y. (2015). 'Oh, the places you won't go as an LGBT expat!' A study of HRM's duty of care to lesbian, gay, bisexual and transgender expatriates in dangerous locations. *European Journal of International Management, 9*, 737–765.

Moeller, M., Maley, J., Harvey, M., & Kiessling, T. (2016). Global talent management and inpatriate social capital building: A status inconsistency perspective. *The International Journal of Human Resource Management, 27*, 991–1012.

Moeller, M., & Reiche, B.S. (in press). Inpatriates – A review, synthesis and outlook of two decades of research. In Y. McNulty and J. Selmer (Eds.), *Research handbook of expatriates*. Cheltenham: Edward Elgar.

Napier, N. K., Schert, J. M., Raney, G., Petersen, C., Lokken, B., Kemper, D., … Cooper, J. (2015). *Wise Beyond Your Field*. Boise, ID: Boise State University Press.

Neu, D., Warsame, H., & Pedwell, K. (1998). Managing public impressions: Environmental disclosures in annual reports. *Accounting, Organizations and Society, 23*, 265–282.

Peng, M. W., Wang, D. Y., & Jiang, Y. (2008). An institution-based view of international business strategy: A focus on emerging economies. *Journal of International Business Studies, 39*, 920–936.

Perry, R. W., & Mankin, L. D. (2005). Preparing for the unthinkable: Managers, terrorism and the HRM function. *Public Personnel Management, 34*, 175–193.

Powers, M., & Choi, S. W. (2012). Does transnational terrorism reduce foreign direct investment? Business-related versus non-business-related terrorism. *Journal of Peace Research, 49*, 407–422.

Ramirez, J., Madero, S., & Muñiz, C. (2015). The impact of narcoterrorism on HRM systems. *The International Journal of Human Resource Management, 27*, 2202–2232.

Reade, C. (2009). Human resource management implications of terrorist threats to firms in the supply chain. *International Journal of Physical Distribution & Logistics Management, 39*, 469–485.

Saha, S., & Yap, G. (2014). The moderation effects of political instability and terrorism on tourism development: A cross-country panel analysis. *Journal of Travel Research, 53*, 509–521.

Scullion, H., Colling, D., & Gunnigle, P. (2007). SGHRM in the 21st century. *Human Resource Management Journal, 17*, 309.

Shaver, K. G. (2015). *Principles of social psychology* (Vol. 28). Oxford: Psychology Press.

Shore, L. M., & Coyle-Shapiro, J. A. M. (2003). New developments in the employee–organization relationship. *Journal of Organizational Behavior, 24*, 443–450.

Spich, R., & Grosse, R. (2005). How does homeland security affect U.S. firms' international competitiveness? *Journal of International Management, 11*, 457–478.

Stahl, G. K., & Björkman, I. (2006). *Handbook of research in international human resource management*. Cheltenham, UK: Edward Elgar Publishing.

Steen, J., Liesch, P. W., Knight, G. A., & Czinkota, M. R. (2006). The contagion of international terrorism and its effects on the firm in an interconnected world. *Public Money and Management, 26*, 305–312.

Suchman, M. C. (1995). Managing legitimacy: Strategic and institutional approaches. *Academy of Management Journal, 20*, 571–610.

Takeuchi, R., Wang, M., Marinova, S. V., & Yao, X. (2009). Role of domain-specific facets of perceived organizational support during expatriation and implications for performance. *Organization Science, 20*, 621–634.

Victoroff, J. (2005). The mind of the terrorist: A review and critique of psychological approaches. *Journal of Conflict Resolution, 49*, 3–42.

Wang, X., & Kanungo, R. N. (2004). Nationality, social network and psychological well-being: Expatriates in China. *The International Journal of Human Resource Management, 15*, 775–793.

Williamson, O. (1981). The economics of organization: The transaction cost approach. *American Journal of Sociology, 87*, 548–577.

Protecting expatriates in hostile environments: institutional forces influencing the safety and security practices of internationally active organisations

Anthony Fee, Susan McGrath-Champ and Marco Berti

ABSTRACT

The operations of internationally active organisations continue to encroach on hostile locations that are vulnerable to the negative consequences of crises such as political upheaval, terrorist attacks or natural disasters. Yet research into how firms ensure the physical and psychological safety and security of international staff in these locations is limited. This article reports an empirical study exploring the expatriate safety and security practices of 28 internationally active organisations from three industries that commonly operate in hostile environments. We unveil starkly different approaches across the three industries, and label these approaches 'regulatory' (mining and resources), 'informal mentoring' (news media) and 'empowering' (international aid and development). We use institutional theory to propose that these configurations reflect legitimacy-seeking choices that these organisations make in response to the various institutional environments that affect each sector. Our results provide a platform for initial theory building into the interrelated elements of organisations' safety and security practices, and the institutional factors that shape the design of these.

Creating a global workforce brings benefits but comes with costs. International mobility increases exposure of expatriates to threats that range from individual misadventure to terrorist attacks (e.g. Claus, 2009; Czinkota, Knight, Liesch, & Steen, 2010). These threats are becoming more salient to organisations with operations in multiple countries ('internationally active organisations') as the number of expatriates working in locations which present substantial danger to health and security grows (Bader, 2014).

This article reports an empirical investigation that identifies and explains the characteristics of the expatriate safety and security approaches of internationally active organisations from three industries, all operating in particularly dangerous environments. We examine this phenomenon through the lens of institutional theory, a perspective that foregrounds the influence of the institutional environments in which organisations configure and enact their HR practices, and the various stakeholders that legitimise those institutions. Our research builds on recent empirical studies that have begun to unpick the HR implications of expatriates' safety and security in particular sectors (Fee & McGrath-Champ, 2016) and settings (Bader & Schuster, 2015). Further, we contribute towards theory development by documenting similarities and differences across the three sectors, and offer propositions for understanding how institutional pressures may contribute towards this pattern of practices. Our study is the first, to our knowledge, to apply an institutional perspective to the HR practices of internationally active organisations in hostile environments. This sample represents an interesting case of organisational activity occurring at the intersection of different institutional fields. Until recently, institutions have been conceptualised as relatively independent social arenas, thus underplaying the relations linking different fields (Furnari, 2016). However, organisations operating in alien settings must negotiate institutional logics of home, host and sectoral environments. Substantial differences between these discursive realms increase complexity and can prompt new configurations at myriad levels, including the potential of 'outsider driven' institutional change (Maguire & Hardy, 2009, p. 148). Indeed, our results suggest a range of institutional forces that contain remnants of different organisational fields shape these organisations' practices and philosophies: home country, host country and specific industry. Underpinning this theoretical contribution is our aim to better understand internationally active organisations' responses to the HR challenges of operating in hostile environments. In doing so, we approach HR management as a devolved set of practices that extend beyond the confines of the HR function (Kulik & Bainbridge, 2006) to include those critical HR services and activities undertaken by operational staff and line managers.

We commence by summarising the theoretical landscape of institutional theory, and the existing empirical base from which our research questions are developed. This is followed by coverage of the methodology and results of our exploratory study. We conclude by using institutional theory as a lens through which to discuss the implications for international human resource practitioners and researchers.

Theory and literature

We define a hostile environment to include any environment perceived to be vulnerable to events or circumstances that present a threat to expatriates' safety and security (McPhail & McNulty, 2015). At least three types of distinct threats exist. First, myriad natural or medical emergencies tend to be indiscriminate in whom they affect (e.g. typhoons, medical emergencies like Zika or Ebola outbreaks). Organisations can cushion expatriates to some extent against these threats (e.g. prophylactic agents); however, preventing or responding to such threats is contingent to a large extent on local conditions and institutions (health, education) and so are, to a large extent, *infrastructure-dependent*. A second type of threat involves direct and indirect targeted criminal and political violence. Such threats are more *legitimacy-dependent* in that they may relate directly to the way in which local actors perceive expatriates and their employers; e.g. targeted kidnappings of foreigner workers in Nigeria in June 2016 (Cuddihy, 2016). A third and related category of risk emerges from expatriates' contextual or cultural ignorance and incompetence (*knowledge-dependent threats*). While these are untargeted, expatriates' lack of awareness of, or experience in, the host-country, can amplify exposure to and consequences of threats that range from climatic (e.g. dangers to health of particular weather conditions or events) to cultural (e.g. hostility arising from breaching cultural mores) to specific contexts (e.g. risks posed by particular road conditions). In general, hostile environments provide conditions that make all three types of crises more frequent and/or potentially more severe.

Researchers examining the way organisations 'manage' threats from their external environment have catalogued a range of generic checklists, guidelines and tools to assist organisations plan or coordinate crisis response (e.g. Bernstein, 2011). From this, researchers have distilled several elements that are central to ensuring expatriate safety and security (Fee, McGrath-Champ, & Liu, 2013), including developing robust policy frameworks, evaluating threats, establishing processes and know-how for managing crises, and providing training, resources and post-crisis support for affected staff. A comprehensive study of the HR practices of internationally active organisations from the international development sector showed that their approaches were centred on strong organisational cultures supported by a suite of HR practices and competencies (Fee & McGrath-Champ, 2016). A feature of these organisations was their use of elements of 'acceptance' within the local community as a means to buffer expatriates against threats, apparently in contrast to approaches preferred by corporate multinationals (Harvey, 1993). The authors suggested that future studies examine the extent to which this configuration of practices might be comparable with and/or transferable to other sectors (Fee & McGrath-Champ, 2016). Hostile environments provide an especially valuable context for this because, by definition, they present elevated threats to staff as well as distinct institutional environments that influence organisations' operations. In this context, 'institutions' are the assorted internal and external structures and practices that collectively create stability and meaning (Scott, 1995) and which constitute the 'rules' in which organisations operate. Directly and indirectly, these can be sources of threat or protection to international staff and can place myriad demands on the ways in which expatriate safety and security is managed.

To understand how and why the practices of internationally active organisations, including HR policies and practices, interact with their external environments in the ways that they do, we draw on *institutional theory* (DiMaggio &

Powell, 1983; Greenwood, Oliver, Sahlin, & Suddaby, 2012; Lepoutre & Valente, 2012). Institutional theory posits that organisations face pressure to conform in order to attain or retain legitimacy within a given institutional context, characterised by sets of 'cognitive, normative, and regulative elements' that have become accepted as taken for granted facts (Maguire & Hardy, 2009, p. 149). *Organisational legitimacy* (Suchman, 1995) refers to the acceptance of the organisation by the prevailing institutions and its social actors (Kostova & Zaheer, 1999). The legitimacy of an organisation's practices is seen as central to its success within a particular environment. Researchers argue that this process of firms seeking legitimacy leads to institutional homogeneity, as organisations feel pressure to adopt norms, copy, or respond to external pressure to be more alike via a process of 'isomorphism'. Three distinct isomorphic pressures have been articulated (DiMaggio & Powell, 1983): *coercive* isomorphism stems from the need to comply with social rules and regulations, notably 'institutional agencies' present in the organisational environment (Westney, 1993, p. 49); *mimetic* isomorphism results from implicit pressures to imitate or innovate as a result of competition from other organisations within the field, and *normative* isomorphism derives from the professionalisation of labour creating a 'pool of almost interchangeable individuals who occupy similar positions (…) and possess a similarity of orientation' (DiMaggio & Powell, 1983, p. 152). Empirical studies have shown that isomorphism helps to legitimise an organisation in the eyes of both regulators and the public (Deephouse, 1996), and the concept is often used to examine the diffusion of homogeneous human resources practices (Gooderham, Nordhaug, & Ringdal, 1999; Rosenzweig & Nohria, 1994; Zhang et al., 2016). It therefore offers a solid theoretical lens for understanding similarities in the practices of organisations that operate in the same institutional environment. That is, it enables our research to go beyond descriptive accounts of expatriate protection measures that earlier studies have reported (Fee & McGrath-Champ, 2016) to *explain* pattern of practices.

Institutional theory acknowledges the socially constructed nature of concepts like 'safety' and 'hostility' (Gherardi, 2006; Gherardi & Nicolini, 2000). From this perspective, organisations do not simply devise strategies to suit a set of objective environmental threats, as contingency theory would predict (Donaldson, 2001). Rather, organisations co-produce a process involving 'people, technologies, and textual and symbolic forms assembled within a system of material relations' (Gherardi & Nicolini, 2000, p. 10). In such a process legitimacy issues are central to organisational practices (Lindøe, Engen, & Olsen, 2011).

Understanding these practices in internationally active organisations is especially pertinent given the diverse layers of institutions that shape their operations (Kostova, Roth, & Dacin, 2008). These include national institutions in parent- and host-countries, as well as the organisational fields existing within an industry (Kostova et al., 2008). On the one hand, the importance of legitimacy for internationally active organisations is exacerbated by the substantial barriers that they must overcome; notably, liability of being 'foreign' (Kostova et al., 2008). At the same time, informal institutional forces like cultural, linguistic and geographic barriers, and the diversity of legitimating bodies, may impede legitimation efforts (Kostova & Zaheer, 1999). The result is that these organisations' responses to their institutional environments are 'unique and unpredictable' (Kostova et al., 2008, p. 999).

For organisations that operate in hostile international environments, legitimacy pressures feed directly into issues associated with expatriate safety and security. By definition, hostile environments tend to be characterised by weak formal institutions in the guise of poorly enforced rules of law, unreliable infrastructure, high levels of political instability, and low levels of economic development (Institute for Economics & Peace, 2014). Against such a backdrop, legitimacy from host institutional actors in the form of support for an organisation's operations and acceptance of international staff within a host community can provide a 'safety net' for expatriates through access to information and physical and emotional support. Indeed, such an *acceptance* approach has been shown to be a viable alternative to more defensive *protection* strategies that separate expatriates from host actors (Fee & McGrath-Champ, 2016). This form of legitimacy builds on cognitive and normative acceptance that tend to be more 'tacit' and thus potentially problematic than (formal and explicit) regulatory institutions (Kostova & Zaheer, 1999).

Viewed holistically, hostile environments present organisations with formal institutions that may be unreliable and social actors that may be sources of either threat or protection. These factors elevate the need for legitimacy to ensure expatriates are protected from indiscriminate or targeted threat. However, the empirical and theoretical literature provides little guidance; indeed, it suggests forces of convergence and divergence may operate simultaneously on the way in which expatriates might be protected. On the one hand, the weak formal institutions may provoke similarly abundant practice among organisations irrespective of their internal characteristics or industry. In these cases we would expect to find evidence of firms deploying a suite of common 'good practice' solutions to protect expatriates that are designed to offset the uncertainties and institutional weaknesses prevalent in hostile locations. On the other hand, industry-level demands and entrenched norms may lead to different responses being used in particular sectors (Bjerkan, 2010; Watson, 2005), even in identical host-institutional environments. Irrespective, the few studies in business and management in this domain remain directed at expatriates' work attitudes and performance (Bader, 2014; Bader & Berg, 2013) rather than how organisations can protect expatriates' physical and psychological safety. Consequently, the ways in which the various institutional forces influence policies and practices of internationally active organisations in hostile environments remains poorly mapped.

The empirical research reported here takes steps to remedy the soft empirical and theoretical underbelly of this phenomenon by examining how these competing institutional forces influence the HR practices of internationally active organisations. We do this by examining the deployment of practices and philosophies for managing expatriate safety and security by organisations from three sectors conditioned to operating in hostile environments.

Methodology and research context

The study used an inductive (interpretivist) research design. This approach is suited to studying phenomena with limited empirical foundations because it avoids the potentially misleading descriptions and conceptual models that deductive (positivist) research might produce (Edmondson & Mcmanus, 2007; von Krogh, Rossi-Lamastra, & Haefliger, 2012). Our aim was to produce robust empirical foundations that would allow propositions about explanatory relationships between variables to be generated for future testing or refutation.

We approached this task via a multiple case design, centred on examining 'extreme' cases (Farquhar, 2012) in the form of organisations with vast experience operating in hostile environments. Case study research has a long tradition in business and management research (Farquhar, 2012). While not associated with a particular epistemology, our interpretivist perspective was consistent with theory-building research drawing on observations *in situ* (Dul & Hak, 2008), seen to be one of the strengths of the approach (Yin, 2003).

Sample

The sample comprised twenty-eight internationally active organisations from industries that commonly operate in hostile environments: (a) mining and resources (M&R, 12 organisations), (b) news media (media, 6 organisations), and (c) international aid and development (IAD, 10 organisations). Combined, the case study organisations had assignees in more than 31 nations rated by the risk consultancy firm *Control Risks* as being a high or extreme risk threat.

Case selection involved a combination of purposive and convenience sampling drawing mainly on the authors' professional contacts, supplemented by snowball sampling and—in a minority of cases—direct approaches. We sought cases that would provide diversity in terms of variables like parent country, size, and type, remaining cognisant of the pragmatic need to access a suitable depth of data regarding the phenomenon (Gerring, 2007). Table 1 profiles the 28 organisations as well as the breadth and extent of data collected.

Research context

The operating conditions, objectives and nature of expatriate placements being managed by the case study organisations varied within and across sector. M&R organisations are increasingly operating in inherently unstable 'frontier' regions in order to access available and cheap natural resources. However, their exposure to threat is imbued by the nature of M&R work irrespective of destination—e.g.

Table 1. Industry source profile.

Respondent organisation characteristics	Mining & resources	News media	International aid & development[a]
Organisation characteristics			
Number of organisations	12	6	10
Parent country of respondent organisations	Australia, Japan, Netherlands, Norway, Switzerland, UK, USA	Australia, UK, USA	Australia, Germany, UK, USA
Number of expatriates (per organisation)			
• Average	1,780	296	2,250
• Range	60–3,500	20–1,200	190–8,600
Expatriate location/s	Africa, Asia-Pacific, Europe, Middle East, North America, South America	Africa, Asia-Pacific, Europe, Middle East, North America, South America	Africa, Asia-Pacific, Europe, Middle East, North America, South America
Source Information			
Policy documents	59	9	104
Interviews			
• Number	9	7	11
• Respondents' roles	6 × security/risk manager 3 × HR manager	2 × manager (non HR) 3 × HR manager 2 expatriate	4 × security/risk manager 2 × manager (non HR) 1 × HR manager
In-text organisation reference	R1-12	M1-6	A1-10

[a]Data relating to the 10 organisations in this sector have been used in prior published research (Fee & McGrath-Champ, 2016).

capital intensive and highly hazardous via the use of potentially dangerous plant and chemicals. Organisations in this sector tend to have high levels of standardisation and tightly coupled systems, characterised by invariant sequences leading to production goals (Perrow, 2011). The sector also experiences high levels of resentment and mistrust from local communities, manifest through a series of recent legitimacy-dependent threats directed at local and international workers (Newenham-Kahindi, 2011). In most nations the licence to operate for organisations requires stringent safety standards. These organisations use expatriates for myriad roles, from highly skilled (management, engineering) to semi-skilled (e.g. machinery operators). It is common for expatriates in various roles to be co-located on-site. Indeed, a feature of most (not all) M&R placements is their geographic remoteness and fixedness; that is, the work usually revolves around fixed sites defined by access to natural resources.

In contrast, the media's use of expatriates tends to be via small numbers of foreign correspondents and special event reporters. The role requires high levels of mobility and so their work 'space' encompasses site visits, frequent ground or air travel, and makeshift offices. It also involves a high degree of reliance on the local knowledge and contacts of host-country national (HCN) informants, technicians and staff. Expatriates tend to operate in-country alone or in small teams (e.g. correspondent, producer, camera operator). On the whole, their relative mobility and the nature of events they cover in hostile environments (i.e. natural disaster, war) provide opportunities to interact regularly with expatriates from their profession. In this loosely coupled context, strategies, policies, employees' decisions and outcomes are linked while still preserving elements of independence and indeterminacy (Orton & Weick, 1990). As a consequence the influence of others within this informal 'community of practice' (Wenger, 2000) is strong, relative to directions from a distant parent organisation.

The nature of IAD placements varies greatly. Some circumstances require teams of tightly knit expatriates operating in temporary shelter for limited periods (e.g. emergency relief), while others involve large numbers of dispersed individuals embedded in host-country organisations (typically longer term development-focused projects). Importantly, the capacity development objectives of this sector usually require collaboration and cooperative partnerships with local communities (Cornwall & Brock, 2005), necessitating high levels of interaction (and interdependence) with HCNs. Consequently, IAD expatriates are likely to be conditioned both by the policies and directives of host organisations and by the broader community of practice (incorporating local agencies and members of other IAD organisations) to which they belong.

All three sectors used a range of casual and permanent staff (as well as external contractors, excluded from our analysis). Placements generally ranged from 6 to 24 months, although all sectors made use of more flexible assignment designs (e.g. dispatching large numbers of short-term expatriates to cover major events, fly-in-fly-out placements). A mix of internally and externally recruited expatriates was common in all sectors.

Data collection

Empirical materials were collected via two complementary sources: (a) in-depth interviews with internal stakeholders and (b) various internal policy documents.

Interviews

Interviewees included international HR managers, line managers, security experts and expatriates (Table 1), all with at least three years' experience in the organisation. In total, 27 internal stakeholders from 15 of the sample organisations were interviewed. Interviews lasted from 45 to 120 min. While questions were customised to the specific experiences of interviewees, a standard interview 'template' was used, with questions relating to interviewees' roles, responsibilities, and experiences at the pre-, during- and post-crisis stages. All interviews except one were recorded and later transcribed in full. Notes were taken at all interviews and cross-referenced with transcripts.

Policy documents

We analysed 172 separate policy documents from 24 of the 28 organisations (Table 1). These exceeded 1,000 pages in total and included codes of 'best practice', security charters, country-specific security briefings, training programmes and activities, travel protocols, evacuation hierarchies, flow charts, risk rating systems and procedures for safe travel.

Data analysis

Content analysis of documents and transcripts involved a process of coding, categorising and comparison. Multiple cases from multiple sectors allowed us to examine the phenomenon in different settings and compare policies and practices across organisations and across industries.

The analytical process comprised four stages adapted from Farquhar (2012). First, data were coded to descriptive categories in order to create tabulated case files for each organisation. These ranged from 5 to 17 pages and contained a summarised, cross-referenced catalogue of organisations' activities across stage (pre-, during and post-crisis), participants (actors involved and/or affected), and data source, as well as holistic case notes. This initial within-case analysis triangulated interview and document data and was built primarily on a priori codes.

Next, second-level thematic categories were sketched through a process of open and axial coding focusing on prominent and repeated themes. By way of example, activities relating to collecting and managing information were identified across all stages of the crisis lifecycle and so were mapped for each of the 28 organisations along three dimensions: environmental scanning, staff profiling and incident reporting.

Once a complete set of case files was built, cross-case pattern searches were used to compare and contrast themes. This was done at multiple levels–within and across cases and sectors, between interviewees' experiences and written policies, and between our summarised case files and the original data. This process necessitated some follow up communications with interviewees to confirm detail. It involved the creation of numerous tables and matrices, several of which quantified or categorised the presence, extent and type of HR practices by organisation and sector. It was from these tables that several overarching assertions were devised at the sample- and industry-levels, and compared against individual case notes. Finally, our results were confirmed through member checks (Seale, 1999).

Results

Our analysis unearthed a number of patterns that provide the basis for theory development. Most prominently, we identify strong within-sector similarities regarding approaches to managing expatriate safety and security, to the point where clear philosophical distinctions existed between the three sectors. Indeed, our analysis showed that for these organisations it was sector, rather than organisation size, parent or host country, number of expatriates, or years of operation, that defined differences in their philosophical approach to managing expatriate safety and security. This led us to develop a nomenclature, expanded below, to convey the clear sectoral tendencies that emerged empirically. At the same time, we also identify some underpinning principles that appear common to all 28 organisations irrespective of sector, suggesting that 'core' practices were deemed necessary for all hostile-exposed organisations irrespective of the industry in which they operate.

These similarities and differences are summarised in Tables 2 and 3 and elaborated below.

Core principles that foreground local responsiveness and context

Viewed holistically, the data show that all 28 organisations took seriously the human—not just the business–implications of operating in hostile destinations. All invested time and resources beyond 'standard' duty of care concerns (Claus, 2010). All exceeded what is suggested in the literature in areas ranging from training (Chien & Law, 2003) to policy development (Crandall, Parnell, & Spillan, 2010) and post-crisis support (Raphael, 1986). Also commonplace was investment in strategic redundancy (e.g. multiple communication channels and/or information sources), and in-housing activities like post-crisis psychological support which are typically outsourced (Claus, 2010).

As exemplars of this comprehensiveness, we focus on three features prioritised at multiple stages of the expatriate management process by the sample organisations: (1) the information intensity of their expatriate support mechanisms, (2) the investment in customising policies and practices to suit on-the-ground conditions, and (3) the degree of (within-sector) collaboration and information sharing, to the extent where collaboration tended to take precedence over competition.

Information intensity

Prominence was placed on collecting and managing quality and timely information relating to conditions in which expatriates were operating. This involved triangulating information from multiple related activities. Ongoing 'environment

Table 2. Common expatriate safety and security practices used in hostile environments.

Common feature	Common characteristics
Information intensity	• Strategic use of multiple information sources • Ongoing 'environmental scanning' of on-the-ground conditions • Central internal clearinghouse to process and analyse data • Triangulation of data sources and types
Customisation	• Customisation of HR practices, including recruitment and selection, to suit local conditions • Compulsory in-country safety and security briefings • Independent security evaluations for specific cities, sometimes at odds with home government recommendations • Customised evacuation procedures supported by comprehensive policies
Collaboration	• Formal and informal intra-sector networks to collaborate in response to threats, crises, and expatriate safety and security issues • Sharing of information among security personnel relating to expatriate safety and security, including policies, training programmes, and minimum standards

Table 3. Sample sector characteristics and expatriate safety and security practices in hostile environments (summary of differences by sector).

	Mining and resources	Media	International aid and development
Sector characteristics	• Geographically remote and fixed • Concentrated expatriate deployments • Relative isolation from host actors • Capital intensive and inherently hazardous work • Highly standardised and tightly-coupled operations	• Small and dispersed expatriate deployments • Regular networking and interaction with host actors but irregular work patterns • Opportunities for regular interaction with expatriates in the sector	• Variable placements often via embedding expatriates in host communities • Substantial interactions with and reliance on host actors through capacity building
Overarching philosophy	Regulatory (compliance with formalised standard)	Informal mentoring (tacit knowledge-exchange)	Empowering (shared-responsibility based on local knowledge)
Expatriate screening criteria	Technical competence, formal crisis qualifications/accreditation	Technical competence, inherent 'street smarts' and experience	Technical competence, cultural intelligence
Expatriate training	Extensive, compulsory and multi-modal, emphasising verification and portability	Primarily informal mentor-protégé exchange on the job from expatriates and host-country nationals	Extensive, compulsory and multi-modal, with a strong focus on cultural awareness
Expatriate housing	Designated compounds to reduce interactions with host communities	Varied; based on recommendation from incumbent and informants	Embedded in host community where feasible
Crisis management procedures	Comprehensive and formalised, well resourced	Ad hoc, negotiated between expatriate and line manager	Comprehensive and formalised, drawing on expertise and goodwill from host community
Post-crisis support	Externally sourced from specialists	Evacuee-initiated, informal, restricted by occupational culture of 'endurance'	Comprehensive psychological and medical support from specialists

scanning' was used to evaluate perceived threats–both indiscriminate and targeted, emanating from the local environment–via safety/security updates from a diverse mix of sources including publicly available media (e.g. CNN, Global Disaster Alert and Coordination System website), contracted security analysts, personal contacts (e.g. military, security or embassy personnel), in-country operatives, and local and expatriate staff. In the M&R sector where funding was abundant, nearly half the organisations sustained the substantial cost of contracting multiple external security firms to supplement information updates. In IAD and media organisations, where resources were more limited, accessing experts more typically involved personal contacts, freely available information, and trained on-the-ground personnel including expatriates themselves. The bulk of organisations across all three sectors also maintained comprehensive electronic databases to collate information on incidents and individuals (although mechanisms to review this data were more sporadic).

The priority given to information extended to the use of internal experts as a clearinghouse to manage and interpret data, a practice seldom used in multinational corporations (Claus, 2011). This typically comprised small teams of security specialists and/or regional security managers based at head office, although at least four organisations from the M&R sector also deployed in-country security experts (less common in IAD and media).

Customising practices

A second characteristic of all 28 organisations was a commitment to customising expatriate safety and security plans to take account of on-the-ground conditions. All organisations provided compulsory in-country security briefings of varying durations, customised to anticipated threats, placement type and specific locations. Recruitment and selection processes (e.g. psychological and physical screening), evacuation triggers and procedures, communication devices and protocols, alert notifications, and incident monitoring and reporting all underwent substantial and expensive customisation to suit specific host conditions (not just risk ratings).

We heard of several cases in which in-house security experts made country risk evaluations that differed from the formal advice provided by home governments (an issue of great sensitivity for some interviewees). By way of example, organisation R11 produced a 70-page safety and security plan for one West African country. The plan includes six discrete evacuation plans for various circumstances using different air, land and sea evacuation points, emergency contact details, as well as maps, images and GPS coordinates of evacuation craft, meeting points and safe houses. In 10 organisations, typical of all 3 industries, risk evaluations addressing context-specific details were undertaken for specific cities as well as countries. Most organisations also customised contingencies to cope with perceived inadequacies in host institutions (e.g. multiple evacuation routes and safe house options in case of emergency).

Collaborating, not competing

Arguably the strongest indication of these organisations' investment in expatriate safety and security comes from the extent of collaboration in which they chose to engage. Twelve of the 15 organisations in which staff could be interviewed participated in semi-formal national or international networks that discussed and exchanged safety/security knowledge. Pertinently, however, none of these networks included organisations from outside the sector. Collaboration was most evident in the IAD sector. Policy documents and interviewees cited publicly available information from multiple think tanks, policy institutes and interest groups. Ad-hoc *Security Management Teams*, convened in-country as a crisis begins escalating, as well as permanent networks of security experts were used to share knowledge across the sector.

In a similar vein, M&R organisations commonly reviewed crisis plans against those of international and regional bodies, leading to the sharing of formalised 'standards'. The sector also had a practice of sharing elaborate in-house training and diagnostic activities, including live military-style scenarios involving affiliated operations (*'It's quite clear that there's an appetite to share'*, R5). The sector has gone as far as developing accredited training programmes that facilitate within-sector staff mobility. Likewise, media firms have begun offering expatriates standardised industry-specific training, and a recent collaborative, industry-wide initiative led to formal media-specific hostile environment training being established.

A distinctive aspect of this collaboration is that it tended to over-ride competition between organisations in the same sector. All nine interviewees from the M&R sector spoke about their experiences and willingness to share resources, information and HR practices with others in the sector (*'It's one area where you're not bound by industry secrecy'*, R4). Similarly, a HR manager from the media sector explained that they:

> *... never collaborate on writing or legal (issues), but in the case of safety, it's safety before competition. We'll suspend competition for safety* (M3).

Three sector-specific philosophies for managing expatriate safety and security

Against this backdrop of commonalities and comprehensiveness, our analysis also led us to articulate three sector-specific approaches to managing the safety and security of expatriates in hostile destinations. Each involved a system of HR practices underscored by a central philosophy, shared to varying degrees by organisations in the sector and which served as key points of between-sector differentiation (Table 3). The approach of organisations in the M&R sector is *'regulatory'*–highly structured, formalised, licence-driven and heavily regulated. We label the media industry organisations' approach as *'informal mentoring'*, intentionally informal, heavily person-based, relying on the tacit know-how of key individuals (expatriates and HCNs) and shaped distinctly by occupational identity and their (primarily in-country) community of practice. The IAD sector's approach is designated as *'empowering'*, focused on building organisational culture and capacity that is trained, empowered and nestled within support received from host communities.

Mining and resources

In the M&R sector's *'regulatory'* approach, safety and security onus rests on all operating personnel, enforced by strong CEO support and led by centralised security teams of former military, police and emergency services workers, complemented by in-country managers. Licensing, regulation and the tightly coupled nature of their operating systems imbue this sector with an imposed 'policing' emphasis; comprehensive, documented and externally verifiable. Several firms, for example, require expatriates in specific locations to have seven days' emergency food and water provisions and a 'grab' bag of essential items (cash, passport etc.). Mine sites typically have their own local evacuation plans, security policies, health and safety team, codes of conduct, and even hospitals. Housing expatriates in gated compounds as a means of separating them from the local community is common;

cultural awareness training linked to expatriates' safety and security is less so. In general, non-essential interaction between expatriates and HCNs outside work is discouraged and mitigated through a policy of separation rather than education (*'No-one leaves camp after 10:00 at night, drug and alcohol policies (are) enforced ...'* R11, interview). Training, formally accredited and thus transferable, aims to verify hazard and crisis competence rather than improve cultural awareness. In short, crisis management is strategically important and part of the fabric of these organisations. The cost is considerable (R1, R2, R11 interviews) but willingly borne by these firms, which have substantial financial capacity and unwavering conviction that such cost is a necessity.

Media

While the approach of organisations in this sector is more variable than in the other two, the hallmark of the media industry is its deliberately individual-centred, '*informal mentoring*' approach. Formal policies are comparatively ad hoc, and the nascent tendency towards policy formulation continues to be countered by the remarkably strong, individualistic occupational culture of news journalism. These individuals make decisions about, for example, whether to travel with an organised security convoy, or to deploy less obtrusively and thus be less formally protected. In-country safety and security rests largely with the individual, founded in experientially gained knowledge from on-the-job observations and semi-formal discussions with more experienced colleagues, HCNs or desk editors (usually former expatriates). In this regard, the expatriates' informal community of practice is a prominent influence on their decision-making, carrying greater credibility than formal organisational policies. Thus, the networks, local informants and 'street smarts' of individual journalists and their mentors become critical to their safety and security. This approach, which positions interpersonal relationships with HCN informants and confidants as a necessity to be encouraged, can be contrasted with the M&R attitude of quarantining expatriates.

Consistent with the informal approach of this sector, ad hoc person-focused and experience-based teaching, akin to a journey-'man' or mentor-protégé relationship still comprises a large part of expatriates' pre-departure 'orientation'. Post-crisis support also reflects the sector's informal, evolving approach.

Our findings suggest that, above all, the professional culture predisposing foreign correspondents towards independence and enduring hardship (*'When everyone else is flying out of a crisis zone, the journalists are flying in'*, M4 interview) remains dominant (Feinstein, 2006). This was exemplified most strongly by an anecdote shared by a foreign correspondent who had been evacuated from a conflict zone for a period of rest; soon after returning home a white feather, recognised within the sector as a symbol of cowardice, was anonymously posted to his home letter box.

International aid and development

The most prominent feature of the sector's '*empowering*' approach is organisations' efforts to build-in awareness of, and capacity for, safety and security management. This multifaceted commitment is oriented towards developing a culture in which staff are trained and empowered to be pro-active in assuming responsibility for the safety and security of themselves, others and the organisation.

Central to the culture-building endeavours is compulsory training for all staff (including non-operational and casual staff) that emphasises safety awareness, decision-making and personal responsibility. Expatriates are expected to be pro-active in two ways: via responsibility that 'our individual actions affect the safety and security' of everyone (A4, policy document), and by monitoring and sharing safety-related information.

Underpinning this approach is the importance placed on integrating expatriates into their host communities. This is the only industry to explicitly view expatriates' assimilation in the local community as 'a preferred security strategy' for the individual (A3, policy document), and 'by extension, the reputation of [the organisation] itself' (A4, policy document). To this end, improving cultural awareness, modifying behaviour and developing strong relationships within the host community, are central features of expatriates' security agenda.

This sector's embedded, community-founded, resource-constrained, empowering approach contrasts markedly with M&R's licensing imperative, formalised qualification accreditation, overtly coordinated safety operations, and seemingly open-ended resourcing of hazard/emergency management. Flowing from this, the tendency towards an 'acceptance' approach (Fee & McGrath-Champ, 2016) differs from M&R firms' preference for a 'protection' strategy (van Brabant, 2001), focusing on reducing vulnerability through protection devices and barriers. The media sector's glimmers of growing training and policy systematisation sit juxtaposed with the individualism of journalists' occupational identity and the on-going necessity of embedded, locally attuned knowledge and information. The generally sporadic placement and short-term presence of media journalists in host locations limits 'acceptance strategy' opportunities while simultaneously defying the development of comprehensive prescriptive systems, yielding a distinctive policy and practice mix presently in a state of transition.

Discussion

We focus our interpretation by offering tentative explanations for the patterns documented in the *Results* section, and articulate a series of testable propositions that link the practices of internationally active organisations, via institutional theory, with the empirical results of our investigation.

Sector isomorphism and legitimacy-seeking behaviour

Arguably the most prominent finding is the unified pattern of philosophies and practices that emerged at the sector level, and the related between-sector differences. The three distinct philosophies (regulatory, informal mentoring and empowering) represent starkly different responses to (host-country) institutional environments with similar conditions. We note that this difference is particularly prominent in relation to legitimacy-dependent threats emanating from host communities. For instance, IAD organisations' explicit framing of HCNs as sources of information, support and protection can be contrasted with M&R organisations' tendency to define HCNs as avoidable threats.

While multiple interpretations are possible, institutional theory leads us to propose that these configurations may reflect pragmatic choices an organisation makes about the form of legitimacy that best suits the sector-specific features of its work and its relationships with host communities (Kostova et al., 2008). To explain, organisations like those in the IAD sector, whose core business produces effects that are generally perceived as being favourable for the local community, have a higher chance of achieving legitimation from relevant host stakeholders provided this 'positive externality' is acknowledged by host institutional actors (Fast, 2014). We term this *intrinsic legitimacy*, whereby organisations' activities are perceived as congruent with the interests of a large proportion of local stakeholders, and as contributing directly or indirectly to the local field. On the other hand organisations like those in the M&R sector whose activities serve predominantly the interests of non-local constituencies must resort to ad hoc actions aimed at demonstrating (either rhetorically or factually) compliance with local norms (O'Faircheallaigh, 2013). In these cases, *extrinsic legitimacy* must be achieved by means of specific legitimation strategies, since the activities of the organisation are neither aligned nor beneficial for the majority of local constituencies (Newenham-Kahindi, 2011).

A second feature influencing these organisations' practices relates to the actual need for host legitimation based on the extent to which organisations operate interdependently with host institutional actors. Industries like M&R enable expatriates to operate autonomously, in relative isolation from host social environments. In such circumstances, technologies, know-how and practices can, if desired, be readily imported to create 'self-contained' task environments requiring minimal levels of host acceptance and relatively weak isomorphic pressures from local institutions (Perrow, 2011). In contrast, sectors like IAD and media require organisations to actively interact and engage with the host field to achieve their core 'business'. This is not just an issue of higher exposure to local institutional forces, but also of higher legitimation requirements, since these organisations must actively collaborate with locals and integrate practices with local conditions in order to succeed. These features open the organisation to normative isomorphism (DiMaggio & Powell, 1983) via routines and approaches more inclusive of local input, and thus are oriented to seeking a higher level of legitimation.

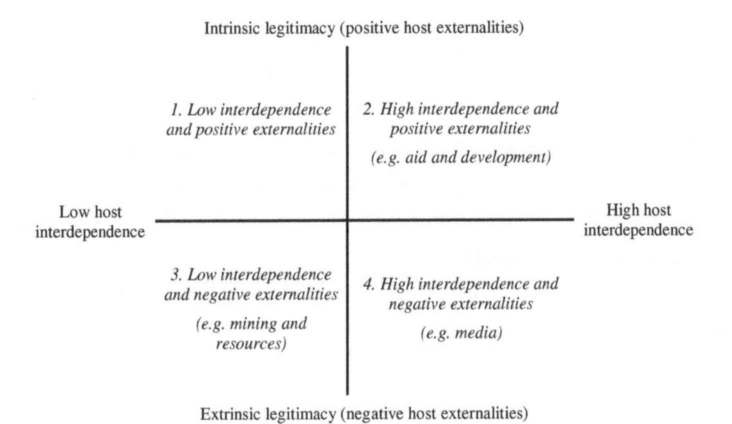

Figure 1. Framework of options for supporting expatriate safety and security (host interdependence and host externalities).

Combining these dimensions, we propose a tentative 2 × 2 framework presented in Figure 1 that articulates four possible legitimation 'spaces' for preserving expatriate safety and security in hostile environments. These are based on two overarching dimensions: the extent to which the organisations' operations may be perceived as congruent with interests of host institutional actors (intrinsic/extrinsic legitimacy), and the extent to which the organisation needs to work interdependently with host institutional actors (high/low host interdependence). We expect organisations with *high intrinsic legitimacy and high host interdependence* (quadrant 2 in Figure 1) to be best placed to capitalise on host-country legitimacy in ensuring expatriate safety and security by being highly sensitive to local institutional conditions and exploiting the goodwill from their positive contribution to the local community. For these organisations, the risk of legitimacy-dependent threats is low, and knowledge-dependent threats can be offset through cultural and contextual awareness (e.g. selection, training). The IAD sector's 'empowering' approach is an example of this. In contrast, organisations with *low interdependence and extrinsic legitimacy* (quadrant 3) confront challenges achieving host legitimacy. In this space, 'separation' approaches typical of M&R organisations in our study may be rational and efficient responses that minimise exposure to legitimacy- and knowledge-dependent threats.

More problematic is the case of organisations whose activities are not intrinsically legitimate from the perspective of host institutions but which still need high host interdependence to operate (quadrant 4). This may be the case for the international media organisations in our study. For these organisations, the high cost of acquiring 'blanket' legitimacy may lead them to deploy a more agile position that enables individual expatriates to negotiate the level of host legitimation (in the form of personal social capital) that is necessary for their operations. Such an approach requires high levels of tacit knowledge and local expertise to avoid knowledge-dependent threats, and so may lend itself towards the informal mentoring approach evident in media organisations.

Finally, quadrant 1 represents an 'ideal' space where intrinsic legitimacy is feasible but legitimacy needs are actually low. While no organisations in our study fell into this category, one example may be faith-based organisations operating in destinations that are receptive to the core principles (e.g. Catholic missionaries in predominantly Catholic countries).

On the basis of the preceding discussion and the framework in Figure 1 we make the following proposition:

> **Proposition 1:** *The expatriate safety and security approaches used by organisations in hostile environments will be determined, in part, by the nature of the organisations' interactions with host institutions; specifically, the degree of interdependence and the perceived local externalities that are created in the performance of their business.*

The 'hostility' of uncertain institutional environments

While the preceding discussion seeks to explain between-sector differences, the question of what institutional forces have contributed to the distinctive similarities in each sector is more complicated. An overwhelming picture that emerged from our analysis, and confirmed by interviewees, was the willingness of organisations to commit substantial time, energy, resources and effort well beyond 'standard operating procedures' to ensure expatriates in hostile environments were safe. All 28 organisations exhibited a strong foundation of normative duty of care, exemplified in Table 2, that exceeds the breadth and depth of practices evident in studies of 'mainstream' multinational corporations across several decades (Claus & Giordano, 2013; Howard, 1991; Harvey, 1993). As our results show, much of this energy focused on understanding and seeking to mitigate on-the-ground conditions in the host environment via collating and sharing local intelligence, and customising responses to this (Table 2).

We propose that these measures represent organisations' responses to the uncertainty associated with perceived elevated threat to expatriates emanating from the (hostile) host institutional environment. From an institutional perspective, the lack of robust *formal institutions* such as stable political and legal systems and reliable social welfare infrastructure, combined with organisations' relative unfamiliarity with host-countries' *informal institutions* (i.e., the safety and security 'liability' of foreignness), represent highly uncertain environments and make expatriates vulnerable to all three types of threats (infrastructure-dependent, legitimacy-dependent, knowledge-dependent). Viewed this way, organisations' use of mechanisms like sourcing copious amounts of local knowledge, elaborate and customised security plans, and sharing information with competitors, represent efforts to offset the ambiguity emerging from the generally weak and unfamiliar host institutional environments. Consequently, we propose:

Proposition 2a: *In order to support the safety and security of expatriates in hostile environments, organisations will seek to overcome perceived institutional weaknesses by employing practices that go beyond minimum 'duty of care' requirements.*

Proposition 2b: *In order to support the safety and security of expatriates in hostile environments, organisations will seek to overcome perceived institutional weaknesses by investing in highly customised and information-intensive HR practices.*

Beyond this, our analysis suggests an intricate mix of industry-dependent institutional forces also shape organisations' responses. The professional cultures that dominate the industries (normative forces) are prominent in all three sectors. In news media, foreign correspondents' reputation for combining independence and resilience with professional camaraderie (Feinstein, 2006) was strongly evident in our data and suggests a highly institutionalised domain (DiMaggio & Powell, 1983). Likewise, the core principles and motivations of IAD professionals, including their emphasis on host community empowerment and development, were also evident in the approaches preferred by the sector (Fast, 2014; Fee & McGrath-Champ, 2016).

However, other institutional forces were also apparent and acknowledged by interviewees. For instance, interviewees from the M&R sector confirmed that State licensing/regulatory requirements and trade union activity arising from incidents in home-country contexts constituted strong coercive forces (DiMaggio & Powell, 1983). In the IAD sector, coercive influences from funding bodies that specify minimum organisational safety and evacuation capabilities were identified as increasingly powerful. In the media sector, despite occupational resistance by expatriates in the field, greater awareness of welfare issues for expatriates have been prompted by fatalities, duty of care insurance, and legal counsel. Recent major crisis events were also acknowledged as important determinants in that sector. It was also apparent that in all three sectors the high degree of within-sector staff mobility–facilitated in M&R by accredited training programs–contributed to strengthening similarities via normative forces (DiMaggio & Powell, 1983).

In short, isomorphic tailwinds for these organisations comprised a complex mix of path dependence, professional culture and stakeholder engagement, all of which contributed to the idiosyncratic sector approaches. From this we propose that:

Proposition 3: *In relation to expatriate safety and security in hostile environments, sector- and industry-based differences emerge from different prevailing institutional forces.*

Sector homogeneity and collaborative behaviour

Institutional theory posits that *mimetic isomorphism* typically emerges from *competition* between organisations (DiMaggio & Powell, 1983). Indeed, for most corporate practices conformity within a sector is attributed primarily to intensive competition-driven benchmarking and imitation (Farndale & Paauwe, 2007). However, even though HR practices reflect firm-specific competencies and organisational knowledge (Clark & Lengnick-Hall, 2012), in hostile environments this does not seem to be transferred to expatriate safety and security practices. In fact, our results show that these practices are more aligned with shared human values and driven by genuine welfare issues, evident in sharing/collaborating on these issues rather than competing. One theoretical explanation for this 'consented mimicry' may relate to *legitimacy spillover*, whereby counterproductive actions of one organisation may taint perceptions of legitimacy towards all organisations that are seen to be alike because of their similarity on salient features (Kostova & Zaheer, 1999). For instance, an incident at a mining facility or a death of an aid worker has the potential to hamper operations of all similar organisations in the region (Fast, 2014). Thus, by sharing information organisations may be acting to minimise potential negative impacts on their own expatriates by assisting other firms within their sector.

A second way our findings are inconsistent with institutionalism is via the extensive in-country networking and information sharing of these organisations, which contrasts with the limited inter-organisational contact and subsequent weak organisational fields that are believed to characterise internationally active organisations (Kostova et al., 2008). While alternative explanations are possible, the practice of formal and informal information sharing networks appears to have been a mechanism for offsetting uncertainty provoked by the weak host institutions (Kostova & Zaheer, 1999). In short, hostile environments appear to encourage rather than deter inter-organisational contact, even in circumstances that make this challenging (e.g. limited communication infrastructure). It is likely that the 'cauldron' of the local conditions and perceived proximity of particular types of threats may help to forge a more collaborative, rather than competitive, mindset in the same way that external economic threats can coalesce industry-level collaborations. One outcome of these networks is the strengthening of the organisational field through socially constructed cognitive norms. On this point, it is worth noting that while almost all case organisations participated in this practice, no organisations networked or shared information with individuals or organisations from outside the sector.

These findings go some way to addressing the question of which institutional pressures become most prominent during times of stress. Whereas 'formal' coercive (regulatory) forces are generally recognised as influencing HR practices most prominently (Ferner, 1997), the hostile environments experienced by the case study organisations appears to have given prominence to a form of *consented mimicry*. Our final proposition, therefore, is:

Proposition 4: *In relation to expatriate safety and security, the organisational fields of internationally active organisations in hostile environments produce isomorphic forces that tend to emerge from collaborative rather than competitive mimetic forces.*

Theoretical implications

Our study extends earlier empirical research (Fee & McGrath-Champ, 2016) in several important ways. First, our empirical materials collected across multiple sectors allow the mapping of clear between- and within-sector patterns of HR practices. Indeed, arguably the most prominent implications from the data relate to the clear sectoral differences in expatriate safety and security practices. All 28 organisations have experience managing expatriates in hostile settings and strong internal and external incentives to mitigate and quickly resolve crisis events. Yet three distinct approaches exist, reflecting a complex interplay of isomorphic influences such as the nature and legitimacy of the core business, occupational norms, and external factors like exposure to regulators or benefactors. In short, when it comes to expatriate safety and security practices, industry does appear to matter. While research in domestic contexts has identified industry-level patterns in several HR practices, including occupational health and safety (Bjerkan, 2010), international research in this domain has overlooked the potential for expatriates' industry to predict salient outcomes like perceived stress levels (Bader & Berg, 2013) or sensitivity to threats (Bader, 2014) when working in high risk locations; our research foregrounds its importance as an explanatory variable in future studies. Pertinent to this, we also introduce the notion of 'legitimating space' – a product of an organisations' perceived externalities and interdependence with the host community - as a metaphorical landscape within which an organisations' expatriate safety and security approaches may flourish or flounder.

As well as expanding descriptive accounts reported in earlier studies, the use of institutionalism as a theoretical lens allows us to posit a series of testable propositions explaining these patterns. Specifically, unlike earlier studies which describe in detail the patterns of HR policies and practices of hazard-exposed organisations (Fee & McGrath-Champ, 2016), our theoretically grounded propositions elucidate the HR practices and configurations deployed by the sample organisations. In combination with Figure 1, they provide a theoretical foundation that begins to map the relationship between the HR practices and the institutions that either heighten or mitigate the threats to personal safety and security. In doing so, we introduce theoretical underpinnings to both explain the results of earlier studies (Fee & McGrath-Champ, 2016), and advance understanding of strategic HR choices beyond 'acceptance' and 'protection' approaches to safety and security (van Brabant, 2001) to incorporate the way that these strategies interact with hostile (and complex) institutional fields.

Building on this, by foregrounding the social construction of the legitimation process (Figure 1), our theorising reinforces the importance of symbolic practices and a deep understanding of the nuances of the host institutional context (Gherardi, 2006). By highlighting interactions between internationally active organisations and their host communities as an important consideration in understanding expatriate safety and security approaches, our study balances earlier work that emphasises the role of an organisation's (internal) culture in solidifying a coherent safety and security platform (Fee & McGrath-Champ, 2016). This would seem to be especially relevant given the complex genealogy of threats that expatriates confront; notably, those derived from socially constructed realities (legitimacy-dependent threats), or the strongly relational elements inherent in knowledge-dependent threats.

To the extent that these relationships are dynamic, we would expect to see organisations respond by taking steps to either 'manage' these relationships (e.g. encouraging greater intrinsic legitimacy) or to adjust their expatriate safety and security approaches. For instance, evidence that organisations in the IAD sector appear to be using protective security approaches more frequently in recent years (Fast, 2014; Fee & McGrath-Champ, 2016) may reflect changing perceptions in some host communities about the legitimacy of their work (from positive to negative externalities; hence a shift from quadrant 2 to quadrant 4 in Figure 1). Similarly, the evidence we document about the formalisation of practices within large media organisations may reflect decreasing interdependence with host actors (quadrant 4 to quadrant 3), perhaps due to technological changes and/or increasing use of freelancers. Used this way, Figure 1 represents not just a tool to map and understand the HR practices of internationally active organisations, but a framework for anticipating how changing institutional dynamics may affect these organisations' HR practices. These findings are consistent with the notion that the level of mutual dependence between fields affect the likelihood that actors in both fields will collaborate in creating new shared institutional practice (Furnari, 2016).

Beyond this, our results provide impetus for a reassessment of how the practices of internationally active organisations are configured to their complex institutional environments. Challenging earlier assertions (Kostova & Zaheer, 1999) we found that, in hostile environments, mimetic isomorphism can emerge as a form of consented mimicry (rather than competitive isomorphism), and that organisational fields can be strengthened rather than weakened (proposition 4). To some extent these findings may reflect the discretionary freedom that internationally active organisations have to respond to their institutional environments (Kostova & Zaheer, 1999). The results, however, do point to the benefits of studying organisation–institution interactions in extreme conditions like those presented by hostile environments. At the same time, this may also reflect a broader tension between 'top down' formal policies, on the one hand, and emergent practices stemming from professional communities. The practices and policies of the case study organisations suggest that the relative influence of formal 'authorities' may be mediated by the relative 'tightness' of systemic interdependence between policies, actions and consequences (Orton & Weick, 1990; Perrow, 2011) characterising different types of organisations. Our analysis highlights that the different practical modes of dealing with hostile environments are not determined by universal good practices or by objective characteristics of the dangers, but emerge from an interaction between materiality (e.g. types of threats, technology at hand), institutional forces (e.g. isomorphism, pursuit of legitimacy) and the relative weight of organisational and community-of-practice influences. More specifically, it shows how environmental dangers add to the existing (high) level of institutional complexity that internationally active organisations face. The practical solutions they develop when coping with this complexity contribute to transformation in field-level logics (Smets & Jarzabkowski, 2013) shaping different industry-specific institutional approaches to safety and security. As such it shows how embedded agency (Garud, Hardy, & Maguire, 2007) operates at the intersection of different institutional fields, and thus contributes to a more nuanced picture of inter-field institutional transformation (Furnari, 2016).

Practical implications

At a practical level, the unifying features in Table 2 represent, we posit, a baseline of HR practices that internationally active organisations in hostile (and non-hostile) environments could benchmark. These findings refine and support—but also give credence to the cross-sector transferability of—a core set of 'hostile-exposed' practices (Fee & McGrath-Champ, 2016).

Yet our results show that these practices alone are insufficient. While they represent mitigating responses to the perceived threat and uncertainty of locations deemed as hostile, they fail to take into account how the patterns of interaction and interdependence with host institutions lead organisations to curate divergent configurations of practices. In this regard, Figure 1 provides a framework for understanding how the characteristics of internationally active organisations might determine the approach, and related suite of HR practices, that best enables them to protect their expatriates. Organisations producing positive externalities (quadrants 1 and 2) can benefit from the goodwill imbued in their operations by using host institutional actors as resources of information and protection thus increasing legitimacy. These firms can reinforce their philosophies by ensuring their positive intentions are understood and accepted by local stakeholders, and are deployed in culturally- and socially-sensitive ways. On the other hand, firms whose operations result in primarily extrinsic externalities may choose to direct resources towards minimising legitimacy- and knowledge-dependent threats (e.g. quarantining expatriates in gated compounds) or to seek to make attitudes of HCNs more favourable by, for instance, promoting the ways in which their operations benefit host institutional fields. Importantly, the framework makes clear that a one-size-fits-all solution to expatriate safety and security may not work. Rather, organisations must understand, and take advantage of, the various institutions emanating from the sector, professions and host countries in which their activities exist. Our findings therefore challenge the wisdom–from our experience common in the mainstream business community - of relying entirely on outsourced service providers to manage expatriates' safety and security via off-the-shelf solutions.

The framework also provides a template for understanding the complexity of legitimacy-seeking practices used by internationally active organisations when it comes to expatriate safety and security. Of pertinence is the need for these organisations to juggle legitimacy demands from geographically and culturally diverse groups of stakeholders (Kostova et al., 2008), all of which may differ in their interests in expatriate safety and security and perceptions about the organisation's externalities. We found tensions emerging in organisations from all three sectors that may be reflective of this. The IAD sector, for instance, faces pressure from some donors for a more hardened 'protection' approach to security (van Brabant, 2001) that is at odds with, and would likely undermine, the acceptance approach that underpinned the organisations' shared philosophy (Fast, 2014). We also heard accounts from informants in news media organisations about resistance of more experienced foreign correspondents to change emerging from the top (following crises like those of 11 September 2001). Such patterns appear consistent with isomorphic resistance that has been documented by institutional theorists (Ramanath, 2008). Competing demands like these may be explained as contrasting perceptions among stakeholders about the nature of the threat stemming from the organisations' externalities. Such differences of perspective highlight the need for organisations to collect evidence about how their operations are perceived by host institutional actors, an information activity that currently none of the organisations in our study undertake with any vigour. At a minimum, devising an appropriate expatriate safety and security approach requires organisations to be cognisant of how their operations are viewed by, and interdependent with, salient host institution actors. In turn, we suggest that this necessitates a base level of in-house expertise in host-culture awareness, perception monitoring, perception management and/or symbolic image building by associating with other bodies that have higher levels of legitimacy (Kostova et al., 2008).

From this platform, Tables 2 and 3 plus Figure 1 indicate areas where organisations – and HR departments in particular – might focus efforts to develop greater awareness and expertise, and consequently play a more prominent role in supporting expatriate safety and security. The results may also assist organisations to diagnose strengths and weaknesses, or to meld key crisis management operations with broader strategic objectives. In a similar vein, our results hint at opportunities for across-the-board improvements by increasing cross-sector knowledge and resource sharing. International HR managers may be well positioned (Welch & Welch, 2012) to instigate discussions with counterparts from different sectors about the possibility of formal or informal exchange of information, resources, policies, or programs (e.g. training modules) as a means of cross-fertilising knowledge and achieving economies of scale.

Limitations and future research

Like all studies, the research we report here has limitations that constrain the transferability of the results, most notably the need for deductive verification of our propositions. Beyond this, broadening the range of sample organisations and operating environments will enable more nuance regarding the features we have unveiled. In particular, expanding empirical investigations to encompass additional sectors–including others that operate in hostile locations (e.g. government diplomatic corps)–may lead to more thorough typologies of industry responses that build on the work reported here. Similarly, while we actively sought interviewees able to provide diverse perspectives, research that includes informants with other experiences (e.g. pre-departure expatriates, external government stakeholders, specialist service providers, host-country community members) is worthwhile. Moreover, while the parent countries of our case study organisations were varied, all were based in developed nations from the 'Global North'. Thus, studies that investigate the practices of internationally active organisations from developing countries, where similarities between home and host institutional environments may be stronger, might unearth new insight.

Beyond the sample, our theoretical lens for this study (institutional theory) led our analysis to focus on external factors. New understanding into how and why expatriate safety and security practices are configured the way they are is likely to emerge from a range of alternative, equally valid, perspectives. On this issue, we make a final observation. Our focus for this special issue article was on *hostile environments*, and how the various institutional forces influence the HR practices of internationally active organisations. However, it is pertinent that the operations of internationally active organisations themselves are not always neutral and may, in fact, create environmental risks. That is, through their operations, practices and attitudes, organisations may introduce threats to otherwise benign institutional environments that create or exacerbate hostility for local communities (Baram, 2009). This may be especially true of economically, socially and politically fragile contexts, susceptible to the introduction of activities that pose physical, environmental, political, and/or social hazards (e.g. activities that disrupt biological equilibrium, challenge the political status quo, or reflect different cultural values). In this regard, the practice of internationally active organisations in *enacting* hostile environments, while not addressed here, is worthy of further investigation.

Disclosure statement

No potential conflict of interest was reported by the authors.

References

Bader, B. (2014). The influence of terrorism on expatriate performance: A conceptual approach. *The International Journal of Human Resource Management, 25*, 539.

Bader, B., & Berg, N. (2013). An empirical investigation of terrorism-induced stress on expatriate attitudes and performance. *Journal of International Management, 19*, 163–175.

Bader, B., & Schuster, T. (2015). Expatriate social networks in terrorism-endangered countries: An empirical analysis in Afghanistan, India, Pakistan, and Saudi Arabia. *Journal of International Management, 21*, 63–77.

Baram, M. (2009). Globalization and workplace hazards in developing nations. *Safety Science, 47*, 756–766.

Bernstein, J. (2011). *Manager's guide to crisis management*. New York, NY: McGraw-Hill.

Bjerkan, A. M. (2010). Health, environment, safety culture and climate—analysing the relationships to occupational accidents. *Journal of Risk Research, 13*, 445–477.

van Brabant, K. (2001). *Mainstreaming the organisational management of safety and security: Humanitarian policy group report 9*. London: Overseas Development Institute.

Chien, G. C. L., & Law, R. (2003). The impact of the severe acute respiratory syndrome on hotels: A case study of Hong Kong. *International Journal of Hospitality Management, 22*, 327–332.

Clark, K., & Lengnick-Hall, M. L. (2012). MNC practice transfer: institutional theory, strategic opportunities and subsidiary HR configuration. *The International Journal of Human Resource Management, 23*, 3813–3837.

Claus, L. (2009). *Duty of care of employers for protecting international assignees, their dependents, and international business travelers*. Philadelphia, PA: International SOS.

Claus, L. (2010, February). *International assignees at risk: Employers have a duty of care for workers around the globe*. Alexandria: HR Magazine.

Claus, L. (2011). *Duty of care and travel risk management: Global benchmarking study*. Philadelphia, PA: International SOS.

Claus, L., & Giordano, E. (2013). Global employer duty of care: Protecting the health, safety, security and well-being of employees crossing borders. In L. Claus (Ed.), *Global HR practitioner handbook* (pp. 3813–299). Portland, ME: Global Immersion Press

Cornwall, A., & Brock, K. (2005). What do buzzwords do for development policy? A critical look at 'participation', 'empowerment' and 'poverty reduction. *Third World Quarterly, 26*, 1043–1060.

Crandall, W., Parnell, J. A., & Spillan, J. E. (2010). *Crisis management in the new strategy landscape*. Thousand Oaks, CA: Sage.

Cuddihy, M. (2016, June 23). *Australian workers at engineering giant Macmahon kidnapped in Nigeria*. Ultimo: Australian Broadcasting Corporation. Retrieved from http://www.abc.net.au/news/2016-06-23/australian-south-african-mining-workers-kidnapped-in-nigeria/7535308

Czinkota, M. R., Knight, G., Liesch, P. W., & Steen, J. (2010). Terrorism and international business: A research agenda. *Journal of International Business Studies, 41*, 826–843.

Deephouse, D. L. (1996). Does isomorphism legitimate? (includes appendices). *Academy of Management Journal, 39*, 1024–1039.

DiMaggio, P., & Powell, W. W. (1983). The iron cage revisited: Institutional isomorphism and collective rationality in organizational fields. *American Sociological Review, 48*, 147–160.

Donaldson, L. (2001). *The contingency theory of organizations*. Thousand Oaks, CA: SAGE.

Dul, J., & Hak, T. (2008). *Case study methodology in business research*. Burlington, MA: Butterworth-Heinemann.

Edmondson, A. C., & Mcmanus, S. E. (2007). Methodological fit in management and research field. *Academy of Management Review, 32*, 1155–1179.

Farndale, E., & Paauwe, J. (2007). Uncovering competitive and institutional drivers of HRM practices in multinational corporations. *Human Resource Management Journal, 17*, 355–375.

Farquhar, J. D. (2012). *Case study research for business*. Thousand Oaks, CA: SAGE.

Fast, L. (2014). *Aid in danger: The perils and promise of humanitarianism*. Philadelphia, PA: University of Pennsylvania Press.

Fee, A., & McGrath-Champ, S. (2016). The role of human resources in protecting expatriates: Insights from the international aid and development sector. *The International Journal of Human Resource Management*, 1–26, doi:10.1080/09585192.2015.1137617.

Fee, A., McGrath-Champ, S., & Liu, H. (2013). Human resources and expatriate evacuation: A conceptual model. *Journal of Global Mobility, 1*, 246–263.

Feinstein, A. (2006). *Journalists under fire: The psychological hazards of covering war*. Baltimore, MD: The John Hopkins University Press.

Ferner, A. (1997). Country of origin effects and HRM in multinational companies. *Human Resource Management Journal, 7*, 19–37.

Furnari, S. (2016). Institutional fields as linked arenas: Inter-field resource dependence, institutional work and institutional change. *Human Relations, 69*, 551–580.

Garud, R., Hardy, C., & Maguire, S. (2007). Institutional entrepreneurship as embedded agency: An introduction to the special issue. *Organization Studies, 28*, 957–969.

Gerring, J. (2007). *Case study research: Principles and practices*. Cambridge: Cambridge University Press.

Gherardi, S. (2006). *Organizational knowledge: The texture of workplace learning*. London: Blackwell.

Gherardi, S., & Nicolini, D. (2000). The organizational learning of safety in communities of practice. *Journal of Management Inquiry, 9*, 7–18.

Gooderham, P. N., Nordhaug, O., & Ringdal, K. (1999). Institutional and rational determinants of organizational practices: Human resource management in European firms. *Administrative Science Quarterly, 44*, 507–531.

Greenwood, R., Oliver, C., Sahlin, K., & Suddaby, R. (Eds.). (2012). *Institutional theory in organization studies*. London: SAGE.

Harvey, M. G. (1993). A survey of corporate programs for managing terrorist threats. *Journal of International Business Studies, 24*, 465–478.

Howard, P. D. (1991). Circle of impact: HR professionals respond to war, riot, terrorism. *Employment Relations Today, 18*, 29–38.

Institute for Economics and Peace. (2014). *Global terrorism index: Measuring and understanding the impact of terrorism*. Retrieved from http://static.visionofhumanity.org/sites/default/files/Global%20Terrorism%20Index%20Report%202014.pdf

Kostova, T., Roth, K., & Dacin, M. T. (2008). Institutional theory in the study of multinational corporations: A critique and new directions. *Academy of Management Review, 33*, 994–1006.

Kostova, T., & Zaheer, S. (1999). Organizational legitimacy under conditions of complexity: The case of the multinational enterprise. *Academy of Management Review, 24*, 64–81.

Kulik, C. T., & Bainbridge, T. J. (2006). HR and the line: The distribution of HR activities in Australian organizations. *Asia Pacific Journal of Human Resources, 47*, 541–558.

Lepoutre, J. M., & Valente, M. (2012). Fools breaking out: The role of symbolic and material immunity in explaining institutional nonconformity. *Academy of Management Journal, 55*, 285–313.

Lindøe, P. H., Engen, O. A., & Olsen, O. E. (2011). Responses to accidents in different industrial sectors. *Safety Science, 49*, 90–97.

Maguire, S., & Hardy, C. (2009). Discourse and deinstitutionalization: The decline of DDT. *Academy of Management Journal, 52*, 148–178.

McPhail, R., & McNulty, Y. (2015). 'Oh, the places you won't go as an LGBT expat!' A study of HRM's duty of care to lesbian, gay, bisexual and transgender expatriates in dangerous locations. *European Journal of International Management, 9*, 737–765.

Newenham-Kahindi, A. M. (2011). A global mining corporation and local communities in the Lake Victoria zone: The case of barrick gold multinational in Tanzania. *Journal of Business Ethics, 99*, 253–282.

O'Faircheallaigh, C. (2013). Community development agreements in the mining industry: An emerging global phenomenon. *Community Development, 44*, 222–238.

Orton, J. D., & Weick, K. E. (1990). Loosely coupled systems: A reconceptualization. *The Academy of Management Review, 15*, 203–223.

Perrow, C. (2011). *Normal accidents: Living with high risk technologies*. Princeton, NJ: Princeton University Press.

Ramanath, R. (2008). Limits to institutional isomorphism: Examining internal processes in NGO–government interactions. *Nonprofit and Voluntary Sector Quarterly, 38*, 51–76.

Raphael, B. (1986). *When disaster strikes: A handbook for the caring profession.* London: Unwin Hyman.

Rosenzweig, P. M., & Nohria, N. (1994). Influences on human resource management practices in multinational corporations. *Journal of International Business Studies, 25*, 229–251.

Scott, W. R. (1995). *Institutions and organizations.* Thousand Oaks, CA: SAGE.

Seale, C. (1999). *The quality of qualitative research.* London: SAGE.

Smets, M., & Jarzabkowski, P. (2013). Reconstructing institutional complexity in practice: A relational model of institutional work and complexity. *Human Relations, 66*, 1279–1309.

Suchman, M. C. (1995). Managing legitimacy: Strategic and institutional approaches. *Academy of Management Review, 20*, 571–610.

von Krogh, G., Rossi-Lamastra, C., & Haefliger, S. (2012). Phenomenon-based research in management and organization science: When is it rigorous and does it matter? *Long Range Planning, 45*, 277–298.

Watson, G. W. (2005). Dimensions of interpersonal relationships and safety in the steel industry. *Journal of Business and Psychology, 19*, 303–318.

Welch, C. L., & Welch, D. E. (2012). What do HR managers really do? HR roles on international projects. *Management International Review, 52*, 597–617.

Wenger, E. (2000). Communities of practice and social learning systems. *Organization, 7*, 225–246.

Westney, D. E. (1993). Institutionalization theory and the multinational corporation. In S. Ghoshal, & D. E. Westney (Eds.), *Organization theory and the multinational corporation* (pp. 47–67). Basingstoke: Palgrave.

Yin, R. K. (2003). *Case study research: Design and methods* (3rd ed.). Thousand Oaks, CA: SAGE.

Zhang, M. M., McNeil, N., Bartram, T., Dowling, P., Cavanagh, J., Halteh, P., & Bonias, D. (2016). Examining the 'black box' of human resource management in MNEs in China: Exploring country of origin effects. *The International Journal of Human Resource Management, 27*, 832–849.

In the line of fire: managing expatriates in hostile environments

Judie Gannon and Alexandros Paraskevas

ABSTRACT
This study explores best practice in the preparation and protection of strategic HRs deployed by Multinational corporations (MNCs) in hostile environments. By building on the literature from the areas of strategic and IHRM, expatriation, as well as risk and crisis management, the limitations and gaps of the extant research are highlighted. This provides a foundation for our investigation through a series of in-depth interviews with corporate executives, and insurers and relocation specialists with professional expertise in protecting and supporting HRs. This represents the first time such a detailed picture of the partnerships between MNCs and the specialists, required to deliver preparation and protection in hostile environments, has been depicted in the IHRM literature. The findings identify the challenges MNCs face when protecting their HRs and highlights the importance of specialist expertise, knowledge, and management. A framework for managing HRs within international hostile environments is subsequently developed offering an opportunity to systematically consider some of the ethical and strategic issues associated with the contemporary challenges of international mobility.

Introduction

Multinational corporations (MNCs) typically coordinate and control their international operations through the varied use of expatriates, inpatriates, and traveling executives (Edström & Galbraith, 1977; Harzing, 2002; Welch, Steen, & Tahvanainen, 2009). The IHRM literature has explored in depth the deployment and development of these strategic HRs and acknowledged the range of practices used by organizations to select, train, develop, reward, and support these managers (Dabic, González-Loureiro, & Harvey, 2015). There is recognition in this literature of an increased level of complexity in the supporting practices considered as part of IHRM, where issues beyond the workplace become part of HRM provisions for international staff, for example, in terms of housing, schooling, and wider total reward concerns (Baruch, Dickmann, Altman, & Bournois, 2013; Brewster, Bonache, Cerdin, & Suutari, 2014; Dabic et al., 2015). Significantly less research has been conducted on the HRM support and practices developed when the deployment of strategic HRs takes place in hostile (i.e. politically and socially unstable, violent) environments (Fee & McGrath-Champ, 2016; Harvey, 1993). Where there has been research on people management in hostile environments there is a tendency to focus on individual managers' experiences and their perspectives of the treatment and support they receive and their concerns associated with their locations. This emphasis on the individual managerial standpoint has been at the expense of the organizational assessment of the challenges and practices of managing employees in hostile environments (Fee, McGrath-Champ, & Liu, 2013; Harvey, 1993; Ramirez, Madero, & Muñiz, 2015; Wernick & Von Glinow, 2012).

There is then a specific gap in knowledge regarding corporate HR executives' views on the specific risks their assignees face in hostile environments and the support and arrangements required for international managers operating in such challenging locations. While the literature abounds with evidence of environmental and organizational factors which influence the use of local or international managerial resources (Chang, Gong, & Peng, 2012; Edström & Galbraith, 1977), there is limited evidence of how hostile environments shape such appointment decisions (Bader et al., 2015). As such, the aim of this study is to explore the awareness of the risks, and the approaches taken to support managerial resources operating in hostile environments from the perspective of corporate executives. We do this by first examining the specific nature of the risks which organizations' managers are exposed to when deployed in hostile environments, and then by scrutinizing the specific practices and actions for the support and protection of these strategic HRs during different stages of expatriation. Many of these practices, such as extended duty of care, assisted relocation, personal self-defense, hibernation, and evacuation, have received minimal attention in the existing literature (Fee & McGrath-Champ, 2016; Fee et al., 2013) and little is known about their development, utilization, and review in international organizations operating in hostile environments. Yet, these organizations are continuously called to deal with challenges and threats to their deployed HRs (Fox-Koob, 2016; Fuller, 2015; MND, 2016) which require rigorously planned responses based on clear and detailed policies and standards.

In addition, existing research fails to examine whether companies differentiate the risks and the practices deployed between specific groups of strategic HRs or adopt blanket approaches which cover the mobility of all managers. For example, while traveling executives (frequent flyers) and expatriates may be exposed to similar risks in hostile locations, and will both typically lack local knowledge, the intensity of the risks and comprehensiveness of support required may differ where frequent flyers are temporarily located and do not develop identifiable routines that increase their risk exposure. By building upon the expatriate cycle (Bianchi, 2015; Bonache, Brewster, & Suutari, 2001) and the model developed by Fee and McGrath-Champ (2016), and by further addressing the limited coverage of organizational perspectives on the risks and support practices provided to international managers operating in hostile environments, this article provides new evidence on the expanding remit of corporate HRs and the know-how they seek from specialists with risk, security, and insurance expertise. We also advance Fee and McGrath-Champ's (2016) conceptualization by investigating the international hotel industry, which depends on extensive mobility among its managers at both the corporate and operational levels (Gannon, Roper, & Doherty, 2010) to deliver its global services. This sector offers a compelling focus due to its role in suggesting safe havens for international executives in hostile environments (Paraskevas, 2013; Wernick & Von Glinow, 2012). New implications and contributions emerge for HRM executives and academic researchers considering the findings and framework developed.

At the outset, this article explores the literature on the approaches taken to managing key HRs before evaluating what is meant by hostile environments. The existing literature on managing people in crisis/hostile environments is then appraised. The setting in which this study takes place, the international hotel industry, is subsequently described. The research design is outlined together with a rationale for the in-depth interview method deployed with international hotel company executives, insurance brokers, and security relocation consultants. The findings from the interviews are analyzed in relation to the extant research on the practices deployed to protect HRs operating across international hostile environments. This paper proposes a comprehensive framework for the preparation, support, and protection of HRs when deployed in such environments. Finally, a discussion of the main contributions and limitations of this study as well as the theoretical and research implications, conclude this article.

Literature review

Managing international HRs

This domain of research has adapted its focus over the years depending upon the challenges and issues facing organizations (Dabic et al., 2015; Harvey & Moeller, 2009); however, international subsidiary managers have typically been identified as the linchpins in successful MNCs where they coordinate, control, and sustain organizations' interests and augment the transfer of knowledge across national boundaries (Chang et al., 2012; Welch et al., 2009). While the literature has focused on expatriates and their management, researchers (Baruch et al., 2013; Elango, Graf, & Hemmasi, 2007) have also deployed the term 'expatriate' in the broadest sense to embrace 'the full range of international assignees, international business travelers and their dependents' (Fee et al., 2013, p. 247). This encompassing conception of the term expatriate is also often associated with the 'strategic human resources' label used by some commentators (Boxall & Purcell, 2011; Marchington, 2015). Such HRs arguably allow firms to capitalize on their proprietary knowledge and transfer it effectively across their operations to achieve competitive advantage (Boxall & Purcell, 2011). However, there are problems with this interpretation of strategic HRs as there is little differentiation between whether they are talented, aspiring subsidiary managers, experienced regional cluster managers, or senior executives representing the organization overseas. This absence of clarity in the literature referring to expatriates is captured eloquently by McNulty and Brewster (2016a, 2016b) who evaluate the confusion and complexity of the term, to provide consistency and coherency to empirical investigations. They recognize the growing myriad of terms, depending on various criteria applied such as, length of stay, (flexpatriates, business travelers, frequent flyers), cultural and national origins (inpatriates or expatriates of host country origin (EHCOs)), to organizational versus self-assignment (company assigned or self-initiated expatriates) and highlight why terminology matters but is equally challenging to accomplish (McNulty & Brewster, 2016a, 2016b). How companies differentiate in their management of these different forms of the wider term 'expatriate' is unclear, and ripe for further investigation (Dabic et al., 2015; McNulty & De Cieri, 2011). As such, there is no empirical evidence of whether there is any variation in terms of the strategic value of some 'strategic human resources' or how the practices and support, protecting these HRs operating in hostile environments, may differ.

What constitutes a hostile environment?

Within the expatriation literature, there has been long-term recognition of hardship locations which provide international assignees with significant challenges for their working and personal lives (Bader, 2015; Harvey & Moeller, 2009). These hardship factors have often been associated with remoteness, adverse conditions, limited facilities, extensive cultural differences, political instability, and developing economies (Fee & McGrath-Champ, 2016; Suutari & Brewster, 1999). To this list 'countries or regions that suffer from terrorism, severe crime or other forms of violence' (Bader, Berg, & Holtbrügge, 2015a, p. 1) can be added.

Hostile environments have more recently become strongly associated with terrorism; which is problematic to characterize (Glazzard & Pantucci, 2015). Williams' (2004, p. 7) definition suggests terrorism can be understood as 'politically [including ideologically, religiously or socially – but not criminally] motivated violence, directed generally against non-combatants, intended to shock and terrify, to achieve a strategic outcome'. However, there are challenges to differentiating between terrorism and criminal activity across the different sides of political, social, economic, and religious divides (Institute of Economics & Peace, 2015). A quandary for MNCs and managers is that while the threat of terrorism may appear to be higher in specific locations, international assignees are still more likely to be victims of violent crime (Elango et al., 2007; Institute of Economics & Peace, 2015). Accordingly, there is a growing focus on the implications of living, and managing businesses, in environments where hostility (violent crime and terrorism) is seen as a contemporary fact of life (Bader, Berg & Holtbrügge, 2015a; Fee et al., 2013; Fee & McGrath-Champ, 2016; McNulty & De Cieri, 2011; Ramirez et al., 2015).

IHRM in hostile environments

Several factors, including the extent of national and international business travel (Elango et al., 2007; Kraimer, Takeuchi, & Frese, 2014; Welch, Welch, & Worm, 2007), increasing variety in length and type of work assignments (Baruch et al., 2013), growing numbers of, and variations in, subsidiary ownership (Slangen & Van Tulder, 2009), further attention on risk factors and concerns over crisis management and business continuity (Czinkota, Knight, Liesch, & Steen, 2010), have seen HRM professionals extend their expertise in the related areas of health, safety, and security (Mankin & Perry, 2004). After Harvey's (1993) seminal article, there was an absence of research in this area until the early 2000s with the resurgence in interest apparently prompted by the events of 9/11 (Howie, 2007; Mankin & Perry, 2004). There is also evidence of a clear split between conceptual articles and those based upon empirical investigations. Conceptual articles typically involve the use of versions of risk or crisis management models (Fee et al., 2013; Liou & Lin, 2008; Wang, Hutchins, & Garavan, 2009), in relation to specific HRM practices and approaches.

These models are akin to the cycles of expatriation and repatriation as advocated by various authors (Bianchi, 2015; Bonache et al., 2001; Brewster et al., 2014; Harvey, 1982) with their phases of expatriation planning, pre-expatriation, expatriation, and repatriation. These four phases focus upon different aspects of managing those on international assignments. In the initial planning stage, attention is centered on analysis by determining the nature of the assignment in relation to the organization and the location and selecting assignees (Bianchi, 2015; Dabic et al., 2015). The second stage, pre-expatriation involves an emphasis on preparation through awareness raising, communication of assignee objectives and performance criteria, language and location training for the assignee and their families (Bianchi, 2015; Bonache et al., 2001). The expatriation or during assignment phase concentrates on issues of engagement on the assignment via expatriation performance and compensation, and offering sufficient support to the assignee and their families to pre-empt any shock or early return issues (Bianchi, 2015; Bonache et al., 2001). This third phase will also ideally involve planning for repatriation building on the experiences gained through the assignment. The final phase of repatriation or re-entry focuses on managing re-adjustment, family re-orientation, organizational updates for the assignee, and career management for future international and domestic roles (Bianchi, 2015; Bonache et al., 2001).

These four phases of the expatriate cycle can be seen to mimic the models often adopted by organizations operating in uncertain or adverse political, economic, and social conditions (Salter, 1997; Smith, 1990). For example, the risk management model known as PPRR: prevent, prepare, respond, and recover (Salter, 1997) offers four stages. The two Ps (prevent and prepare) concern those activities and support provided by the organization in the pre-crisis stage of a potential incident's life cycle whereas the two Rs (respond and recover) concern the other two stages, respectively, i.e. during and post-crisis (Fee et al., 2013; Sawalha, Jraisat, & Al-Qudah, 2013). In the context of relocation to a hostile environment, the pre-crisis stage would refer to the time before the actual expatriation (pre-expatriation) but also the period in expatriation without an incident. Consequently, the 'during crisis' period refers to expatriation disrupted by a crisis event and the response to it; and the post-crisis refers to the resolution of the crisis that would entail repatriation, recovery, evaluation, and possibly planning for re-expatriation in the same or other location, thus feeding into a new pre-expatriation period. These staged models of expatriation and crisis management offer useful possible routes to further understanding of the process of managing international HRs (Figure 1).

Several empirical studies focus on specific national contexts as part of their investigations of hostile environments, for example, Papua New Guinea (Bhanugopan & Fish, 2008); Sri Lanka (Reade & Lee, 2012); Mexico (Ramirez et al., 2015) and Afghanistan, India, Pakistan, and Saudi Arabia which were identified as terrorism endangered countries (Bader & Schuster, 2015). Further scrutiny of the extant literature identifies the paucity of researchers undertaking empirical studies from the organizational perspective (Fee et al., 2016; Harvey, 1993; Ramirez et al., 2015; Wernick & Von Glinow, 2012). Instead, there is a profusion of quantitative studies engaging with individual

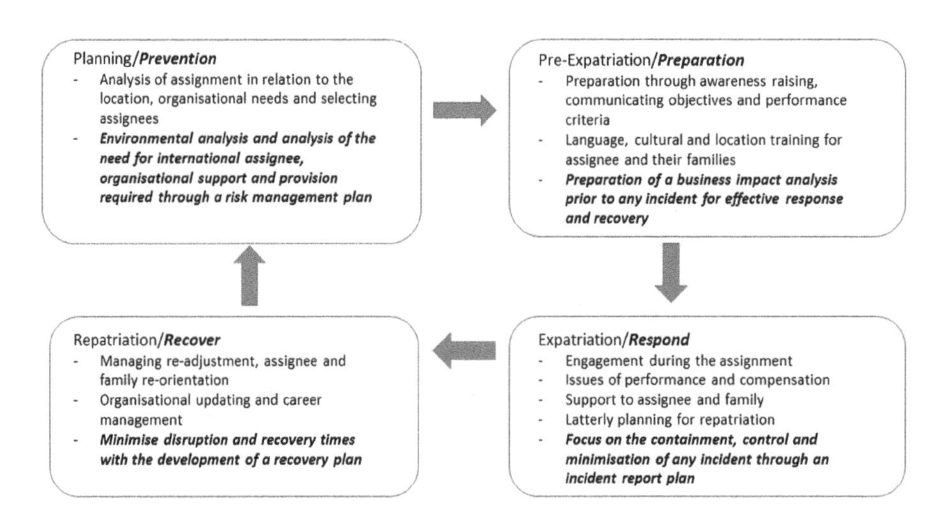

Figure 1. The expatriate cycle with risk management considerations. Source: (adapted from Harvey (1982), Bianchi (2015) and Salter (1997))

expatriates' experiences of being managed in hostile environments (Bader, 2015; Bader, Berg, & Holtbrügge, 2013; Bader & Schuster, 2015; Bader et al., 2015; Bhanugopan & Fish, 2008; Reade & Lee, 2012). Key implications for organizations arise from these studies of individual expatriates' responses to people management practices in hostile environments, which include the perceived value of; organizational support, protection, and assistance programs for expatriates (Bader, Berg, & Holtbrügge, 2013; Reade & Lee, 2012) and their families (Bader, Berg & Holtbrügge, 2013; Bader et al., 2015), the merits of awareness, crisis, and evacuation training (Bader, Berg & Holtbrügge, 2013) and organizational interventions developing social networks with colleagues and engagement with locals (Bader & Schuster, 2015).

Of those studies adopting an organizational stance, Harvey's (1993) investigation provides insights on the corporate mindset for managing terrorism threats highlighting that the key concerns for those MNCs which did have programs were the protection of assets, investments in security to limit threats, and the training of executives. The investigation of domestic and international firms (Danish, Brazilian and US MNCs) operating in Mexico and the impact of this narco-terrorism environment on the HRM practices and approaches focus on the firm rather than the corporate level (Ramirez et al., 2015). It exposes the direct and indirect impact which this hostile national setting has on HRM practices and how employees at different levels, locals through to expatriates, are supported and protected, physically and emotionally. The authors also comment on the importance of the companies' adherence to managing the 'balance between stability and flexibility', in relation to the dilemmas of SHRM, in such an environment (Ramirez et al., 2015, p. 22).

Using the resource-based view (RBV) approach alongside theories of the psychological contract and duty of care, Fee et al. (2013) developed a conceptual model focused on crisis management and the evacuation of expatriates, highlighting the value of integrating training for high risk locations into wider talent management practices in international organizations. Developing their original model, Fee and McGrath-Champ (2016, p. 7) interviewed relevant HRM specialists on their approach to managing the "safety and security of their expatriates" as well as scrutinizing relevant policy documentation. Their groundbreaking work provides crucial insights into the extensiveness and range of HRM policies and practices which protect expatriate aid workers, and go beyond the measures typically instigated by other international corporate entities. They suggest three service areas and the overall organizational culture (strategy, philosophy and policies about safety and security) which capture the HRM remit. The service areas are People services (screenings, training housing and employee well-being), Communication services (internal and external networks and locating and communicating with staff), and Information services (data collection and monitoring, evaluating and organizational learning). Fee and McGrath-Champ (2016) also attest to the pressures to adopt a hardened or 'protection' approach to managing these valued workers while simultaneously experiencing demands to embrace an 'acceptance' approach. An 'acceptance' strategy tries to reduce or remove threats by increasing the acceptance (the political and social 'consent') for an organization's presence and work in a location (politicians and the military call this 'winning hearts and minds'). A 'protection' strategy uses protective devices and procedures to reduce the vulnerability of the agency, but it does not address the threat. In technical jargon, this is called 'hardening the target' (Childs, 2013; Van Brabant, 2000). The authors also draw parallels between this 'acceptance' and 'protection' predicament and those faced by HRM when resolving the coinciding demands "for local responsiveness and global integration" associated with managing international HRs (Fee & McGrath-Champ, 2016, p.21).

Each of the studies adopting an organizational (corporate or firm level) perspective, when studying hostile environments, remarks upon the challenges of gaining access and winning the confidence of managerial representatives to ensure participation in their research (Fee & McGrath-Champ, 2016; Harvey, 1993; Ramirez et al., 2015). This underscores the importance of studies with an organizational focus in this area of IHRM where opportunities to gain access and further understanding are limited. The extant literature emphasizes that while several studies have concentrated on the views of individual expatriates (Bader, 2015; Bader et al., 2015b; Bhanugopan & Fish, 2008; Reade & Lee, 2012) there has been more limited evidence of researchers adopting organizational level interpretations (Fee & McGrath-Champ, 2016; Harvey, 1993; Ramirez et al., 2015). This article specifically sets out to address the gap in our understanding of the organizational perspective by exploring corporate HR and risk and security executives' views on the support and practices provided to international hotel managers operating in hostile environments. The research also provides additional knowledge of the support corporate executives access through specialist advisors, from the world of risk and security, insurance brokers and relocation specialists, to protect these HRs.

The international hotel industry and management of its international managers

The international hotel industry provides a valuable setting for a study of this nature due to its global reach, complex ownership structures, and the people intensive nature of its core services (Gannon, Roper, & Doherty, 2015; Gannon et al., 2010; Melissen, van Ginneken, & Wood, 2016). At the global level the largest hotel corporations have thousands of properties, stretching across more than 100 countries and employing more than 150,000 employees (Gannon et al., 2015; ILO, 2010). Such extensive portfolios are achieved via asset light market entry modes where ownership of a hotel property is split from the operational responsibilities, typically through arrangements such as management contracts and franchise agreements, among other dealings (ILO, 2010; Melissen et al., 2016). Properties in hostile environments have increasingly become part of these expanding hotel portfolios presenting a dilemma for companies where operating in such locations can offer attractive, competitive, and political opportunities but also present significant operational and HR challenges (Gannon et al., 2015; Sawalha et al., 2013).

The asset light market entry modes adopted mean that local investors shoulder the financial burden and the Western hospitality services associated with these organizations offer refuge and recuperation for influential local residents and visiting politicians, media, and non-governmental agencies (Paraskevas, 2013; Sawalha et al., 2013). However, international brand names, which epitomize Western values and appear ostentatious compared to local services, may become targets for aggression (Wernick & Von Glinow, 2012). Furthermore, the clientele who patronize international hotel brands, and the international hotel managers who deliver their services may also be the victims of hostile behavior (Paraskevas, 2013; Sawalha et al., 2013). This dilemma is difficult to resolve where hotels are typically open public spaces, involve people intensive services delivery, have high levels of footfall, and are consequently cited as soft targets for aggression (Malik, Abdullah, & Uli, 2014; Paraskevas, 2013). Examples such as the attack on the Radisson Blu hotel in Bamako, Mali in November 2015 and other incidents in recent years (Fee et al., 2013; Wernick & Von Glinow, 2012) suggest that international hotel firms require comprehensive strategies and practices to prepare, support, and protect their HRs in such environments. However, the asset light expansion arrangements also have implications for people management practices where hotel level employees are normally employed by a firm representing the investor/owner but are managed by expatriates, who are employed by the parent MNC (Gannon et al., 2015; Hodari & Sturman, 2014; ILO, 2010). Such hotel managers are viewed as strategic HRs (Gannon et al., 2010, 2015). This suggests that for international hotel companies managing their HRs operating in hostile environments their focus is likely to be on those occupying, or destined for, managerial roles rather than those working at operative levels, who are the responsibility of the local investor/owner.

Research design

This study adopted a qualitative approach to explore MNCs' management of HRs deployed in hostile environments. Due to the recognized issues with gaining access to executives about these topics discussed previously, the authors used their own professional networks to invite participants from the global hotel sector. Initially, HRM executives from four of the largest international hotel companies were invited to participate. In the process of the study, it became apparent that the management of expatriates in hostile environments took place in collaboration with risk and internal security managers as well as external insurance brokers and relocation service providers. Therefore, a snowball sampling technique was used to expand our sample with the external experts these companies were engaging. We interviewed nine HRM and risk and security executives from four international hotel groups (respondents HE1 to HE9) to gather insights of the challenges faced and the HRM practices used to protect personnel in hostile environments. This group then introduced us to, and we interviewed, six insurers and brokers specializing in people risks (respondents IB1 to IB6) and three relocation service consultants (respondents RC1 to RC3) all of whom worked with the hotel companies (see Table 1 – Participants). The participating hotel companies account for approximately 38 percent of the total branded hotel market in terms of open rooms, and 65 percent of the development pipeline (hotels in planning and under construction but not yet open). These are also the international hotel companies that normally operate in environments characterized as 'hostile', driven there by their corporate clients. Smaller international hotel companies usually do not have the risk appetite to operate in such environments. The participating insurers/brokers were from the leading companies in people risk coverage representing over 50% of the relevant market share. Similarly, the three relocation service providers came from the leading companies in their sector.

The exploratory nature of the study led us to choose in-depth interviews as a data collection technique to secure the richest possible response from the specialists in this topic and to bracket any personal biases (Creswell, 2007). Participants were asked the question: 'Based on your experience, what would constitute best practice in preparing and protecting strategic human capital deployed internationally in hostile environments?' This type of interview was chosen to allow respondents to talk about what they see as important, an insight that could be compromised with a semi-structured interview. The respondents were encouraged to expand their answers in a non-leading manner by probing, 'Tell me more about this,' or, 'Can you give me an example of that?' In this way, we could gain a detailed understanding of the way the respondents made sense of their world and continued until we felt that the participants had nothing more to add. The interviews were conducted in UK, France, and the US either in person (face-to-face) or via Skype and lasted on average between one to one and a half hours (min. 48 minutes; max. 112 minutes; mean 82 minutes). Transcriptions were offered back to participants for member-checking, 'the most crucial technique for establishing credibility' in a study (Lincoln & Guba, 1985, p. 314).

The transcripts were analyzed thematically using the conventions of template analysis which involves the development of a coding 'template' which summarizes the themes and organizes them in a logical manner (King, 2004). The first criterion for the coding template development was temporal, i.e. the stage at which a particular service is provided by HRM to the expatriates. Following Fee et al. (2013), the original template involved three stages: pre-crisis; during the crisis; and post-crisis. In the process, however, it emerged that the codification should be done in four temporal stages: pre-expatriation, expatriation, crisis response (in expatriation), and crisis resolution (in expatriation or repatriation). The second criterion for the coding template development was the types of services provided by HRM, i.e. people services, information services, communication services, and the company's organizational culture as it is reflected by its HRM policy and

Table 1. Research participants.

Participant Code	Participant job role	Company's activity	No of hotels/employees	Reach
HE1	Head of HR in hotel operations	International hotel company A	>5000 hotels/	100+ countries
HE2	SVP global risk management	International hotel company A	>5000 hotels	100+ countries
HE3	Vice president global safety	International hotel company A	>5000 hotels	100+ countries
HE4	Director global security	International hotel company B	>500 hotels	50+ countries
HE5	Vice president human resources	International hotel company B	>500 hotels	50+ countries
HE6	Vice president human resources	International hotel company C	>5000 hotels	80+ countries
HE7	Director of security & safety	International hotel company C	>5000 hotels	80+ countries
HE8	Vice president human resources	International hotel company D	>2500 hotels	100+ countries
HE9	VP global security	International hotel company D	>2500 hotels	100+ countries
IB1	Client services director, major risks practice	Insurance broker	>20000 empl.	Global
IB2	Client executive	Insurance broker	>60,000 empl.	Global
IB3	Account executive	Insurance broker	>15,000 empl.	Global
IB4	Account executive; international liability	Insurance broker	>5000 empl	Global
IB5	Partner; credit, political & security risks team	Insurance broker	>10,000 empl.	Global
IB6	Casualty underwriter	Insurance broker	>30,000 empl.	Global
RC1	Relocation account manager	Relocation services	>2500 empl.	Global
RC2	Expatriate assignment consultant	Relocation services	>2500 empl	180+ countries
RC3	Senior global mobility consultant	Relocation services	>6000 empl.	170+ countries

standards as well as its risk and safety philosophy and strategy (Fee & McGrath-Champ, 2016). During the piloting of the interviews, the need for a fifth category emerged from the respondents' examples: the risks to which an international manager is exposed in a hostile environment. The transcripts were analyzed and coded by the authors separately, following the use of hierarchical coding (by temporal stage, by type of service and by detailed service offered). This enabled the interviews to be analyzed at different levels resulting in broader higher order codes describing the support offered whereas detailed lower order codes went deeper into the distinctions. The resulting coding did not show significant differences from one another. The reliability of the coding process was ensured with a test-retest reliability check, where the authors performed the same task for a second time, four weeks later. Inter-coder reliability was calculated to 83.5% which is higher than generally accepted as the norm for a good reliability test 80% (Hayes & Krippendorff, 2007).

Findings and discussion

The scrutiny and analyses of the interview data uncovered various issues that appear to offer important explanations of the approaches and practices involved in managing expatriates in hostile environments. Four areas emerge within this section centering on the themes of; an expanded understanding of hostile environments, minimizing the risk exposure of strategic HRs, the HRM practices associated with the temporal dimensions, and key service areas. Alongside the four key themes, the existing literature will be deliberated to further demonstrate the theoretical implications and emerging themes.

An expanded understanding of 'hostile environment'

From our first engagement in our fieldwork, it was apparent that corporate HR departments feel that they do not have all the knowledge and experience needed for managing the preparation and protection of expatriates deployed in hostile environments. They therefore develop 'specialist' knowledge networks internally with the risk and security departments and externally with relocation service providers who have unique destination expertise. In order to minimize both the expatriates' and the organization's risk exposure in such environments, they add to these networks the services of insurers or brokers, normally specialists in political insurance cover. These services may vary from simple asset insurance and medical/life policies to more complex services, such as staff evacuation, hostage negotiation, ransom/facilitation payments, hostage exfiltration and rehabilitation, alongside all relevant public and media relations activities and are often labeled as 'specialty products' (IB4, IB5). Although the levels of coverage vary depending on what services are included in the policy, policies against these risks are pretty much the same for all types of insured clients (IB4, IB5).

An immediate result of this expanded knowledge network is the much broader perception of what constitutes a 'hostile environment'. During the interviews, the participants identified several possible adverse incidents that expatriates could face in a hostile destination not all of which are discussed in the extant academic literature. To gain an insight of the risks that concern the participants, the researchers recorded the total number of mentions of these risks (Table 2).

As was expected the risks related with political instability (war/terrorism and civil disorder) were the ones mentioned the most and, notably by all participants. The fact that the interviews were conducted in a period, autumn/winter 2015, when terrorist attacks and political violence events were making headlines may be a contributing factor but also the literature (Elango et al., 2007; Ramirez et al., 2015; Reade & Lee, 2012) shows that perceptions of 'hostile environments' are mostly related with politically unstable locations.

Crime and theft, in general, are also a concern for the participants. However, there are particular risks associated with this category that are seen and, at times, are managed separately. One of these is the risk of kidnap. Interestingly, the word 'abduction' also came up in the interviews several times. An explanation that was given was that 'abduction' is normally referring to children of expatriates taken by deceit or forcibly whereas 'kidnap' involves adults taken by force. When prompted about possible support offered in such cases all executives were reluctant to respond, with some of them saying that this is a law enforcement matter. This reluctance may also be attributed to the special clauses that 'kidnap and ransom' insurance policies have forbidding open disclosure of such policies (Fink & Pingle, 2014; Lang, 2012).

Other risks identified in the study that could also be associated with criminal behavior were the wrongful detention and the extortion of expatriates, risks that are again not necessarily related with politically unstable and violent countries. Wrongful detention was associated with the expatriates' 'unlawful detention or imprisonment by the country's authorities or by an insurgent group' (IB3). Two hotel executives mentioned this risk because their hotel groups experienced this situation recently in Libya and Mali. Extortion is a risk which is not mentioned in the literature. This is probably attributed to the fact that this type of risk is covered by specific policies and is not so widely known or discussed.

> Often, we have cases where expatriate or even domestic personnel of multinationals are receiving payment demands by local criminals threatening to injure or kill them or a member of their family, cause damage to their properties, contaminate products, harm hotel guests, etc. These are difficult cases to verify and negotiate and our cover provides specialist consultants to assist in handling. (IB5)

The most accepted definition of 'hostile environment' by Bader et al (2015) talks about "terrorism, severe crime or other forms of violence" (p. 1). This study confirms this definition and shows that crime is even of more concern than terrorism and political instability, as it collectively received the most mentions (76 mentions collectively of crime, theft, kidnap, detention, extortion and cyber; and

Table 2. Risk exposure in hostile environments ($n = 18$ interviews).

Participant Code	War/terrorism/ civil disorder	Health & medical	Transport accidents	Natural disas-ters	Crime/theft	Kidnap/abduc-tion	Wrongful detention	Personal/Prop-erty extortion	Cyber extor-tion
HE1	4	3	3	2	2	0	0	0	0
HE2	2	3	0	4	1	1	0	0	0
HE3	5	0	2	3	2	3	0	0	0
HE4	3	2	2	3	3	2	0	0	0
HE5	2	3	4	2	1	0	0	0	0
HE6	2	3	3	2	1	1	1	0	0
HE7	1	2	2	2	2	2	0	0	0
HE8	4	3	3	3	2	1	0	0	0
HE9	5	2	3	2	2	2	1	0	0
IB1	2	3	4	2	2	3	3	2	2
IB2	4	3	1	2	2	2	1	0	2
IB3	1	2	3	0	3	1	1	3	0
IB4	4	2	3	2	1	1	1	1	1
IB5	5	1	2	0	2	2	2	1	0
IB6	2	2	1	3	2	0	0	0	0
RC1	2	3	2	2	2	0	0	0	0
RC2	2	3	0	0	1	0	0	0	0
RC3	4	2	3	0	1	1	0	0	0
Total mentions	54	42	38	34	32	22	10	7	5

54 mentions of war/terrorism/ civil disorder). However, our study revealed that there are many other risks, alongside the ones mentioned above, that also concern the participating organizations, such as health and medical, transport accidents, and natural disasters. As these risks are not necessarily related to politically unstable or high violence countries, the above definition of 'hostile environments' appears too narrow, especially for destinations that are vulnerable to such hazards as epidemics and natural disasters or with weak transport and other infrastructure and prone for transport accidents. As a result of our findings, we propose a new definition for a 'hostile environment' as;

> the work environment in a location where the organization's human resources and assets are exposed to severe, pervasive or persistent levels of risk originating from a variety of man-made or natural threats and hazards.

HRM services for expatriates in hostile environments

The practices shared by the respondents fall largely into the three types of services identified by Fee and McGrath-Champ (2016), namely information services, people services, and communication services. One further HRM activity that does not fall into these three categories is the development of policies and standards, which Fee and McGrath-Champ (2016) include under the label 'organizational culture'. However, there is also an important temporal dimension to these policies and standards which mean they sit alongside the three services, so that our findings indicate four areas, as opposed to the three identified elsewhere (Fee & McGrath-Champ, 2016; Fee et al., 2013) of managing HRs in hostile environments. Figure 2 outlines the temporal aspects as they emerged from the analysis of the interviews and how the stages of expatriation and crisis management coalesce.

HRM services for pre-expatriation planning (crisis prevention)

The support activities and types of services provided for expatriates' preparation for expatriation, shared by the participants in this and the next stage, broadly confirm features suggested in the extant literature (Fee & McGrath-Champ, 2016). It was also evident that this stage created the foundation for all the other phases and what was mentioned in this stage, across the four areas identified by our respondents, was then adapted to be relevant to the situation in subsequent stages.

Information services. Most participants emphasized as a first step here the need to make corporate decisions on the expansion of their activities in hostile environments based on in-depth intelligence gathering using expert professional sources, threat landscaping for risk identification, and risk assessment procedures (Czinkota et al., 2010; Ramirez et al., 2015). 'Moral obligation to the employees who will take the assignment' was unanimously mentioned and more times than any other reason (i.e. legal necessity, due diligence, and business sense) for

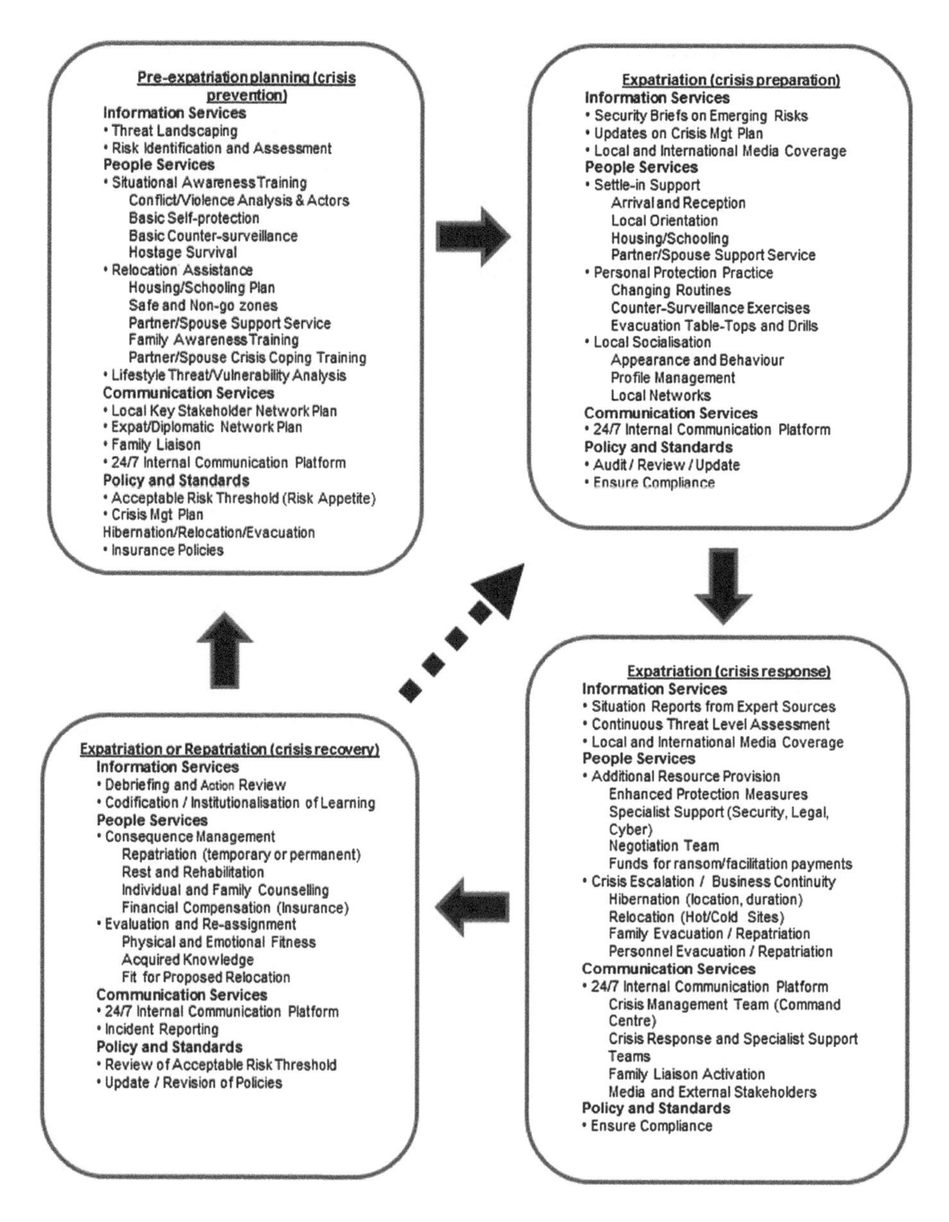

Figure 2. HRM services across expatriation stages.

collecting this information. Clearly, this is the information that will be fed into all other services at this stage and will determine the overall expatriation strategy.

People services. There was strong consensus that the information collected should provide the foundation for the assignee's pre-expatriation training (Fee et al., 2013; Wernick & Von Glinow, 2012). This training may range from a 'one-day briefing' (HE2, HE4 and RC3) on the political, social, and cultural issues of the destination, the associated risks, and possible mitigation strategies, to more sophisticated 'on-boarding' *training* (HE5, IB2, IB3, RC1) that would include a full analysis by expert advisors of the political violence and crime levels at the destination, the main actors involved, and basic self-protection practices to minimize risk exposure. According to some participants (IB5, RC1), depending on the severity of risk in a destination, this training may also include more sophisticated training on basic counter-surveillance and hostage survival practices (Bader, Berg & Holtbrügge, 2013; Fee et al., 2013). This level of training was mentioned only by one hotel company executive and only to express his skepticism:

> Having a military background myself, I am aware of more 'intense' survival training courses in the market. [...] These perhaps are useful for NGO workers on war-zone assignments or war correspondents not hotel managers! (laugh) [...] Participants in such courses know well that they will not be killed, and therefore do not get the experience that will prepare them for a real situation. These courses, in their less extreme commercial versions are, at their best, good team-builders. (HE7)

This view appears to be shared by the other hotel executives who, in their responses were happy with the assignees being able to '... understand the threat, understand the [terrorist/criminal] attack cycle and not becoming a target ...' (HE9).

Training aside, another service offered by HR departments (most often in collaboration with relocation service providers) is the assistance package for relocation in hostile environments. The practices shared were not significantly different from those reported (Elango et al., 2007; Harvey, 1993). It appears that in such assignments most companies (HE1, HE4, HE5) have tended to move away from the standard of a relocation lump sum to a more 'managed and controlled housing process' (HE4, RC2) where the relocation consultant is given a budget and arranges housing according to the organization's safety and security standards. Relocation consultants will also provide advice on 'safe' and 'non-go' zones in the destination. Some hotel company executives (HE5, HE9) also suggested that for their high-value human assets who may be more likely targets for kidnap and ransom situations, a 'life pattern threat and vulnerability analysis' (HE9) should be undertaken to identify vulnerabilities in their daily routines to develop the necessary risk mitigation strategies and practices (Fee et al., 2013; Ramirez et al., 2015). In the rarer cases where families relocate together additions to the standard family/spouse support packages (Bader et al., 2015), i.e. settling-in advice, career support and counseling, retraining, assistance to the trailing spouse in finding work and arranging childcare, were evident. Several participants (H7, H9, IB3, RC2) required 'family awareness training' [H9] i.e. a 'light' version of the assignee's on-boarding program, and if not relocated, the spouse/partner should undergo specific training to cope with possible crisis situations at a distance.

Communication services. Most hotel executives and all relocation consultants emphasized the need to carefully plan the development of social networks in the host country (H6 and RC1 consider this planning as an 'imperative pre-deployment [expatriation] activity') (Bader, 2015; Bader & Schuster, 2015; Reade & Lee, 2012). Although the understanding of these networks varied among the participants, they broadly suggested two types: (a) with the local expatriate and diplomatic community, mainly for intelligence sharing on safety and security matters but also for potential collaboration in emergency situations (Bader & Schuster, 2015); and (b) with local key stakeholders, primarily local authorities and law enforcement but also with all sides of religious and political actors (Bader, 2015; Ramirez et al., 2015). However, what is missing is the recognition that social networks organized by employers can be valuable in increasing perceived organizational support, where this is seen to tackle some of the results of the indirect impact of terrorism threats, namely organizational commitment, performance, and positive work attitudes (Bader, Berg & Holtbrügge, 2013; Bader & Schuster, 2015; Reade & Lee, 2012). Another type of contact rather than a network suggested by participants from all three groups (H1, H8, IB2, IB6 and RC3) was the 'family liaison' *aspect.* However, their views as to where this liaison should be located and what exactly their role would be were mixed and in some instances unclear, which broadly supports the work of Bader et al. (2015). The consensus was that this person should 'act as the company's designated contact person for the family' (H1) in case of emergency situations.

A relatively surprising finding was that the provision of an open communication platform between expatriates and the corporate offices was an element perhaps taken for granted by most respondents, and not mentioned at this stage, unless prompted. It emerged as a response in the crisis stage and the word 'platform' was underscored by most of them (HE3, HE5, HE6, HE8, IB1, IB3, RC1, RC2, RC3) meaning that a 'line' is not sufficient and multiple means of 24/7 communication are needed.

Policies and standards. Participants HE3, HE7, HE9, IB1, and IB5 suggested that the intelligence available for the hostile environments considered for expatriation should provide the foundation for the organization's 'acceptable risk threshold' (some used the term 'risk appetite'), i.e. amount and type of risk the organization is willing to take by expanding in and relocating HRs to a hostile environment (Driffield, Jones, & Crotty, 2013). The articulation of a clear risk appetite statement is the basis for the development of any expatriation strategy, the networks of partners that will support it, and the policies that will protect it. Another unanimously agreed element of the pre-expatriation support is the development of a detailed crisis management plan (Harvey, 1993; Mankin & Perry, 2004; Wang et al., 2009). The hotel executives with risk and security management roles (HE3, HE4, HE5, HE6, HE7, HE9) went into more detail than the other participants, indicating different levels of escalation for this plan but broadly agreeing that it should look at: 'hibernation' during a crisis situation which refers to sheltering the persons in place until the threat is over or further assistance is rendered; 'relocation' which is the withdrawal of HRs from a location to a safer one but normally within the same country; an 'evacuation' which is the withdrawal of HRs to another country. While the academic literature does mention evacuation (Bader et al., 2015; Fee et al., 2013; Wang et al., 2009) it does not mention hibernation. Most participants also emphasized that these plans need to be rehearsed and evaluated at least once in this (pre-expatriation) stage.

HRM services for expatriation (crisis preparation)

As identified in Figure 2, this stage involves building upon the previous stage covering aspects of pre-expatriation and expatriation notably, the settling-in of the deployed HRs, and the support they need to implement their 'acceptance' and 'protection' security strategies.

Information services. Participants from both the HE and RC participant groups also underscored the importance of continuous communication and intelligence flow between HR corporate departments and deployed expatriates on safety and security issues, new emerging risks, and possible updates or changes on agreed security procedures or crisis management plans, from either side. Depending on the strategic value of the deployed HRs, HE and IB participants recommend the monitoring of media coverage of the company and of the specific persons deployed both locally (at the hostile destination) and internationally. The information collected from this activity will facilitate the expatriate's 'profile management' (HE2, HE3, IB4, IB5) discussed later in this section.

People services. According to the participants, the HR support at this stage should focus on assisting the expatriate settle-in with clear 'arrival and reception processes' (HE3, RC1) (meeting points, contact persons, transport to accommodation) and 'local orientation' (HE1, RC2) which can range from a simple city tour to a more detailed orientation on dealing with authorities, banks, public services, and a reminder of safe and non-go zones. This orientation can be conducted by an experienced local member of staff or a relocation agent (Bader & Schuster, 2015; Briscoe & Schuler, 2004). Although most of the participants talked about the role of HR, at this stage, as facilitating the implementation of housing and schooling plans as well as ensuring the partner/spouse support plan developed in the previous stage, HE4 and HE9 placed increased emphasis on the need for the corporate HR department to adopt a rigorously structured approach for relocated staff in implementing the personal protection training they had received at the pre-expatriation stage:

> We need to ensure that they are changing regularly the routines that render them vulnerable to terrorists and criminals, that they practice basic counter-surveillance and that they test their evacuation plans. Complacency is not an option! (HE4)

Finally, there is a need for management (often based on new intelligence) of the expatriates' 'local socialization' (RC3) process. 'Appearance and behavior are crucial in hostile environments. The less attention one attracts the less chances of becoming a target they have' (HE7). Interestingly HE6, HE9, and RC2 also spoke about the avoidance of attracting, 'the "wrong" kind of attention'. Quite often, in order to achieve an appropriate level of community acceptance there is need for corporate HR departments to 'manage the public profile of an expat with the assistance of a PR [public relations] agency' (HE3). An important element of this local socialization is also the active development of the social networks with key local stakeholders as well as the expatriate and diplomatic communities (HE6, RC1, RC2, RC3).

Communication services. In common with the previous stage, the participants did not make any particular comment on communication but instead mentioned the use of pre-existing communication mechanisms to ensure robust and redundant internal communication systems between corporate headquarters and internationally deployed staff was in place.

Policy and standards. The actions associated with this particular stage focused upon the pre-expatriation knowledge and plans in place, so *audits* and *tests* for compliance (HE4, HE5, HE7) and periodic maintenance i.e. *periodic review* and *update* of policies (HE2, HE5) were ongoing.

HRM services for expatriation (crisis response)

This is the stage of expatriation where the expatriate is becoming to a large extent dependent on the support provided by the corporate HR department, which may vary according to the crisis situation (Wernick & Von Glinow, 2012). The security strategy at this stage shifts from 'partial acceptance' to 'full protection' but can go further. HE7, IB3, and IB5 identified examples in Iraq and Libya where severe threat levels and strategic HRs led to the change of the security strategy to 'deterrence' i.e. hardening the hotel and the security detail of the general manager with armed security guards (Childs, 2013; Van Brabant, 2000).

Information services. HE1 suggested that this is one of the most important functions of corporate HR in expatriation since as it becomes the hub of information collection and dissemination, and determines the course of the expatriation not only during but also after the crisis. Participants showed minimal variance in their responses referring mainly to monitoring and gathering information and data from local and international media; collecting situation reports from expert sources; facilitating threat level assessment; and enabling the Crisis Management Team (CMT) to make crisis response decisions.

People services. HRM support in a crisis situation will aim to enhance the employees' and the organization's resilience in the hostile environment. Such resilience can be achieved by ensuring both business and human continuity through the provision of additional measures and resources, depending on the context and the level of threat. Some indicative responses included: enhanced protection measures with 'extra security personnel at higher levels of threat' (HE7); specialist support such as 'expert legal advice in the case of wrongful detention' (IB6), 'cyber security specialists dealing with cyber extortion' (HE2) or even 'negotiation team in the case of kidnap' (IB3); and additional financial resources such as 'funds for facilitation payments or the payment of ransom' (IB4). HE9 warned that this support needs to be commensurate with the crisis situation and the local conditions:

> We do not want situations such as the case of Dr [XXXX] who was kidnapped from the [XXX] Complex in XXXX and was killed in XXXXXXX during a rescue effort by the local Citizens-Police Liaison Committee. It is important that we are able to retain highly specialized negotiators and extraction teams that can handle effective such a crisis. (HE9)

The participants also suggested that the most important support that can be provided by corporate HRM is the coordination of the crisis management plan's implementation. Accordingly, most participants acknowledged that although the personnel 'on the ground' will execute the plan, they agreed that the escalation of the crisis management plan is subject to corporate decision-making. 'It is the corporate headquarters that will normally activate the plan and decide on the staff's hibernation duration and location' (HE3). Again, the decision on 'how and when family members will be evacuated while staff is still in 'hibernation' will typically be made at corporate level rather than at local' (HE6). In the case of relocation within the country '[...] the decision may be made at local level but the relocation sites whether "hot" or "cold" will be provided by the corporate headquarters who will also decide the "how and when" a full-scale "evac" and repatriation will take place' (HE6).

Communication services. Clearly, since a large part of the crisis response decision-making is made by the corporate team the need for abundant and redundant communication lines between the CMT and the deployed expatriates is obvious. However, HR is responsible also for open and continuous communication between the CMT and its extended network of support specialists (often provided by the insurers and/or the relocation consultants) and the crisis response team that may be 'on the ground' (HE8, IB6, RC1, RC2).

Almost all participants underscored the role of corporate communication with external stakeholders and the media but, in the clear majority of responses, it was suggested that this communication should be handled by an expert team and not just the HRM department. HE3 and HE7 were the only HR executives who felt confident in handling this task as they had received special 'media spokesperson' training. H1, H8, IB2, IB6, and RC3 also referred to the role of the 'family liaison officer' who should be activated at this stage and acts as the link between the expatriate's family and the organization.

Policy and standards. Unlike the previous stage where the role of HR was more dynamic with regard to policy, in the stage of crisis response, the participants who explicitly or implicitly (HE3, HE4, HE9, IB1, IB3, IB4, IB5) alluded to the role of HRM used the words 'compliance', 'conformance', and 'adherence' once again confirming the role of 'policy police'. This demonstrates how important the previous stages, and the associated service areas, are in executing the effective management of expatriates when crises occur.

HRM services for expatriation or repatriation (crisis recovery)

At this stage, the participants discussed the support activities and practices related to the recovery of the repatriated staff after a crisis situation and what HE1 and HE2 eloquently termed 'consequences management'. Many of the participants, (HE3, HE4, HE6, HE8, IB2, IB3, IB6, RC1) however, noted that this stage is not necessarily connected with the end of expatriation in the specific hostile environment. 'It is not a total recall, repatriation may be temporary and only for a short while or it may not be needed if the deployment [expatriation] environment gets back to what we accept as normality' (HE3). It was, therefore, implied that many of the practices described at this stage can take place while the expatriates continue their deployment at the same destination.

Information services. The participants stressed the importance of managing the 'learning' from the crisis experience and using it for the re-design of the entire process based on this learning. HE1 suggested that a 'debriefing and an action review' needs to take place where the organization and its stakeholders will have the opportunity to evaluate plans, actions, and responses, identify potential weaknesses, and re-design the whole process based on these new insights. HE3 and HE7 also suggested that this new learning should be 'codified' by corporate HR and 'become a source for new policies and standards, new training and permeate the entire organization'. These views are consistent with the literature on crisis knowledge governance where emergent 'crisis' knowledge complements or replaces already institutionalized knowledge until itself becomes obsolete (Paraskevas, Altinay, McLean, & Cooper, 2013).

People services. As already discussed, repatriation may be temporary or not take place at all. The participants suggested 'paid rest and rehabilitation' (in the case of injuries sustained during the crisis or the evacuation) as well as 'individual and family counseling' (HE1, HE2, IB2, IB4, RC3) to address any post-traumatic disorder (Liou & Lin, 2008; Ramirez et al., 2015). HE5 and all the IBs also talked about 'claims management and the payment of compensations via insurance covers', whereas HE1 and HE2 talked about 'other consequences management' explaining that in case of fatalities there is always a need for the organization to arrange the identification and repatriation of bodies and their personal effects.

One very important activity at this stage is the evaluation of the expatriate's 'level of recovery' (HE3, HE4), 'acquired new knowledge' (HE8), and 'appropriateness' (HE1) or 'fit-for-redeployment' (RC3) in order for 're-assignment' decisions to be made (HE1, HE2).

> Decisions for re-assignment should not be only based on the company's business needs but also on a rigorous assessment of the candidate's 'physical and emotional fitness' and their 'fit' for the proposed destination. (RC3)

The assessment of whether the individual is emotionally and physically fit for repatriation in the same or other work environments places particular onus on corporate HR departments to ensure the care and support packages created are suitable and effective (Mankin & Perry, 2004).

Communication services. The role of HR as a 'communication hub' (HE7, HE9) or 'conduit' (HE2) at this stage was also discussed in the study. As before, all people and information services imply open, 24/7 communication as an HR support service. The participants suggested that although it is not HR's direct responsibility to have an incident reporting system, it plays a major role in establishing one. As all HR participants were operating in networks with the risk and security managers in their organization, they took this as granted. There was only one HR executive, (HE5), who stated that incident reporting and claims management was in their remit.

Policy and standards. One of the major outcomes of this stage as noted by HE7, HE9, and IB5 is that the knowledge created by the debriefing and action review will enable the corporate HR department to re-assess and perhaps modify the organization's 'threshold of acceptable risk', something that will impact the entire expatriation strategy. Also, the crisis knowledge that will emerge from this evaluation process, as pointed out earlier, can be used to review, enrich, and perhaps amend the policies and standards that support this strategy. This is part of closing the loop to more effectively prepare and protect HRs deployed in hostile environments.

Minimizing the risk exposure of strategic HRs

What also emerged from the interviews was that the focus of all these activities is the minimization of risk exposure for both the deployed expatriates and the organizations concerned, especially with regard to financial and reputational costs. Hence, the creation of extended networks that manage together such types of expatriation: the relocation partners offering deeper local knowledge which will protect the deployed staff; and the insurers/brokers with who, in a sense, a large part of the risk exposure is 'shared'. The focus on risk exposure minimization is evident by the increasingly adopted practice, emphasized by both the hotel executives group and the relocation consultants group (HE1, HE3, RC2), of the development and deployment of only local HRs in both hostile and non-hostile environments as inpatriates (Collings, 2014; Gannon et al., 2010; Harvey, Novicevic, & Speier, 2000).

> As we expand internationally, we are trying to nurture leaders from within the ranks of in-country employees, something that in the long run will result in fewer expatriate assignments, particularly when it comes to geopolitical hotspots. (HE1)

> We sign up the 'best and brightest' from these destinations and give them short-term assignments in 'strong' properties where they can be fully exposed and 'indoctrinated' to our company's culture, standards and policies, [...], interact with senior management and mentors before re-allocating them to the countries they are already familiar with. [HE3]

However, as the pool of strategic HRs is still relatively limited and the speed of hotel brand expansion fast, expatriation in certain hostile environments is inevitable. Again, however, risk exposure minimization dominates decisions with regard to how this expatriation takes place:

> In such situations [hostile environments] we encourage the 'split family' approach. Normally these locations are inhospitable for families – they do not have international schools, don't offer family-friendly housing and accessibility to amenities and are, of course, unsafe. However, we realize that this is not a long-term solution and have to compensate accordingly with an increased number of home leave trips. [HE1]

An important role in this decision is played also by the insurers. An expatriate with a family in a hostile environment represents higher risk exposure and therefore policy cover and premiums will reflect this increased exposure. Participants recalled cases where insurers have not insured expatriates where they were escorted by their families in certain countries [IB4, IB6]. This is not though a very common issue as, notably, many participants [HE2, HE6, HE7, RC2 and RC3] claimed that there is an increased trend for expatriate assignees in general, and not only those assigned in hostile environments, to not relocate with their families: '[...] with dual-career families, extended family responsibilities and children's education needs, the "trailing spouse" tends to become a pattern of the past' [RC3].

The role of the insurers in the management of expatriation process is becoming evident also in other aspects. As Fee and McGrath-Champ (2016) identify, there may be a 'partial acceptance' security strategy which blends elements of 'acceptance' with 'protection' and our findings suggest that since the risk exposure result of an acceptance strategy is shared with, if not completely transferred to an insurer through a policy, the latter may influence this approach. As revealed in the interviews, depending on the insurance policy, the level of risk exposure, and the value of the protected HRs, the security strategy may move from 'partial acceptance' to outright 'protection' and even reach the level of 'deterrence' (Childs, 2013; Van Brabant, 2000).

We identified in the literature review that there has been limited consideration of how the differences in risk exposure of international managers, due to the variety in their established routines and length of stay in hostile environments, may impact on their management by corporate HRM executives. The loss or compromise of any one of these HRs (traveling senior executive, regional cluster manager or assigned expatriate) would be dreadful for those concerned but the impact for the organization is likely to be more ruinous if it is the senior executive. However, the participants did not differentiate between managerial resources on this basis despite their focus on risks associated with specific environments. For all the respondents, their focus was very clearly upon the widest use of the term expatriates as those who managed their international properties and the corporate and regional executives who coordinate business across their hotel portfolios. The synonymous treatment of these different forms of strategic HRs derives from the coverage of insurance policies which also do not vary between them. This highlights again that rather than company policies driving HRM practices and support, for deployed resources in hostile environments, insurance policies lead to a 'one-size-fits-all' approach with limited differentiation between non-native executives.

While local hotel employees were mentioned, they were seen to be the prime responsibility of their direct employers, the franchisees, or investors/owners of the property. The four international hotel companies provided support to their business partners on risks, security, and the protection of their hotels (customers and staff), but the focus of the corporate HR executives' attention was very clearly on direct corporate employees.

From the outset of our initial fieldwork invitations, we were surprised by the introductions to the wider support networks offered by our initial research participants (the corporate HRM executives) who we had anticipated would be the primary sources for our investigation. There was also evidence that the corporate executives, both HRM and risk and security, had in place mechanisms and practices (for example, training, specific crisis management plans, communication platforms and support services) which constitute best practice in managing their HRs in threatened locations. This apparently matches the 'table stake' best practice SHRM approach where there are people management activities which all organizations in an industry will use and legitimize their industry membership (Boxall & Purcell, 2011). The unanimous employment of specialists in the fields of relocation and insurance further indicate that table stake best practice approaches were manifest in hotel MNCs' approaches to managing their HRs.

Conclusions and recommendations

This article has attempted to identify and address the limitations in the existing literature on the missing organizational voice around managing people in hostile environments, specifically explore the approaches taken to managing expatriates in hostile environments, and examine the practices involved. By drawing upon the theoretical literature on SHRM and existing evidence of HRM practices, it provides a more comprehensive definition of hostile environments and a detailed depiction of the ways managerial resources are managed by their corporate employers in such locations. The growth and importance of this IHRM area resulted in our targeted corporate respondents introducing us to the external specialists who augment the corporate approaches and practices with their knowledge and expertise. This business partnering of corporate executives, amid increasingly challenging competitive, social, and political conditions, highlights the significance of relationship building for an organization's survival and reputational success. As such our study fills a gap in the literature where few have been able to provide the corporate perspective on managing HRs across international commercial operations in difficult surroundings.

Theoretical contributions and limitations

We contribute to the literature in four specific ways. First, this study is the first to explore the awareness of the risks, and the approaches taken to support managerial resources operating in hostile environments from the perspective of corporate executives and the specialists who support them (relocation consultants and insurers). Second, as part of our findings we provide a new definition of hostile environments which captures more broadly the way corporate HRM executives and specialists in the fields of risk, security, relocation, and insurance view the concept. Whereas Bader et al., (2015) focused upon different forms of violence (terrorism, crime etc.) our definition takes a broader perspective and considers a variety of man-made or natural threats and hazards. Third, we further developed Fee et al., (2013, 2016) models on HRM services for expatriates to better reflect the key practices HR departments implement, at the different stages of expatriation, in order to prevent a crisis, prepare expatriates to face a crisis, respond to a crisis, and recover from a crisis. This is one of the few occasions corporate executives have contributed to the area of expatriation under duress, and we not only captured their approaches to supporting HRs in hostile environments but the specialist expertise they rely upon to deliver such policies and practices. One particular feature of the new model is that it distinguishes different sets of support services in what Fee et al., (2013, 2016) call the pre-crisis stage. We identified a set of practices and services taking place pre-expatriation that aim at minimizing the risk exposure of the expatriate and another set of practices and services which take place during expatriation and prepare the expatriate to face a crisis but before a crisis incident. The findings also highlight that the focus for these HRM executives is very much based on ensuring the preparation for expatriation and crisis situations is comprehensively planned. The extensive nature of the initial stage of the model is crucial for all other subsequent stages. The proposed model also reinforces the importance of continual organizational learning from minor and major crisis incidents, and sustained business continuity. This is a sizable challenge where ownership is devolved, multiples of properties exist, and there is substantial geographical dispersion (Gannon et al., 2015; Paraskevas et al., 2013).

The final distinctive contribution identifies how the lack of differentiation in the support of different strategic HRs (traveling executives to expatriates on three year assignments) in hostile environments is founded on a blanket approach taken by the companies as dictated by the insurance policies available to them. This means that companies are forced to offer the same support to all expatriates in spite of their strategic importance, in all countries regardless of the types of risks each location may have. This indicates the strategic importance of external stakeholders, such as insurance brokers, in developing support strategies, which is a novel contribution to the literature. It also shows the need for a better understanding of specific categories of risks that are present in hostile environments so that these strategies may be tailored for specific locations.

The research was undertaken with corporate executives from international hotel corporations which only represent a small percentage of MNCs. Although international hotel groups are among the most credible examples of multinationals, we recognize perhaps research in other sectors would derive different results. We also interviewed hotel executives, insurers, and relocation service providers associated with only four international hotel companies. The focus on respondents associated with the international hotel industry constrains the extent to which the results of this investigation can be generalized. However, as a truly international industry focused upon the mobility of people, the hotel sector still provides a pertinent setting for an investigation of corporate approaches and practices associated with managing HRs in hostile environments. Our hotel companies sample represent 40 percent of the total branded hotel sector, however, a larger, or perhaps a cross-sectoral sample might reveal additional perspectives. Furthermore, the initial corporate respondents were drawn from the researchers' own personal networks and it should be acknowledged that they may not represent all executives' views on the topic.

Practical contributions and further research

The crucial role of HRM executives and their partners in dealing with heightened recognition of the hostile threats is apparent. The continued developments in business travel as well as the trends in international alliances and market expansion, amidst the uninterrupted threat of terrorism and violence does suggest that organizations could actively engage all staff in training in crisis management skills. The findings show it is the less glamorous policy development and enforcement, and the critical information and communication aspects to managing mobility on a grand scale, which appear fundamental to HRM's role. These areas deserve greater attention from the academic community to support the development of effective practices. Undoubtedly, MNCs also have a moral dilemma about the extent to which they can protect their HRs in hostile environments due to the unforeseen nature of threats. Senior executives also therefore need to decide to what extent should their organizations' build in-house capability or customize expertise available elsewhere (Fee et al., 2013). Compared with the internal capacity and expertise of the HR managers in the INGOs studied by Fee and McGrath-Champ (2016), we found limited evidence of the same level of expertise among our sample of international hotel company executives, and a reliance on external specialists brought in to clarify risks, coverage, and provide appropriate support. This highlights that different business sectors are likely to have variations in their approaches to building internal expertise capacity, to manage HRs operating in hostile environments, dependent upon the requirement of their sector to operate in such locations. For example, sectors such as mining and extraction may have no choice in operating in such locations. In addition, we should also recognize the influence of international business formats in shaping where companies operate. The networked and diverse ownership nature of the international hotel industry presents particular challenges here where hotel owners and other partners may be reluctant to engage with the extra costs of enhanced risk expertise and other forms of organizational support (Gannon et al., 2010). As many other industries engage in varied ownership patterns and affiliations, these issues have wider ramifications for the international business world. The overall complexity of addressing these factors highlights how the pressure to minimize business and human risks are leading to changes in the expatriation landscape itself, based upon our participants advocating the wider deployment of inpatriates and more split family relocations.

With regard to future research, this study highlights specific implications for academics and managers. It would be valuable to explore the relationships built between corporate HR and risk and security executives and the external expertise they prize in safely managing their organizations' strategic HRs. The pressure to minimize risk exposure and develop inpatriates presents corporate HRM executives with specific problems in highly diversified and dispersed organizations. All four of the international companies, as well as the other respondents, mentioned the growing use of inpatriates as being safer (lower risk) sources of managerial expertise though it became apparent that companies were inconsistent in their approaches to developing these geographically and culturally dispersed managerial resources. If inpatriates are to be advocated more widely by insurers and corporate executives, then companies will need to improve their talent management and the development of these HRs as part of their attempts to gain advantage through their HRM practices (Collings, 2014; Gannon et al., 2015). The implications of talent spotting and management for specific locations across the globe to satisfy the corporate risk agenda need to be deliberated in far greater detail. More specific investigations of how organizations might support and evaluate their practices supporting managers pre- and post- crisis, and ascertain fitness for subsequent duties, is also warranted. Such studies, where they can capture the perspectives of both the corporate executives and expatriates on the practices deployed, will be particularly appreciated. The overall risk appetite of organizations also suggests a valuable starting point for future investigations of people management practices, how does risk appetite shapes the development of SHRM approaches and the HRM practices which support and protect staff.

Disclosure statement

No potential conflict of interest was reported by the authors.

References

Bader, B. (2015). The power of support in high-risk countries: Compensation and social support as antecedents of expatriate work attitudes. *The International Journal of Human Resource Management, 26*, 1712–1736.

Bader, B., Berg, N., & Holtbrügge, D. (2013). Expatriate performance in high-risk countries: Influence of family-related stress. In Academy of Management Proceedings (Vol. 2013, No. 1, p. 10515). Academy of Management.

Bader, B., & Schuster, T. (2015). Expatriate social networks in terrorism-endangered countries: An empirical analysis in Afghanistan, India, Pakistan, and Saudi Arabia. *Journal of International Management, 21*, 63–77.

Bader, B., Berg, N., & Holtbrügge, D. (2015a). Expatriate performance in high-risk countries: Influence of family-related stress. *Academy of Management Proceedings, 13*, 105–115.

Bader, B. Schuster, T., & Dickman, M. (2015b) CALL FOR PAPERS special issue of international journal of human resource management: Danger and risk as challenges for HRM: How to manage people in hostile environments. Retrieved from http://globaledge.msu.edu/content/uploads/ijhrm_si_baderschusterdickmann.pdf

Baruch, Y., Dickmann, M., Altman, Y., & Bournois, F. (2013). Exploring international work: Types and dimensions of global careers. *The International Journal of Human Resource Management, 24*, 2369–2393.

Bhanugopan, R., & Fish, A. (2008). The impact of business crime on expatriate quality of work-life in Papua New Guinea. *Asia Pacific Journal of Human Resources, 46*, 68–84.

Bianchi, E. M. P. G. (2015). Repatriation: Reflections on organizational practices and its implications on individuals, around the globe. *Gestão & regionalidade (online), 31*, 144–160.

Bonache, J., Brewster, C., & Suutari, V. (2001). Expatriation: A developing research agenda. *Thunderbird International Business Review, 43*, 3–20.

Boxall, P., & Purcell, J. (2011). *Strategy and human resource management.* (3rd ed.). Basingstoke: Palgrave Macmillan.

Brewster, C., Bonache, J., Cerdin, J. L., & Suutari, V. (2014). Exploring expatriate outcomes. *The International Journal of Human Resource Management, 25*, 1921–1937.

Briscoe, D. R., & Schuler, R. S. (2004). International human resource management: Policy and practice for the global enterprise . In *Chapter 13 Health, safety and crisis management in the global enterprise* (Vol. 5, pp. 374–393), New York: Routledge/Psychology Press.

Chang, Y. Y., Gong, Y., & Peng, M. W. (2012). Expatriate knowledge transfer, subsidiary absorptive capacity, and subsidiary performance. *Academy of Management Journal, 55*, 927–948.

Childs, A. K. (2013). Cultural theory and acceptance based security strategies for humanitarian aid workers. *Journal of Strategic Security, 6*, 64–72.

Collings, D. G. (2014). Integrating global mobility and global talent management: Exploring the challenges and strategic opportunities. *Journal of World Business, 49*, 253–261.

Creswell, J. W. (2007). *Qualitative inquiry and research design: Choosing among five approaches.* Thousand Oaks, CA: Sage.

Czinkota, M. R., Knight, G., Liesch, P. W., & Steen, J. (2010). Terrorism and international business: A research agenda. *Journal of International Business Studies, 41*, 826–843.

Dabic, M., González-Loureiro, M., & Harvey, M. (2015). Evolving research on expatriates: What is 'known' after four decades (1970–2012). *The International Journal of Human Resource Management, 26*, 316–337.

Driffield, N., Jones, C., & Crotty, J. (2013). International business research and risky investments, an analysis of FDI in conflict zones. *International Business Review, 22*, 140–155.

Edström, A., & Galbraith, J. R., (1977, June). Transfer of managers as a coordination and control strategy in multinational organizations, *Administrative Science Quarterly, 22*, 248–263.

Elango, B., Graf, L. A., & Hemmasi, M. (2007). Reducing the risk of becoming a victim of terrorism while on international business assignments. *Simulation & Gaming, 39*, 540–557.

Fee, A., & McGrath-Champ, S. (2016). The role of human resources in protecting expatriates: Insights from the international aid and development sector. *The International Journal of Human Resource Management*, 1–26.

Fee, A., McGrath-Champ, S., & Liu, H. (2013). Human resources and expatriate evacuation: A conceptual model. *Journal of Global Mobility, 1*, 246–263.

Fink, A., & Pingle, M. (2014). Kidnap insurance and its impact on kidnapping outcomes. *Public Choice, 160*, 481–499.

Fox-Koob, S. (2016, June 23). Four Australians kidnapped in Nigeria attack, *The Australian*. Retrieved October 18, 2016, from http://tinyurl.com/hr4vwh3

Fuller, E. (2015, January 6). Traveler Safety is Everybody's Business, *Forbes*. Retrieved November 10, 2016, from http://tinyurl.com/j2zu2kc

Gannon, J., Roper, A., & Doherty, L. (2010). The impact of hotel management contracting on IHRM practices: Understanding the bricks and brains split. *International Journal of Contemporary Hospitality Management, 22*, 638–658.

Gannon, J. M., Roper, A., & Doherty, L. (2015). Strategic human resource management: Insights from the international hotel industry. *International Journal of Hospitality Management, 47*, 65–75.

Glazzard, A., & Pantucci, R. (2015). Extreme measures: The challenges and opportunities of measuring terrorism, in the Institute of Economics and Peace *Global Terrorism Index 2015: Measuring and understanding the impact of terrorism*. Retrieved from http://economicsandpeace.org/wp-content/uploads/2015/11/2015-Global-Terrorism-Index-Report.pdf

Harvey, M. (1982). The other side of foreign assignments: Dealing with the repatriation dilemma. *Columbia Journal of World Business, 17*, 53–59.

Harvey, M. G. (1993). A survey of corporate programs for managing terrorist threats. *Journal of International Business Studies, 24*, 465–478.

Harvey, M., & Moeller, M. (2009). Expatriate mangers: A historical review. *International Journal of Management Reviews, 11*, 275–296.

Harvey, M. G., Novicevic, M. M., & Speier, C. (2000). Strategic global human resource management: The role of inpatriate managers. *Human Resource Management Review, 10*, 153–175.

Harzing, A. W. (2002). Of bears, bumble-bees, and spiders: The role of expatriates in controlling foreign subsidiaries. *Journal of World Business, 36*, 366–379.

Hayes, A. F., & Krippendorff, K. (2007). Answering the call for a standard reliability measure for coding data. *Communication Methods and Measures, 1*, 77–89.

Hodari, D., & Sturman, M. C. (2014). Who's in charge now? The decision autonomy of hotel general managers. *Cornell Hospitality Quarterly, 55*, 433–447.

Howie, L. (2007). The terrorism threat and managing workplaces. *Disaster Prevention and Management: An International Journal, 16*, 70–78.

ILO. (2010). Developments and Challenges in the Hospitality & Tourism Sector. Retrieved from http://www.ilo.org/wcmsp5/groups/public/@ed_norm/@relconf/documents/meetingdocument/wcms_166938.pdf

Institute of Economics and Peace. (2015). *Global Terrorism Index 2015: Measuring and Understanding the Impact of Terrorism.* Retrieved from http://economicsandpeace.org/wp-content/uploads/2015/11/2015-Global-Terrorism-Index-Report.pdf

King, N. (2004). Using templates in the thematic analysis of text. In C. Cassell & G. Symon (Eds.), *Essential guide to qualitative methods in organizational research* (pp. 256–270). London: Sage.

Kraimer, M. L. Takeuchi, R., & Frese, M. (2014). The global context and people at work: Special issue introduction, *Personnel Psychology, 67*, 5–21.

Lang, J. (2012, November 26). Kidnap & ransom coverage keeps pace with growing risks around the world. *National Underwriter*, 26.

Lincoln, Y. S., & Guba, E. G. (1985). *Naturalistic inquiry.* Newbury Park, CA: Sage.

Liou, D. Y., & Lin, C. H. (2008). Human resources planning on terrorism and crises in the Asia Pacific region: Cross-national challenge, reconsideration, and proposition from western experiences. *Human Resource Management, 47*, 49–72.

Malik, O. F., Abdullah, H., & Uli, J. A. (2014). The effects of terrorism on work attitudes and behaviors: A literature review and a proposed model. *Journal of Aggression, Conflict and Peace Research, 6*, 143–163.

Mankin, L. D., & Perry, R. W. (2004). Commentary terrorism challenges for human resource management. *Review of Public Personnel Administration, 24*, 3–17.

Marchington, M. (2015). Human resource management (HRM): Too busy looking up to see where it is going longer term? *Human Resource Management Review, 25*, 176–187.

McNulty, Yvonne, & Brewster, Chris. (2016a). The concept of business expatriates. In Y. McNulty & J. Selmer (Eds.), *Research Handbook of Expatriates.* Cheltenham: Edward Elgar.

McNulty, Y., & Brewster, C. (2016). Theorizing the meaning(s) of 'expatriate': Establishing boundary conditions for business expatriates. *The International Journal of Human Resource Management, 28*, 27–61. doi:10.1080/09585192.2016.1243567.

McNulty, Y., & De Cieri, H. (2011). Global mobility in the 21st century. *Management International Review, 51*, 897–919.

Melissen, F., van Ginneken, R., & Wood, R. C. (2016). Sustainability challenges and opportunities arising from the owner-operator split in hotels. *International Journal of Hospitality Management, 54*, 5–42.

MND. (2016, March 14). Businesses plead for extortion strategy. *Mexico News Daily.* Retrieved November 3, 2016, from http://tinyurl.com/zgfsqlb

Paraskevas, A. (2013). Aligning strategy to threat: A baseline anti-terrorism strategy for hotels. *International Journal of Contemporary Hospitality Management, 25*, 140–162.

Paraskevas, A., Altinay, L., McLean, J., & Cooper, C. (2013). Crisis knowledge in tourism: Types, flows and governance. *Annals of Tourism Research, 41*, 130–152.

Ramirez, J., Madero, S., & Muñiz, C. (2015). The impact of narcoterrorism on HRM systems. *The International Journal of Human Resource Management*, 1–31.

Reade, C., & Lee, H. J. (2012). Organizational commitment in time of war: Assessing the impact and attenuation of employee sensitivity to ethnopolitical conflict. *Journal of International Management, 18*, 85–101.

Salter, J. (1997). Risk management in a disaster management context. *Journal of Contingencies and Crisis Management, 5*, 60–65.

Sawalha, I. H. S., Jraisat, L. E., & Al-Qudah, K. A. (2013). Crisis and disaster management in Jordanian hotels: Practices and cultural considerations. *Disaster Prevention and Management: An International Journal, 22*, 210–228.

Slangen, A. H., & Van Tulder, R. J. (2009). Cultural distance, political risk, or governance quality? Towards a more accurate conceptualization and measurement of external uncertainty in foreign entry mode research. *International Business Review, 18*, 276–291.

Smith, D. (1990). Beyond contingency planning: Towards a model of crisis management. *Organization & Environment, 4*, 263–275.

Suutari, V., & Brewster, C., (1999). International assignments across European borders. In Brewster, C. & Harris, H. (Eds.), *Chapter 10, International HRM: Contemporary Issues in Europe* .(pp. 183–202). London: Routledge.

Van Brabant, K. (2000). *Operational security management in violent environments*. London: Overseas Development Institute.

Wang, J., Hutchins, H. M., & Garavan, T. N., (2009, March). Exploring the strategic role of human resource development in organizational crisis management. *Human Resource Development Review, 8*, 22–53.

Welch, D. E., Welch, L. S., & Worm, V. (2007). The international business traveller: A neglected but strategic human resource. *The International Journal of Human Resource Management, 18*, 173–183.

Welch, D., Steen, A., & Tahvanainen, M. (2009). All pain, little gain? Reframing the value of international assignments. *The International Journal of Human Resource Management, 20*, 1327–1343.

Wernick, D. A., & Von Glinow, M. A. (2012). Reflections on the evolving terrorist threat to luxury hotels: A case study on marriott international. *Thunderbird International Business Review, 54*, 729–746.

Williams, C. (2004). *Terrorism explained: The facts about terrorism and terrorist groups*. Sydney: New Holland Publishers.

Terrorism and expatriate withdrawal cognitions: the differential role of perceived work and non-work constraints

Anna Katharina Bader, Carol Reade and Fabian Jintae Froese

ABSTRACT

Building on stress theory, this study investigates the mechanism by which terrorism influences withdrawal cognitions of expatriates, namely, via perceived threat as well as perceived constraints in the work and non-work domains. Data from 160 expatriates currently working in African and Asian countries show that the level of terrorism relates to expatriates' perceived threat. Further, we find that the effect of this perceived threat is stronger on perceived constraints in the non-work than in the work domain. While perceived constraints in the work domain have a direct effect on job turnover intentions, perceived constraints in the non-work domain have a direct effect on country leave intentions and an indirect, spillover effect on job turnover intentions. Our study underscores the importance of both work and non-work domains for understanding stress and turnover related to expatriation in terrorism-endangered countries.

Introduction

The global spread of terrorism poses a growing challenge for international business and international human resource management (Czinkota, Knight, & Liesch, 2004; Reade, 2009). While the majority of terrorist attacks are concentrated in a few countries, there has been a noticeable spread worldwide (Institute for Economics & Peace [IEP], 2015). Terrorist activity has also targeted more areas frequented by civilians, as demonstrated by the recent attacks in France, Indonesia, and Turkey. According to the latest data, deaths caused by terrorism increased by 80% over the previous year, the largest increase in 15 years (IEP, 2015, p. 2). Moreover, the percentage of civilian deaths has soared to 172% over the year before (IEP, 2015, p. 2).

Despite the increased risk of terrorism, multinational enterprises (MNEs) continue to expand into terrorism-endangered countries to take advantage of market opportunities. When abroad, MNEs tend to rely on expatriates to control their foreign subsidiaries (Harzing, 2001). Expatriation in itself is a challenging experience for the expatriate because expatriates need to adjust to a new living and working environment. Prior research has accordingly shown that if expatriates fail to adjust they are more likely to show withdrawal cognitions (for a meta-analysis see Bhaskar-Shrinivas, Harrison, Shaffer, & Luk, 2005). Despite disagreement over the definition and magnitude of failure among expatriates (Harzing, 2002), it is generally agreed that failure, e.g. in terms of turnover is costly for MNCs (Harzing & Christensen, 2004). A large body of research has thus investigated the reasons for success and failure during expatriation, largely focusing on adjustment to a foreign culture (for a review see Takeuchi, 2010). Besides the general challenge of adapting to a foreign culture, expatriates in terrorism-endangered countries face additional challenges related to security. Not surprisingly, nascent research in this area reveals that expatriates in such countries suffer from heightened stress and display less positive work attitudes and lower performance (Bader & Berg, 2013, 2014). Due to the challenge of terrorism-induced fear and stress, expatriates in terrorism-endangered countries are likely to exhibit heightened withdrawal cognitions including higher turnover and country leave intentions. The purpose of our study is therefore to develop a model that elucidates the mechanism by which terrorism affects expatriate withdrawal cognitions and to test it with data from 160 expatriates currently working in African and Asian countries.

The current study aims to make the following contributions. First, it adds new knowledge to the scarce literature on expatriates in terrorism-endangered countries (Bader & Berg, 2013, 2014; Bader, Berg, & Holtbrügge, 2015). Drawing from a stress perspective (Lazarus, 1991; Lazarus & Folkman, 1984), we extend this literature by investigating how terrorism influences expatriate withdrawal cognitions, an important indicator of expatriate success (Bhaskar-Shrinivas et al., 2005). Specifically, we link terrorism to expatriates' perception of threat and perceived constraints and investigate their association with job turnover and country leave intentions.

Second, we investigate the differential consequences of terrorism-induced stress by disentangling the effects on the work and non-work domains. Prior related expatriate research suggests that it is important to distinguish between work and non-work domains during expatriation (Bhaskar-Shrinivas et al., 2005; Black, Mendenhall, & Oddou, 1991; Selmer & Fenner, 2009; Takeuchi, 2010; Takeuchi, Yun, & Tesluk, 2002). The work domain refers to experiences in the workplace of the expatriate, while the non-work domain refers to the life of the expatriate outside the job or workplace (Takeuchi et al., 2002). For instance, job responsibilities, workplace culture, and relationships with supervisors and colleagues are part of the work domain, whereas the general living conditions, family issues, and recreational activities outside the workplace are part of the non-work domain.

Prior related research has mainly focused on the different facets (domains) of the cross-cultural adjustment of expatriates. This research differentiates between work (related to the new job requirements in the host country and thus the work domain), interaction (related to social interactions with host-country nationals in the work and non-work domains), and general adjustment (related to the general living conditions particularly in the non-work domain) (e.g. Bhaskar-Shrinivas et al., 2005; Black & Stephens, 1989; Black et al., 1991; Selmer & Fenner, 2009; Takeuchi et al., 2002). Our research extends these studies by investigating the perception of constraints in the work and non-work domains in the context of terrorism-endangered countries. This is important because terrorism poses particular challenges to both the work and private life of expatriates. Regarding the work domain, terrorist attacks can disrupt supply chains and damage infrastructure so that, for instance, there is a delay in shipment of critical office or factory equipment (Sheffi, 2001; Suder, 2006). In the non-work domain, terrorist attacks, especially when relatively frequent, heighten safety concerns (Harvey, 1993) and affect personal movement and lifestyle choices. For instance, in some high-risk countries, expatriates and their families need to be accompanied by security personnel whenever they leave their compound. To capture domain-specific effects, we develop a model illustrating how perceived threat relates to (1) perceived constraints in the work domain and (2) perceived constraints in the non-work domain. We then separately investigate the consequences of these constraints on withdrawal cognitions. In this way, we highlight the differential role of work and non-work constraints on job turnover intentions, i.e. the desire to leave the current job (specific to the work domain), and country leave intentions, i.e. the desire to return home or depart for another country (generalized to the non-work domain).

Third, we investigate spillover effects from the non-work to the work domain (Takeuchi et al., 2002). Spillover effects occur when events or experiences in one domain affect experiences in another domain such as the influence of spouse adjustment on expatriate work adjustment (Bhaskar-Shrinivas et al., 2005). As research has produced inconsistent results, Selmer and Fenner (2009) concluded that the occurrence of spillover effects depends on the specific circumstances of expatriation. In line with prior expatriate studies (e.g. Bhaskar-Shrinivas et al., 2005; Black et al., 1991; Takeuchi, 2010; Takeuchi et al., 2002), we propose that there is likely to be a spillover effect from the non-work to the work domain particularly in the context of terrorism-endangered countries. Accordingly, we investigate the spillover effect from constraints in the non-work domain on job turnover intentions through country leave intentions.

Theoretical background and hypotheses development

Expatriation, stress, and terrorism

Expatriation is an experience that involves stress (Black et al., 1991). This is because expatriates face new environments and need to adapt to a new culture abroad (e.g. Harrison, Shaffer, & Bhaskar-Shrinivas, 2004; Kraimer, Wayne, & Jaworski, 2001; Peltokorpi & Froese, 2009; Stahl & Caligiuri, 2005). As such, the majority of expatriate research has adopted a stress perspective (Bhaskar-Shrinivas et al., 2005; Takeuchi, 2010). Stress is an individual evaluation of and reaction to external circumstances, i.e. stressors (Lazarus, 1991; Lazarus & Folkman, 1984). Stress theory proposes that stress develops in stages, and that stressors can lead to stress depending on individual evaluation of the situation (Lazarus, 1991). In the first stage, the individual makes a primary evaluation of the situation, e.g. a perception of expatriation as positive, neutral, or negative (stressful). In the second stage, the individual evaluates whether he or she has sufficient resources to cope with the stressor. If the individual cannot activate, or draw upon, sufficient resources, stress develops during expatriation (Black & Gregersen, 1991).

We suggest that expatriates in terrorism-endangered countries face specific challenges, or stressors, beyond the need for cultural adaptation. It is reasonable to assume that exposure to terrorism could heighten the overall stress of the expatriate (Bader & Berg, 2014). Research has substantiated that terrorism increases stress (Paton & Violanti, 2007); indeed, terrorism has been referred to as an extreme stressor (Goldberger & Breznitz, 1993). Terrorist acts are designed to elicit fear and anxiety among the general population, and stress reactions reported in the psychology and medical literature include anxiety, irritability, depression, decreased concentration and motivation, and sleeping disorders by those exposed to such acts (Bonger, 2007; Schuster et al., 2001).

Similar stress-related outcomes have been frequently reported as reaction to terrorism. For instance, following the 9/11 attack, employees reported a decline in work concentration and general feelings of disconnectedness with the organization (Mainiero & Gibson, 2003). Other studies have found a negative impact of terrorism, or other forms of political violence. Negative work attitudes include lower work motivation, involvement, and commitment (Bader & Berg, 2013, 2014; Reade, 2009; Reade & Lee, 2012), lower job satisfaction and employee morale (Alexander, 2004; Mainiero & Gibson, 2003), and lower trust in colleagues and top management (Reade, 2009). Negative behaviors includes lower work productivity and higher incidents of withdrawal (Alexander, 2004), as well as expressions of negative emotions toward supervisors and the organization (Mainiero & Gibson, 2003).

Building on these findings, and utilizing a stress perspective, we examine the mechanism by which terrorism influences withdrawal cognitions of expatriates. Figure 1 presents our theoretical model. First, as shown, we investigate whether a perceived threat of terrorism varies with the level of terrorism in the host country. Thus, we measure the individual evaluation of the stressor (Lazarus, 1991). Second, we examine if this translates into perceptions of higher constraints in the work domain (e.g. shortages of goods and equipment due to supply chain disruptions) (Czinkota et al., 2004), and relate this to job turnover intentions (Chen & Spector, 1992; Parasuraman & Alutto, 1984). Third, we investigate whether perceived threat

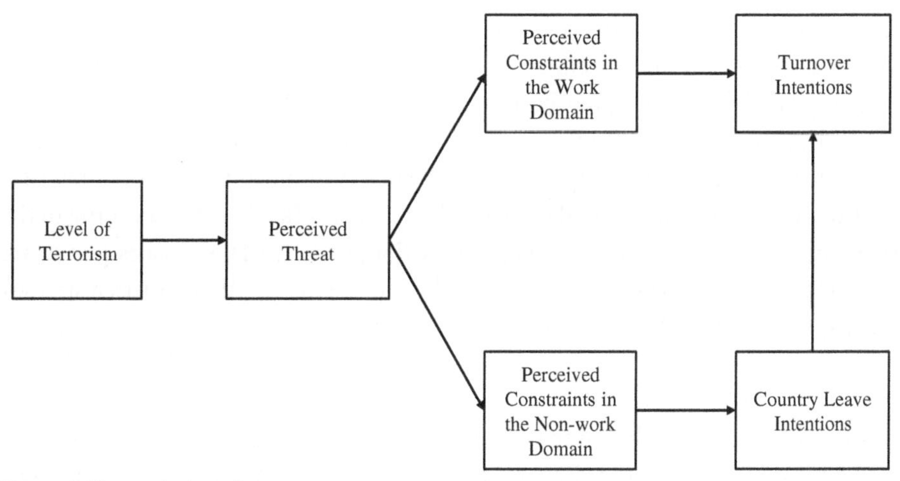

Figure 1. Theoretical model.

of terrorism is associated with perceptions of constraints in the non-work domain of expatriation (e.g. travel constraints due to heightened security measures), and whether this influences intentions to leave the host country. Lastly, we examine a spillover effect from the non-work to the work domain (Takeuchi et al., 2002), by investigating whether non-work constraints relate to job turnover intentions through intentions to leave the host country. In the following sections, we elaborate on our theoretical model and hypotheses.

Level of terrorism and perceived threat

Terrorism involves the threat or use of violence as a means to influence public policy (Alexander, Carlton, & Wilkinson, 1979). It is most prevalent in African and Asian countries with ongoing political conflict, armed conflict, or civil war (Hironaka, 2005; IEP, 2015). These countries are generally characterized by political instability and weak governance which provides fertile ground for the continuance of conflict and terrorist activities (Sakhuja, 2010). As such, the level of terrorism is highest in these countries as defined by the frequency of terrorist incidents, number of people killed or injured, and amount of property damaged (IEP, 2015). Particularly since 9/11, groups of terrorists with international networks have targeted the businesses and civilians particularly of the US and other western countries as a means to undermine or destroy the Western-dominated international economic order and those who support it (Chalk, 2008; Sheffi, 2001). Despite these changes, the frequency of terrorist attacks is relatively low inside Western countries (IEP, 2015). Thus, Western expatriates and their businesses will be more frequently threatened in areas of the world where political instability and weak governance structures provide the opportunity for terrorism to thrive (Sakhuja, 2010). A recent trend has also been for terrorist groups to aim for soft targets like hotels, restaurants, and other public places (Czinkota, Knight,

Liesch, & Steen, 2005; Czinkota et al., 2004), in addition to the traditional targets of embassies and military facilities. The focus on soft targets has resulted in more civilian casualties. Consequently, terrorist attacks have become more unpredictable, indiscriminate, and deadly (e.g. IEP, 2015; Jain & Grosse, 2009). Such attacks generate public fear which ripples through society and produces individual perceptions of personal threat and associated stress (Bar-Tal, 2007). According to the stress literature (Lazarus, 1991; Lazarus & Folkman, 1984), stressors per se are not stressful unless evaluated as such by the individual. In other words, a stressor such as terrorism will only produce stress when an individual feels threatened by the situation and is not able to cope well with it (Goodwin, Willson, & Gaines, 2005; Paton & Violanti, 2007).

Prior literature has shown that the more frequently stressors are perceived the more stressful the situation becomes for the individual (Chen & Spector, 1992; Parasuraman & Alutto, 1984). Therefore, in countries with high levels of terrorism, i.e. those afflicted with a high frequency of terrorist incidents and civilian casualties (IEP, 2015), individuals are more likely to feel threatened because of the probability of attack and their frequent exposure. Thus, while the level of terrorism is an objective measure based on statistics of past incidents, perceived personal threat is a subjective assessment of the probability of a future incident based on those statistics. Added to this is the increasingly unpredictable nature of terrorist attacks, given the recent focus on soft targets, which is likely to heighten perceived threat even more. As a result, individuals are likely to feel a lack of control over the situation and diminished capacity to protect themselves and their family. This leads to our first hypothesis.

> Hypothesis 1: The level of terrorism is positively related to expatriates' perception of personal threat.

Constraints in the work domain

Expatriates are sent abroad to manage business operations in foreign markets. The work domain has thus received much research attention since expatriates need to adjust to a new work environment (e.g. Black, 1988; Firth, Chen, Kirkman, & Kim, 2014; Froese & Peltokorpi, 2013). Most of the extant studies concentrate on the challenges and stress related to adjustment to new job roles and responsibilities within a new cultural and physical context. This increasingly includes assignments in less developed countries (e.g. Okpara & Kabongo, 2011) as MNEs continue to invest in developing and emerging markets. While adjustment to a developing country context may involve challenges associated with poor infrastructure, and a relative lack of goods, services, and medical care, we argue that a terrorism-endangered environment poses additional stressors brought on by the security situation. This is consistent with the findings of a recent study where expatriates in Afghanistan reported that their primary challenge is a lack of security, and secondarily a lack of economic and political development (Suder, Birnik, Nielsen, & Riviere, in press).

A successful business relies on smooth operations. These include basic production and sales functions as well as the supporting and logistical functions of supplier, shipping, and communications networks. Terrorism can disrupt operations through attacks on the organization's supply chain or on the host-country infrastructure. Much has been written on the negative consequences of supply chain disruption by terrorism, for instance, delaying, damaging, or destroying shipments en route to businesses which can result in supply shortages (Czinkota et al., 2004; Reade, 2009; Sheffi, 2001; Suder, 2006). Recent literature on maritime supply chains suggests that a piracy–terrorism nexus may intensify the challenge of protecting sea routes and shipments (Nelson, 2012; Sakhuja, 2010) and heighten the risk to business (Min, 2011). Particularly in situations of intrastate conflict, or civil war, where terrorists aim to undermine the ruling government, attacks may be directed at destroying key infrastructure such as power plants, dams, and airports. In such cases, the government may add additional constraints such as roadblocks to check IDs of people traveling near such infrastructure in order to deter such attacks. Such disruption constrains transportation, access to energy, access to goods and equipment, and business travel and communication and thus might impede expatriates' work abroad.

Terrorism also affects relationships in the workplace (Bader & Berg, 2013, 2014; Lee & Reade, 2015). Research has demonstrated that interpersonal relationships in workplaces located in terrorism-endangered environments are characterized by lower lowered trust and perceived support among colleagues (Kastenmüller et al., 2011; Lee & Reade, 2015; Mainiero & Gibson, 2003; Reade, 2009). Particularly in countries where there is protracted conflict along ethnic, religious, or ideological lines, there may be a tendency for employees to gravitate toward those who are similar to themselves and to form homophilous groups in the workplace (e.g. Lee & Reade, 2015). Such ingroup behavior, emanating from fear, lack of trust, or prejudice toward an outgroup, including foreigners, constrains networking and information sharing across groups, to the ultimate disadvantage of the organization (Kastenmüller et al., 2011).

Such challenges can be considered as stressors and produce what has been referred to as work constraints (O'Connor, Peters, Rudolf, & Pooyan, 1982; Peters, O'Connor, & Rudolf, 1980; Spector & Jex, 1998). Work constraints are defined as aspects of the immediate work situation that can prevent employees from fully performing their job despite individual abilities and motivation. As discussed above, in the terrorism-context, these constraints can be related to safety concerns, but also the lack of equipment or restrained social relationships and accordingly lack of help and support by others. There is research evidence showing a strong positive correlation between employee sensitivity to ethnic-based terrorism and employee frustration over organizational constraints among host-country managers of foreign-invested and domestic firms (Reade & Lee, 2016). Accordingly, we argue that expatriates who report a high level of perceived personal threat due to terrorism are also likely to experience more work constraints. Stated differently, due to the tense situation in their host country, expatriates are likely to experience more work-related disturbances. Accordingly, we hypothesize:

> Hypothesis 2a: Expatriates' perception of personal threat is positively related to their perceived work constraints.

Constraints in the non-work domain

When considering the non-work domain of expatriation, research has mainly focused on general adjustment. This includes adjustment to living conditions such as housing and unfamiliar food in the context of a new culture (Black et al., 1991; Froese, 2012). In terrorism-endangered countries, the adjustment process in private life is all the more challenging. Areas of greatest challenge include security-related constraints on personal movement and travel, and potentially difficult and constrained relationships with host-country nationals (Bader & Berg, 2014; Berger, 2011; Hutchings, Michailova, & Harrison, 2013).

Governments and their embassies will generally post warnings to their nationals about travel to or within countries on terrorism alert lists. Such information may get picked up in the media. However, because expatriates are likely to have less detailed information than locals regarding the current threat in the host country (Bader & Schuster, 2015), they might perceive such news as more threatening than host-country nationals. As a result, they are likely to avoid places deemed to have a high risk of terrorist attack, and may even stay home. Whether or not the potential threat becomes a reality, precautions to restrict movement and travel need to be heeded for the safety of the expatriate and family members. This might also entail changing daily routines, such as taking a different route to the office each day. Changing routines can foil terrorist plans if, for instance, an expatriate is being watched and targeted for kidnapping (e.g. Harvey, 1993).

Relationships with host-country nationals in the non-work domain can be as constrained as those in the workplace, for similar reasons of lowered trust and perceived support (Kastenmüller et al., 2011; Lee & Reade, 2015; Mainiero & Gibson, 2003; Reade, 2009). This is likely to affect interactions with locals in countries with high terrorism. In the non-work domain, one is more vulnerable, especially given the trend toward terrorist attacks on soft targets such as restaurants and shopping centers. Trust is an underlying concern, and interacting with those in the local community in a high terrorism environment can potentially produce stress and perceived personal threat.

From a stress perspective, individuals who experience stressors and interpret them as a personal threat are likely to respond with anxiety, depression, or fear (Brown, Cohen, & Kohlmaier, 2007). Thus, perceived threat can accentuate particular constraints experienced by expatriates. For instance, expatriates will make use of increased safety measures or restrict their traveling. While these precautionary measures are typically applied in order to protect expatriates outside work in terrorism-endangered countries (Bader & Berg, 2013), they nevertheless diminish and limit leisure time activities and personal freedom. Accordingly, because perceived threat is likely to accentuate the experience of constraints in expatriates' private lives, we hypothesize as follows.

> Hypothesis 2b: Expatriates' perception of personal threat is positively related to their perceived non-work constraints.

Additionally, we argue that the perceived threat of terrorism will have a greater impact on the non-work compared to the work domain of expatriates. Organizations invest considerably in protecting their assets and supply chains (Harvey, 1993; Suder, 2006). Furthermore, organizations invest in security measures to protect expatriates at work (Elango, Graf, & Hemmasi, 2008). While companies also provide security measures for expatriates in their private lives such as housing in guarded compounds or cars with special safety features, it is likely that the perceived constraints will be even more salient in the non-work domain. After all, individuals spend a greater percentage of their time in the non-work domain. Thus, there is more room for uncertain conditions, especially when family members have independent schedules and movements. In short, in an environment of terrorism and perceived threat, expatriates (and their families) are likely to become hypervigilant in their private life and even more affected than at work. This leads to the following hypothesis:

> Hypothesis 2c: Expatriates' perception of personal threat is more strongly related to their perceived non-work constraints than work constraints.

Job turnover intentions

Constraints in the work domain have been shown to cause frustration and stress (O'Connor et al., 1982). For instance, insufficient supplies or equipment or the lack of help from others can be barriers to effective work performance, even if the individual is willing and able to perform (Spector & Jex, 1998). Such mismatch between potential and actual ability to perform can cause employees to get frustrated (O'Connor et al., 1982). Workplace constraints have been related to aggression, complaints, and of specific relevance to the current study, intentions to quit the job (Chen & Spector, 1992), and turnover among employees (Parasuraman & Alutto, 1984). These studies were conducted in non-terrorism contexts. Given the above studies, we argue that threats of terrorism will just as likely be associated with perceived work constraints of expatriates, and, moreover, that frustration over perceived work constraints will likely result in expatriate turnover intentions. Accordingly, we hypothesize:

> Hypothesis 3: Expatriates' perceived work constraints are positively related to their job turnover intentions.

Country leave intentions

Kraeh, Froese, and Park (2015) found in their study in Korea that more than 60% of the expatriates were thinking about leaving the country. However, research has not yet placed much attention on this matter. Related research has suggested that some expatriates negatively compare the host with the home cultures (Stahl & Caligiuri, 2005). These negative cognitions can lead to lower adjustment of expatriates (Herman & Tetrick, 2009). As noted above, there are many potential stressors in the non-work domain caused by an environment of terrorism. We propose that these perceived constraints in the non-work domain are likely to be associated with a negative affect toward the host country in general which, together with personal circumstances, will ultimately lead to a desire to leave the country. Consequently, the higher the salience of perceived constraints in the non-work domain, the higher the intention to leave the country. Therefore, we hypothesize:

> Hypothesis 4: Expatriates' perceived non-work constraints are positively related to their country leave intentions.

Spillover effect

Furthermore, we argue that country leave intentions induced by non-work constraints will have a spillover effect on the work domain. Spillover effects are defined as the influence of variables in one domain, such as non-work, on another domain, such as work (Takeuchi et al., 2002). Due to the particular challenges faced by expatriates working in terrorism-endangered countries, specific spillover effects have been identified in prior research such as the influence of security-related restrictions in private life on the work attitudes of expatriates (Bader & Berg, 2013). Accordingly, we argue that the stress resulting from constraints in private life will likewise eventually spillover to the work domain and, similar to our predicted effects of workplace constraints, increase job turnover intentions. We hypothesize as follows:

> Hypothesis 5: Expatriates' country leave intentions are positively related to their job turnover intentions.

> Hypothesis 6: Expatriates' country leave intentions mediate the relationship between their perceived non-work constraints and job turnover intentions.

Methodology

Sampling procedure and sample

To collect data for testing our hypotheses, we developed a questionnaire in English and conducted an international survey. Because the focus of our study is on the effects of terrorism on expatriates, we used a purposeful sampling process to identify potential respondents in African and Asian countries with different levels of

Table 1. Host countries of respondents.

Country	Frequency	GTI score	Country	Frequency	GTI score
Azerbaijan	1	.06	Morocco	5	2.11
Bangladesh	4	5.25	Nigeria	17	8.58
Botswana	1	.00	Oman	1	.00
Cambodia	23	.31	Pakistan	4	9.37
Egypt	1	6.50	Rwanda	2	4.00
India	16	7.86	Saudi Arabia	5	2.71
Israel	4	4.66	Sierra Leone	4	.00
Jordan	2	1.76	Somalia	1	7.41
Kazakhstan	14	2.37	South Africa	3	3.04
Kenya	4	6.58	Tanzania	8	3.71
Kuwait	1	.04	Thailand	19	7.19
Lebanon	5	6.40	Turkey	12	5.98
Malaysia	3	3.04	Total	160	

terrorism. Countries were selected from the Global Terrorism Index (GTI) (IEP, 2014) which assesses the impact of terrorism in terms of total number of terrorist incidents, total number of fatalities, total number of injuries, and the total property damage from terrorist incidents in a given year. Table 1 provides our sample of countries. The sample mainly consists of African and Asian countries ranging from very low terrorism impact such as Azerbaijan to very high terrorism impact such as Pakistan. Information on expatriates in terrorism-affected countries is difficult to find in publicly available databases. Consistent with methodology employed in prior research (Bader et al., 2015), we identified potential respondents in our sample of countries via social networks such as LinkedIn, Xing, and InterNations. We located profiles and email addresses of 1450 potential respondents. We contacted potential respondents via email with individualized survey links in May 2015. Reminders were sent to non-respondents after two weeks and we closed the survey three weeks later. Ultimately, we obtained 160 usable questionnaires resulting in a response rate of 11%. We tested for non-response bias by comparing early and late responses (Armstrong & Overton, 1977). In essence, this procedure uses late respondents as proxies for non-respondents. Significant statistical differences between the two groups in terms of the demographic distribution or the core constructs indicate a non-response bias. However, t-tests showed neither differences in the demographic representation nor in the main variables indicating that our findings are not affected. Furthermore, our procedure resulted in a balanced sample in terms of level of terrorism in the host country (mean = 4.71; SD = 3.04). The countries, number of respondents, and levels of terrorism represented in our study are displayed in Table 1.

Descriptive statistics obtained from our sample are as follows. The average age of respondents was 43 (mean = 42.56; SD = 11.92) and time spent in their current host location was 39 months (mean = 38.60; SD = 42.97). Respondents had on average eleven months of prior experience in countries with a high risk of terrorism and 62.81 months of prior experience as expatriates in total. This is in line with previous studies on expatriates (Bader et al., 2015; Puck, Mohr, & Rygl, 2008;

Takeuchi et al., 2002). The number of females (36%) is somewhat higher than in other expatriate studies for two reasons. Generally, the number of females is rising and female expatriates have increased to up to 25% of the expatriate population (Brookfield Global Relocation Services, 2016). Additionally, our current study is part of a larger research project that investigates not only the effects of terrorism on expatriates, but also the experience of female expatriates in countries with high levels of institutional discrimination against women. Therefore, we purposefully searched for potential female participants during data collection and accordingly received a higher number of female respondents compared with other expatriate studies. The greatest number of respondents (47.5%) was from Germany. This was followed by 11.9% in the UK and 10.6% of US respondents. The remaining respondents were from 18 different home countries.

Measures

Level of terrorism was determined for each of the selected host countries in the study by impact values from the GTI database (IEP, 2014).

Perceived threat of terrorism was measured by three items adapted from Goodwin et al. (2005) to assess expatriates' perception of threat resulting from terrorism in their current host country. A sample item is 'How likely is this attack to directly threaten you or your family?' Items were measured on a scale from 0% (completely unlikely/not concerned at all) to 100% (completely likely/extremely concerned). Cronbach's alpha was .71.

Perceived constraints in the work domain was measured with eight items adapted from Peters et al. (1980) and Spector and Jex (1998). Sample items are 'Please indicate, how often it is difficult (or even impossible) for you to do your job because of inadequate or insufficient equipment/ inadequate or insufficient supplies/ inadequate work environment (heat, dirt, safety …).' These items were measured on a Likert-scale ranging from 1 (= never) to 7 (= several times a day). Cronbach's alpha was .87.

Perceived constraints in the non-work domain was measured on a 6-item Likert-scale derived from prior research (Hutchings et al., 2013). Sample items are 'Please indicate, how often your private life is constrained in your host country in terms of non-work interaction with locals/mobility & travel/leisure time activities' and were also rated on a Likert-scale ranging from 1 (= never) to 7 (= several times a day). Cronbach's alpha was .88.

Job turnover intentions was measured using Zhang, George, and Chan's (2006) three item scale. A sample item is 'I often think about leaving my job.' These items were measured on a Likert-scale from 1 (= completely disagree) to 7 (= completely agree). Cronbach's alpha was .88.

Country leave intentions was measured with items adapted from Zhang et al.'s (2006) scale. While the above job turnover intention items are concerned with leaving the current job, the focus of country leave intentions is on relocation to another country. 'I cannot imagine that I shall live in this country for a long time' is an example of the modified items. In the survey, items measuring job turnover and country leave intentions were separated to avoid cognitive overlap. The items were measured on a Likert-scale from 1 (= completely disagree) to 7 (= completely agree). Cronbach's alpha was .80.

Control variables. Five control variables were included. First, gender was included (0 = male; 1 = female), because studies indicate that gender might influence the perception of terrorism. Females were found to be more sensitive to ethnopolitical conflict, have lower job satisfaction in countries suffering from war (Reade & Lee, 2012), and lower performance in countries with high levels of terrorism (Bader et al., 2015). However, they also have higher work and interaction adjustment during expatriation (Selmer & Leung, 2003). Second, we controlled for age (in years), because older expatriates have more life experience and are thus better able to cope with new challenges and difficult situations (Froese & Peltokorpi, 2013; Peltokorpi & Froese, 2012; Puck et al., 2008). Third, in line with previous studies (Bader et al., 2015; Peltokorpi & Froese, 2012), we controlled for prior experience as an expatriate (in months). In particular, we asked respondents for their experience in countries with a high level of terrorism, as this might help with adjustment to a country with a similar situation (Kraimer et al., 2001). Fourth, we included the respondent's length of stay in the host country (in months), because prior research indicates that adjustment is a time-dependent process (Torbiörn, 1982; Black et al., 1991). Fifth, since the countries in our sample are developing or emerging economies, we controlled for stress that might develop from not being used to living in a country with relatively low economic development (Liu, Spector, & Shi, 2007). To do this, we included the gross domestic product (GDP) per capita in US Dollars (World Bank, 2015).

Results

Table 2 provides an overview of the means, standard deviations, and correlations of the study variables. We used structural equation modeling, and the partial least squares (PLS) latent path model approach (instead of AMOS, Lisrel, etc. which are based on covariance matrices). This type of analysis requires at least 10 times as many observations as the number of indicators for the most predicted construct (Barclay, Higgins, & Thompson, 1995). Even if somewhat small, our sample size ($N = 160$) meets this requirement. Our calculations were conducted with SmartPLS3 software (Ringle, Wende, & Becker, 2015), a program increasingly used in management research. Based on the recommended number, we set the maximum number of iterations to 300. For bootstrapping analysis, we applied individual sign changes and used 5000 bootstrap samples (Hair, Sarstedt, Ringle, & Mena, 2012; Henseler, Ringle, & Sinkovics, 2009). We calculated all results with control variables loading on all variables in our model.

Table 2. Means, standard deviations, and correlations.

	Mean	SD	1	2	3	4	5	6	7	8	9	10
1 Gender	.36	.48										
2 Age	42.56	11.92	–.28***									
3 Prior experience	11.03	26.81	–.15	.25**								
4 Time in host country	38.60	42.97	–.08	.28***	–.01							
5 GDP per capita of host country	12,246.07	12,010.52	–.15	.16*	–.06	–.12						
6 GTI of host country	4.71	3.04	–.10	–.04	.22**	.11	–.14					
7 Perceived threat	25.17	20.10	.04	.01	.16*	.02	.01	.48***				
8 Perceived constraints in the work domain	2.85	1.17	.00	–.04	.17*	.03	–.11	.04	.13			
9 Perceived constraints in the non-work domain	2.51	1.40	.06	–.09	.07	–.08	.16*	.11	.41***	.36***		
10 Country leave intentions	3.16	1.67	.09	.00	.14	–.11	.00	.02	.19*	.19*	.21**	
11 Job turnover intentions	3.06	1.79	.17*	– .06	.10	–.15	.00	–.03	.15	.28***	.16*	.66***

*$p < .05$; **$p < .01$; ***$p < .001$.

Since there is no global goodness-of-fit index for PLS (Henseler et al., 2009), we tested our model following a two-step approach (Chin, 1998; Hair et al., 2012). First, we assessed the outer model. Composite reliability and Cronbach's alpha values were all above the suggested cut-off value of .70 (Nunnally, 1978). All standardized outer loadings were well above the cut-off criterion of .40 (Hulland, 1999), with the lowest value being .65. Furthermore, all average variance extracted (AVE) values were above .50 (Bagozzi & Yi, 1988). Cross-loadings showed that each indicator had the highest loading on the construct it was intended to reflect (Chin, 1998; Grégoire & Fisher, 2006). Additionally, the Fornell–Larcker criterion (Fornell & Larcker, 1981) to assess discriminant validity was met, requiring that the AVE of each latent variable is higher than the squared correlations with all other latent variables (Henseler et al., 2009). Furthermore, the heterotrait–monotrait ratio (HTMT) was below .85 (Henseler, Ringle, & Sarstedt, 2015) which further supports the discriminant validity of our constructs.

To assess the inner model, we examined four criteria (Chin, 1998; Henseler et al., 2009). First, we used blindfolding (omission distance = 7) in order to evaluate the Stone–Geisser criterion. Results indicated sufficient predictive relevance, because this procedure revealed that Q^2 values were greater than 0 for every variable (Chin, 1998; Henseler et al., 2009). Second, we examined the coefficient of determination (R^2) of each latent variable. The highest R^2 values were job turnover intentions ($R^2 = .50$), perceived threat ($R^2 = .25$) and perceived constraints in the non-work domain ($R^2 = .23$). These effects can be considered average to weak, because they meet the cut-off values of .19 and .33 (Chin, 1998). In turn, country leave intentions ($R^2 = .08$) and work constraints ($R^2 = .06$) indicate very weak explanatory power. Third, we assessed the effect size of these latent variables by f^2 values which represent the effect at the structural level (Henseler et al., 2009). This approach showed that the effect of non-work constraints on country leave intentions ($f^2 = .04$) is influential but small, because it exceeds .02 (Henseler et al., 2009), whereas the influence of perceived threat on work constraints does not meet this value ($f^2 = .01$). Fourth, this finding is also supported by the estimates for path coefficients. Bootstrapping analysis shows that while all other paths in the inner model have a significant relationship between constructs (see Figure 2), the path between perceived threat and work constraints is insignificant ($t = 1.39$).

Summary hypotheses test

PLS analysis shows support for hypothesis 1, which stated that a higher level of terrorism in a country is related to higher perceptions of threat ($\beta = .48; p < .001$). While hypothesis 2a, the relationship between perceptions of threat and perceived constraints in the work domain is not supported ($\beta = .09; p > .05$), our data confirm the relationship between perceptions of threat and non-work constraints as predicted in hypothesis 2b ($\beta = .43; p < .001$).

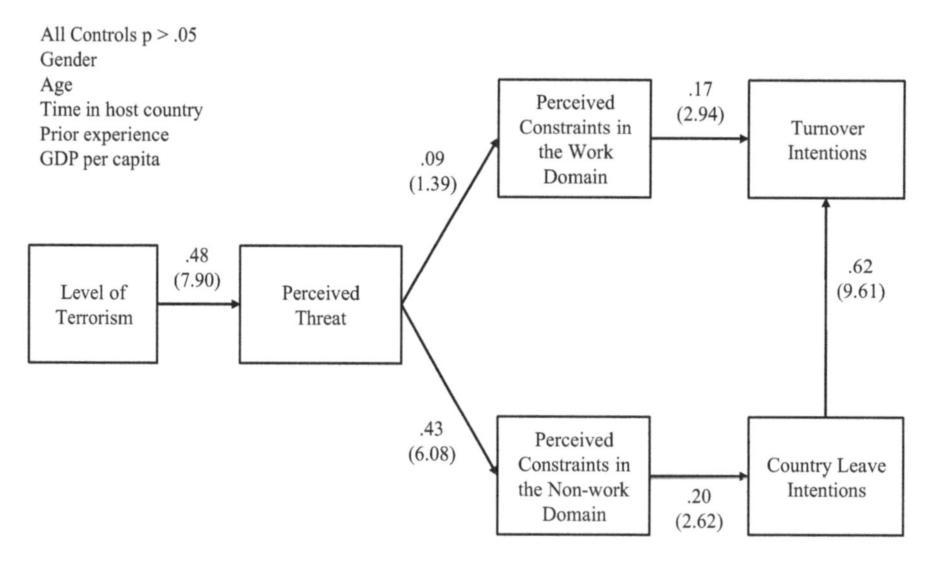

Figure 2. Results of PLS analysis (*t*-values in parentheses).

Because the program SmartPLS does not offer a procedure to test for the significance of differences between regression coefficients, we used SPSS (Version 23) and conducted GLM analysis. We specified a repeated measures model with our two dependent variables representing the two-level within-subject factor using our perceived threat variable as covariate. Results showed that the effects varied significantly ($F(1) = 14.02$; $p < .001$). This provides support for hypothesis 2c, i.e. perceived threat has a more detrimental influence on perceived constraints in the non-work domain than in the work domain.

In support of hypothesis 3, the perception of work constraints is positively related to job turnover intentions ($\beta = .17$; $p < .01$). Supporting hypotheses 4 and 5, perceptions of constraints in the non-work domain are directly related to country leave intentions ($\beta = .20$; $p < .01$), which are then related to job turnover intentions ($\beta = .62$; $p < .001$). Furthermore, bootstrapping analysis provided support for hypothesis 6 regarding spillover effects. The indirect effect of perceptions of non-work domain constraints on job turnover intentions, through country leave intentions, was significant ($p < .05$).

Additionally, we conducted several post-hoc robustness tests. First, we included more control variables which could potentially influence the variables in our model. These included: accompanied by family (dummy coded as 0 = yes; 1 = no), country of origin (dummy coded as 0 = German; 1 = non-German), and position (dummy coded as 0 = non-managerial; 1 = managerial). Out of these additional control variables only accompanied by family was significantly related to perceived threat ($\beta = .14$; $p < .05$) and country leave intentions ($\beta = .17$; $p < .05$). Inclusion of the additional control variables did not affect the significance of results of our original model. Second, we tested our model with an alternate statistical method: regression analysis using SPSS. The results also supported our hypothesized model.

Discussion

Drawing on stress theory, we examined how terrorism influences withdrawal cognitions of expatriates. We found that expatriates in countries with high levels of terrorism perceived greater personal threat than expatriates in countries with lower levels of terrorism. While perception of threat was not related to perceived constraints in the work domain, it was significantly related to perceptions of constraints in the non-work domain. Furthermore, our findings show that perceived constraints at work directly relate to job turnover intentions, while perceived constraints in the non-work domain have a direct effect on country leave intentions and an indirect, spillover effect on job turnover intentions. The following elaborates on our theoretical contributions, practical implications, limitations of our research, and suggested research directions.

Theoretical implications

Our study makes three major contributions to the scarce literature on expatriates in terrorism-endangered countries. First, building on a stress perspective (Chen & Spector, 1992; O'Connor et al., 1982; Peters et al., 1980; Spector & Jex, 1998), our study supports prior research which indicates that expatriates in such countries experience stress as well as exhibit less positive work attitudes and lower performance (Bader & Berg, 2013, 2014). Our findings highlight that operating in terrorism-endangered countries not only has direct costs associated with securing operations and production sites abroad (Czinkota et al., 2004), but also has more indirect costs related to increased withdrawal cognitions and the resulting risk of turnover among expatriates. In particular, our findings suggest that not only host-country nationals (Reade & Lee, 2012), but also expatriates in terrorism endangered countries are strongly affected and show a higher risk of turnover.

Second, we contribute to an increased understanding of work and non-work domains experienced by expatriates in terrorism-endangered countries. We do this by disentangling the stress-induced constraints associated with each domain and their consequences. Prior studies have shown that both domains need to be considered separately during expatriation (Black et al., 1991; Selmer & Fenner, 2009; Takeuchi, 2010; Takeuchi et al., 2002). Our findings support this approach by showing that the experience and outcomes of constraints differ between the domains. We found that perceived threat resulting from higher levels of terrorism in the host country does not produce stressors in the work domain, at least in our sample. Our results differ from the findings of previous studies that showed a positive relationship between terrorist threat and workplace frustration in a terrorism-endangered context (Reade, 2009; Reade & Lee, 2016). Those studies, however, focused on the perceptions of host-country managers, many of whom worked in indigenous organizations. MNEs tend to have comparatively well-developed organizational systems and security protocols, since they invest heavily in the protection of their assets and safety of their employees (Elango et al., 2008; Harvey, 1993; Suder, 2006). Accordingly, our results suggest that such measures reduce perceptions of frustration and security concerns in the work domain among expatriates of MNEs. However, our study also indicates that expatriates feel less protected and more sensitive to terrorist threats outside the workplace.

Further, our data show that the two domains are associated with different outcomes. While constraints in the work domain relate to an increased urge to leave the current job, constraints in the non-work domain are related to a general negative attitude toward the country in which they live, eventually affecting their turnover intentions. These results echo the findings of the meta-analysis by Bhaskar-Shrinivas et al. (2005) which show that non-work factors have the strongest effects on expatriates. In sum, our study highlights the importance of considering the work and particularly the non-work domain when investigating antecedents and outcomes of expatriates' withdrawal cognitions.

Third, we revealed a spillover effect from the non-work to the work domain (Takeuchi et al., 2002). We found that perceived constraints in the non-work domain relate to job turnover intentions through country leave intentions. Our interpretation is that the constraints faced by expatriates relate initially to a negative image of the situation in the host country and the wish to get away from the constraints in private life. This then spills over to the work domain and increases the desire to leave the current job. While prior research has shown that spillover effects do not occur in certain situations, such as expatriation in the public sector (Selmer & Fenner, 2009), our findings are in line with the majority of other studies which indicate the existence of spillover effects (Bhaskar-Shrinivas et al., 2005; Black et al., 1991; Takeuchi, 2010; Takeuchi et al., 2002). Furthermore, by examining these effects, we have underscored the importance of a rather new construct in the non-work domain, intentions to leave the host country (Kraeh et al., 2015), and its explanatory power for job turnover intentions.

Practical implications

Our research findings have implications for the management of expatriate failure. We found that perceived threat and related stress from terrorism-induced constraints does indeed increase employee turnover intentions. To enhance chances for expatriate success, organizations should consider the entire process of expatriation, including before, during, and after expatriation. First, before expatriation, there is a need to develop realistic expectations of what life will be like in the host country (Caligiuri, Phillips, Lazarova, Tarique, & Burgi, 2001). Therefore, organizations should provide expatriates and their families with an orientation to life in a high-risk country. This can be delivered through training or access to previously assigned expatriates in order to obtain first-hand, realistic views. Such training should include stress management techniques. Additionally, because there can be individual variation in response to terrorist threat and development of posttraumatic stress disorder (PTSD) (Brown et al., 2007; Paton & Violanti, 2007), expatriates designated for assignment in high-risk countries should be screened in advance for risk factors for developing PTSD (Brown et al., 2007).

Second, support is crucial during expatriation to terrorism-endangered countries. This can be in the form of personal support networks (Bader, 2015; Bader & Schuster, 2015) and organizational support. Perceived organizational support has been found to lessen the negative impact of ethnic-based terrorism on employee commitment (Reade & Lee, 2012), and the negative effect of terrorism-induced family-related stress on expatriate performance (Bader et al., 2015). Thus, organizations should make efforts to heighten employees' perceptions of support in order to lessen perceptions of perceived personal threat. This might involve making available to expatriates (and their families) in-house counselors or clinical psychologists to monitor and address the stress and mental health issues associated with exposure to terrorist incidents (Reade, 2009). Beyond this, it is important to encourage expatriates to engage in activities that reduce stress. These include meditation and physical exercise, both of which can directly reduce stress (Stoyva & Carlson, 1993). Additionally, these activities can provide a sense of personal control over daily activities in that they provide routine in the face of otherwise unpredictable external events. In particular, our study shows that it is important to support expatriates in the non-work domain. Since perceived threat more strongly affects the private life of expatriates, special assistance such as personal protection, bulletproof windows in cars and homes, and frequent information on current news might help the expatriates develop a stronger sense of security.

Third, additional effort should be placed on the post-expatriation phase. Repatriation has been identified as a phase of high stress and frustration leading to a high turnover among repatriates (Suutari & Brewster, 2003). These challenges are likely to be further magnified when repatriation is from countries with high levels of terrorism. This is because work and particularly daily life experiences in terrorism-endangered countries can be quite stressful due to the security situation. Prior research suggests that expatriates experience a reversed culture shock and long for support to reintegrate in the home country culture even more than the home company culture (Paik, Segaud, & Malinowski, 2002). This is consistent with our findings that show expatriates experience more constraints in their private life and thus are in need of successful reintegration into general living conditions at home. Supporting expatriates to reintegrate in the home country is thus of crucial importance.

Limitations and avenues for future research

As with every study, ours has limitations. First, our sample consisted mainly of European expatriates based in African and Asian countries. Future studies could include a wider range of host countries and expatriates in terms of country of origin. This would allow the investigation of variation resulting from differences in country-of-origin of expatriates and host country. For instance, a promising avenue of research would be to investigate expatriates whose countries of origin range from high to low levels of terrorism, and their experiences in host countries with levels of terrorism ranging from high to low. Such study could potentially aid in expatriate staffing in terror-endangered countries. Further, our sample size was somewhat small; a larger sample would allow conducting multi-level analyses to further deepen our understanding of the effects of different host-country characteristics.

Second, our data, like the vast majority of other studies, are prone to common method bias. Our research was carefully designed in order to counter common method bias ex ante (Podsakoff, MacKenzie, Lee, & Podsakoff, 2003). First, the level of terrorism and several control variables are of an objective nature. Second, we separated the items corresponding to the mediating and dependent variables in the questionnaire. Third, we guaranteed anonymity to respondents. Fourth, respondents were not aware of the research purpose. Furthermore, we conducted ex-post statistical tests, i.e. Harman's single factor test (Harman, 1976) and various PLS tests, which showed that common method variance is not a serious concern in our data. Nevertheless, due to the cross-sectional design of our study, we cannot draw any conclusions on causality, though our hypotheses are driven by prior research. Therefore, future research should conduct longitudinal studies in order to establish causality between the variables. Additionally, stress levels and perceived threat might vary substantially depending on the point in time of measurement. Thus, retrieving data from several points of time, such as immediately after an attack, and at later intervals, would provide a new understanding of time-dependent stress reactions to terrorist attacks, and their outcomes. This would further contribute to the literature on expatriates in terrorism-endangered countries, as well as to the terrorism literature in general.

Third, while we included several demographic and country related control variables in our study, many other factors might affect the variables in our model. Accordingly, future research could include personality traits, such as emotional stability, to investigate, how this affects stress perceptions. Including coping strategies could be another potential path for future research. Furthermore, additional variables from the cultural and institutional environment of the host country which could increase or reduce the stress perceived by the expatriates might also be of great interest for future research.

In conclusion, our study has added novel and important insights into the experiences and consequences of expatriates in high-risk countries, yet much more research is still needed.

Disclosure statement

No potential conflict of interest was reported by the authors.

References

Alexander, D. C. (2004). *Business confronts terrorism: Risks and responses*. Madison, WI: University of Wisconsin Press.

Alexander, Y., Carlton, D., & Wilkinson, P. (1979). *Terrorism: Theory and practice*. Boulder, CO: Westview Press.

Armstrong, J. S., & Overton, T. S. (1977). Estimating nonresponse bias in mail surveys. *Journal of Marketing Research, 14*, 396–402.

Bader, B. (2015). The power of support in high-risk countries: Compensation and social support as antecedents of expatriate work attitudes. *The International Journal of Human Resource Management, 26*, 1712–1736.

Bader, B., & Berg, N. (2013). An empirical investigation of terrorism-induced stress on expatriate attitudes and performance. *Journal of International Management, 19*, 163–175.

Bader, B., & Berg, N. (2014). The influence of terrorism on expatriate performance: A conceptual approach. *The International Journal of Human Resource Management, 25*, 539–557.

Bader, B., Berg, N., & Holtbrügge, D. (2015). Expatriate performance in terrorism-endangered countries: The role of family and organizational support. *International Business Review, 24*, 849–860.

Bader, B., & Schuster, T. (2015). Expatriate social networks in terrorism-endangered countries: An empirical analysis in Afghanistan, India, Pakistan, and Saudi Arabia. *Journal of International Management, 21*, 63–77.

Bagozzi, R. P., & Yi, Y. (1988). On the evaluation of structural equation models. *Journal of the Academy of Marketing Science, 16*, 74–94.

Barclay, D. W., Higgins, C. A., & Thompson, R. (1995). The partial least squares (PLS) approach to causal modeling: Personal computer adoption and use as an illustration. *Technology Studies, 2*, 285–309.

Bar-Tal, D. (2007). Sociopsychological foundations of intractable conflicts. *American Behavioral Scientist, 50*, 1430–1453.

Berger, R. (2011). The golden cage: Western women in the compound in a Muslim country. *Journal of International Women's Studies, 12*, 38–54.

Bhaskar-Shrinivas, P., Harrison, D. A., Shaffer, M. A., & Luk, D. M. (2005). Input-based and time-based models of international adjustment: Meta-analytic evidence and theoretical extensions. *Academy of Management Journal, 48*, 257–281.

Black, J. S. (1988). Work role transitions: A study of American expatriate managers in Japan. *Journal of International Business Studies, 19*, 277–294.

Black, J. S. & Gregersen, H. B. (1991). Antecedents to cross-cultural adjustment for expatriates in Pacific Rim assignments. *Human Relations, 44*, 497–515.

Black, J. S., Mendenhall, M., & Oddou, G. R. (1991). Towards a comprehensive model of international adjustment: An integration of multiple theoretical perspectives. *Academy of Management Review, 16*, 291–317.

Black, J. S., & Stephens, G. K. (1989). The influence of the spouse on American expatriate adjustment. *Journal of Management, 15*, 529–544.

Bonger, B. (2007). The psychology of terrorism: Defining the need and describing the goals. In B. Bonger, L. M. Brown, L. E. Beutler, J. N. Breckenridge, & P. G. Zimbardo (Eds.), *Psychology of terrorism* (pp. 3–12). New York, NY: Oxford University Press.

Brookfield Global Relocation Services. (2016). *2016 global mobility trend survey*. Retrieved June 14, 2016, from http://globalmobilitytrends.brookfieldgrs.com

Brown, L. M., Cohen, D., & Kohlmaier, J. R. (2007). Older adults and terrorism. In B. Bonger, L. M. Brown, L. E. Beutler, J. N. Breckenridge, & P. G. Zimbardo (Eds.), *Psychology of terrorism* (pp. 288–310). New York, NY: Oxford University Press.

Caligiuri, P., Phillips, J., Lazarova, M., Tarique, I., & Burgi, P. (2001). The theory of met expectations applied to expatriate adjustment: The role of crosscultural training. *The International Journal of Human Resource Management, 12*, 357–372.

Chalk, P. (2008). *The maritime dimension of international security: Terrorism, piracy, and challenges for the U.S.* Santa Monica, CA: Rand Corporation.

Chen, P. Y., & Spector, P. E. (1992). Relationships of work stressors with aggression, withdrawal, theft and substance use: An exploratory study. *Journal of Occupational and Organizational Psychology, 65*, 177–184.

Chin, W. W. (1998). The partial least squares approach to structural equation modeling. In G. A. Marcoulides (Ed.), *Modern methods for business research* (pp. 295–336). Mahwah, NJ: Lawrence Erlbaum Associates Publishers.

Czinkota, M. R., Knight, G. A., & Liesch, P. W. (2004). Terrorism and international business. In G. G. S. Suder (Ed.), *Terrorism and the international business environment: The security-business nexus* (pp. 43–57). Northampton, MA: Edward Elgar.

Czinkota, M. R., Knight, G. A., Liesch, P. W., & Steen, J. (2005). Positioning terrorism in management and marketing: Research propositions. *Journal of International Management, 11*, 581–604.

Elango, B., Graf, L. A., & Hemmasi, M. (2008). Reducing the risk of becoming a victim of terrorism while on international business assignments. *Simulation & Gaming, 39*, 40–557.

Firth, B. M., Chen, G., Kirkman, B. L., & Kim, K. (2014). Newcomers abroad: Expatriate adaptation during early phases of international assignments. *Academy of Management Journal, 57*, 280–300.

Fornell, C., & Larcker, D. F. (1981). Evaluation structural equation models with unobservable variables and measurement error. *Journal of Marketing Research, 18*, 39–50.

Froese, F. J. (2012). Motivation and adjustment of self-initiated expatriates: The case of expatriate academics in South Korea. *The International Journal of Human Resource Management, 23*, 1095–1112.

Froese, F. J., & Peltokorpi, V. (2013). Organizational expatriates and self-initiated expatriates: Differences in cross-cultural adjustment and job satisfaction. *The International Journal of Human Resource Management, 24*, 1953–1967.

Goldberger, L., & Breznitz, S. (Eds.). (1993). *Handbook of stress* (2nd ed.). New York, NY: Free Press.

Goodwin, R., Willson, M., & Gaines Jr, S. (2005). Terror threat perception and its consequences in contemporary Britain. *British Journal of Psychology, 96*, 389–406.

Grégoire, Y., & Fisher, R. J. (2006). The effects of relationship quality on customer retaliation. *Marketing Letters, 17*, 31–46.

Hair, J. F., Sarstedt, M., Ringle, C. M., & Mena, J. A. (2012). An assessment of the use of partial least squares structural equation modeling in marketing research. *Journal of the Academy of Marketing Science, 40*, 414–433.

Harman, H. H. (1976). *Modern factor analysis*. Chigaco, IL: University of Chicago Press.

Harrison, D. A., Shaffer, M. A., & Bhaskar-Shrinivas, P. (2004). Going places: Roads more and less traveled in research on expatriate experiences. *Research in Personnel and Human Resources Management, 23*, 203–252.

Harvey, M. G. (1993). A survey of corporate programs for managing terrorist threats. *Journal of International Business Studies, 24*, 465–478.

Harzing, A. W. (2001). Of bears, bumble-bees and spiders: The role of expatriates in controlling foreign subsidiaries. *Journal of World Business, 36*, 366–379.

Harzing, A.-W. K. (2002). Are our referencing errors undermining our scholarship and credibility? The case of expatriate failure rates. *Journal of Organizational Behavior, 23*, 127–148.

Harzing, A.-W., & Christensen, C. (2004). Expatriate failure: Time to abandon the concept? *Career Development International, 9*, 616–626.

Henseler, J., Ringle, C. M., & Sarstedt, M. (2015). A new criterion for assessing discriminant validity in variance-based structural equation modeling. *Journal of the Academy of Marketing Science, 43*, 115–135.

Henseler, J., Ringle, C. M., & Sinkovics, R. R. (2009). The use of partial least squares path modelling in international marketing. *Advances in International Marketing, 20*, 277–319.

Herman, J. L., & Tetrick, L. E. (2009). Problem-focused versus emotion-focused coping strategies and repatriation adjustment. *Human Resource Management, 48*, 69–88.

Hironaka, A. (2005). *Neverending wars: The international community, weak states, and the perpetuation of civil war*. Cambridge, MA: Harvard University Press.

Hulland, J. (1999). Use of partial least squares (PLS) in strategic management research: A review of four recent studies. *Strategic Management Journal, 20*, 195–204.

Hutchings, K., Michailova, S., & Harrison, E. C. (2013). Neither ghettoed nor cosmopolitan. A study of Western women's perceptions of gender and cultural stereotyping in the UAE. *Management International Review, 53*, 291–318.

Institute for Economics and Peace. (2014). *Global terrorism index 2014*. Retrieved March 3, 2015, from http://economicsandpeace.org/wp-content/uploads/2015/06/Global-Terrorism-Index-Report-2014.pdf

Institute for Economics and Peace. (2015). *Global terrorism index 2015*. Retrieved October 30, 2015, from http://economicsandpeace.org/wp-content/uploads/2015/11/Global-Terrorism-Index-2015.pdf

Jain, S. C., & Grosse, R. (2009). Impact of terrorism and security measures on global business transactions: Some international business guidelines. *Journal of Transnational Management, 14*, 42–73.

Kastenmüller, A., Greitemeyer, T., Fischer, P., Tattersall, A. J., Peus, C., Bussmann, P., … Frey, D. (2011). Terrorism threat and networking: Evidence that terrorism salience decreases occupational networking. *Journal of Organizational Behavior, 32*, 961–977.

Kraeh, A., Froese, F. J., & Park, H. (2015). Foreign professionals in South Korea: Integration or alienation? In D'Costa, A. P. (Ed.). *After-development dynamics. South Korea's contemporary engagement with Asia* (pp. 185–200). Oxford: Oxford University Press.

Kraimer, M. L., Wayne, S. J., & Jaworski, R. A. (2001). Sources of support and expatriate performance: The mediating role of expatriate adjustment. *Personnel Psychology, 54*, 71–99.

Lazarus, R. S. (1991). *Emotion and adaptation*. New York, NY: Oxford University Press.

Lazarus, R. S., & Folkman, S. (1984). *Stress, appraisal, and coping*. New York, NY: Springer Publishing Company.

Lee, H.-J., & Reade, C. (2015). Ethnic homophily perceptions as an emergent IHRM challenge: Evidence from firms operating in Sri Lanka during the ethnic conflict. *The International Journal of Human Resource Management, 26*, 1645–1664.

Liu, C., Spector, P. E., & Shi, L. (2007). Cross-national job stress: A quantitative and qualitative study. *Journal of Organizational Behavior, 28*, 209–239.

Mainiero, L., & Gibson, D. (2003). Managing employee trauma: Dealing with the emotional fall-out from 9/11. *Academy of Management Executive, 17*, 130–143.

Min, H. (2011). Modern maritime piracy in supply chain risk management. *International Journal of Logistics Systems and Management, 10*, 122–138.

Nelson, E. S. (2012). Maritime terrorism and piracy: Existing and potential threats. *Global Security Studies, 3*, 15–28.

Nunnally, J. C. (1978). *Psychometric theory* (2nd ed.). New York, NY: McGraw-Hill.

O'Connor, E. J., Peters, L. H., Rudolf, C. J., & Pooyan, A. (1982). Situational constraints and employee affective reactions: A partial field replication. *Group & Organization Management, 7*, 418–428.

Okpara, J. O., & Kabongo, J. D. (2011). Cross-cultural training and expatriate adjustment: A study of western expatriates in Nigeria. *Journal of World Business, 46*, 22–30.

Paik, Y., Segaud, B., & Malinowski, Ch. (2002). How to improve repatriation management: Are motivations and expectations congruent between the company and expatriates? *International Journal of Manpower, 23*, 635–648.

Parasuraman, S., & Alutto, J. A. (1984). Sources and outcomes of stress in organizational settings: Toward the development of a structural model. *Academy of Management Journal, 27*, 330–350.

Paton, D., & Violanti, J. M. (2007). Terrorism stress risk assessment and management. In B. Bonger, L. M. Brown, L. E. Beutler, J. N. Breckenridge, & P. G. Zimbardo (Eds.), *Psychology of terrorism* (pp. 225–246). New York, NY: Oxford University Press.

Pcltokorpi, V., & Froese, F. J. (2009). Organizational expatriates and self-initiated expatriates: Who adjusts better to work and life in Japan? *The International Journal of Human Resource Management, 20*, 1096–1112.

Peltokorpi, V., & Froese, F. J. (2012). The impact of expatriate personality traits on cross-cultural adjustment: A study with expatriates in Japan. *International Business Review, 21*, 734–746.

Peters, L. H., O'Connor, E. J., & Rudolf, C. J. (1980). The behavioral and affective consequences of performance-relevant situational variables. *Organizational Behavior and Human Performance, 25*, 79–96.

Podsakoff, P. M., MacKenzie, S. B., Lee, J. Y., & Podsakoff, N. P. (2003). Common method biases in behavioral research: A critical review of the literature and recommended remedies. *Journal of Applied Psychology, 88*, 879–903.

Puck, J. F., Mohr, A., & Rygl, D. (2008). An empirical analysis of managers' adjustment to working in multi-national project teams in the pipeline and plant construction sector. *The International Journal of Human Resource Management, 19*, 2252–2267.

Reade, C. (2009). Human resource management implications of terrorist threats to firms in the supply chain. *International Journal of Physical Distribution and Logistics Management, 39*, 469–485.

Reade, C., & Lee, H.-J. (2012). Organizational commitment in time of war: Assessing the impact and attenuation of employee sensitivity to ethnopolitical conflict. *Journal of International Management, 18*, 85–101.

Reade, C., & Lee, H.-J. (2016). Does ethnic conflict impede or enable employee innovation behavior? The alchemic role of collaborative conflict management. *International Journal of Conflict Management, 27*, 199–224.

Ringle, C. M., Wende, S., & Becker, J.-M. (2015). *SmartPLS 3*. Bönningstedt: SmartPLS. Retrieved from http://www.smartpls.com

Sakhuja, V. (2010). Security threats and challenges to maritime supply chains. *Disarmament Forum (United Nations Institute for Disarmament Research), 2*, 3–12.

Schuster, M. A., Stein, B. D., Jaycox, L. H., Collins, R. L., Marshall, G. N., Elliott, M. N., … Berry, S. H. (2001). A national survey of stress reactions after the September 11, 2001, terrorist attacks. *New England Journal of Medicine, 345*, 1507–1512.

Selmer, J., & Fenner Jr., C. R. (2009). Spillover effects between work and non-work adjustment among public sector expatriates. *Personnel Review, 38*, 336–379.

Selmer, J., & Leung, A. S. M. (2003). International adjustment of female vs. male expatriates. *International Journal of Human Resource Management, 14*, 1117–1131.

Sheffi, Y. (2001). Supply chain management under the threat of international terrorism. *The International Journal of Logistics Management, 12*, 1–11.

Spector, P. E., & Jex, S. M. (1998). Development of four self-report measures of job stressors and strain: Interpersonal conflict at work scale, organizational constraints scale, quantitative workload inventory, and physical symptoms inventory. *Journal of Occupational Health Psychology, 4*, 356–367.

Stahl, G. K., & Caligiuri, P. (2005). The effectiveness of expatriate coping strategies: The moderating role of cultural distance, position level, and time on the international assignment. *Journal of Applied Psychology, 90*, 603–615.

Stoyva, J. M., & Carlson, J. G. (1993). A coping/rest model of relaxation and stress management. In L. Goldberger, & S. Brenitz (Eds.), *Handbook of stress* (pp. 724–756, 2nd ed.). New York, NY: Free Press.

Suder, G. G. (Ed.). (2006). *Corporate strategies under international terrorism and adversity.* Cheltenham: E. Elgar Publications.

Suder, G., Birnik, A., Nielsen, N. & Riviere, M. (in press). Extreme case learning: The manager perspective on rare knowledge and capabilities development. *Knowledge Management Research & Practice.*

Suutari, V., & Brewster, C. (2003). Repatriation: Empirical evidence from a longitudinal study of careers and expectations among Finnish expatriates. *International Journal of Human Resource Management, 14*, 1132–1151.

Takeuchi, R. (2010). A critical review of expatriate adjustment research through a multiple stakeholder view: Progress, emerging trends, and prospect. *Journal of Management, 36*, 1040–1064.

Takeuchi, R., Yun, S., & Tesluk, P. E. (2002). An examination of crossover and spillover effects of spousal and expatriate cross-cultural adjustment on expatriate outcomes. *Journal of Applied Psychology, 87*, 655–666.

Torbiörn, I. (1982). *Living abroad.* New York, NY: Wiley.

World Bank. (2015). *GDP per capita.* Retrieved September 15, 2015, from http://data.worldbank.org/indicator/NY.GDP.MKTP.CD

Zhang, Y., George, J. M., & Chan, T.-S. (2006). The paradox of dueling identities: The case of local senior executives in MNC subsidiaries. *Journal of Management, 32*, 400–425.

Mind the gap: the role of HRM in creating, capturing and leveraging rare knowledge in hostile environments

Gabriele Suder, Carol Reade, Monica Riviere, Andreas Birnik and Niklas Nielsen

ABSTRACT
Multinational enterprises (MNEs) have increasingly entered markets in less developed regions of the world afflicted with weak institutions and political conflict. Some are characterised by 'extreme' cases of institutional voids and terrorism, creating a hostile environment for the organisation and its people. This in-depth qualitative study of a service company, a European telecommunications joint venture in Afghanistan, seeks to shed light and build theory on the human resource management (HRM) dimension of managerial learning and knowledge acquisition in hostile environments, as part of the MNE's organisational learning process. Specifically, we investigate how knowledge gaps can be addressed through supportive HR practices, and how knowledge classified as 'rare' can be captured and leveraged through HR interventions such as debriefing. We stipulate that HR practices and interventions adapted to hostile environments, together with expatriate willingness to learn and share new knowledge, play a critical role in the creation, capturing and leveraging of rare knowledge for subsequent use by the MNE in other hostile locations. The study has implications for international HRM and organisational resilience, under the proposition that competitive advantage can be gained through exploitation of rare knowledge acquired in hostile environments.

Introduction

Multinational enterprises (MNEs) continue to expand their business operations into developing countries in Asia, Africa and Latin America in the quest for business development (Dewhurst, Harris, & Heywood, 2012; World Investment Report [WIR], 2015). This trend has strategic implications for MNE operations including the deployment and management of human resources. Organisations and their expatriates from more developed countries must learn to adapt to contexts lacking in adequate governance, infrastructure, supplies and amenities to which they are usually accustomed when operating in developed countries. In severe cases of institutional voids, MNEs and their host-country staff need to build what they need for the success of their venture, including infrastructure otherwise provided by the host government. This creates both high cost and high risk for the firm.

Compounding the challenge of institutional voids in certain countries is the simultaneous challenge of violent political conflicts including war and terrorism (Heidelberg Institute for International Conflict Research, 2015). In such contexts, the protection of people and assets becomes paramount, and organisations and their staff need to manage operations whilst learning to adapt to dangerous, high risk environments, also defined as 'extreme' environments. This poses additional high cost and high risk for the firm. We contend that the combination of severe institutional voids and a high security threat, particularly when MNEs and their staff may be targeted, creates an 'extreme' case scenario that goes beyond high risk to what we refer to as a hostile operating environment. 'Extreme' environments are characterised by instability, information ambiguity, and rapid, discontinuous, violent and simultaneous changes in the environment (Brown & Eisenhardt, 1997; Wirtz, Mathieu, & Schilke, 2007). Case studies into such contexts are known as 'extreme' cases (Brown & Eisenhardt, 1997).

Managers in hostile contexts experience the challenges related to severe institutional voids and high security risk, challenges that have implications for the viability of their business. Their perceptions of these challenges illustrate knowledge gaps (hereafter referred to as KGs) that need to be addressed so that both expatriates and local staff can manage operations effectively. Given that challenges in a hostile environment can be particularly confronting or difficult to tackle, we expect to learn from this research how the HR function may support the creation, capturing and leveraging of knowledge, and why this constitutes 'rare' and thus particularly relevant competitive knowledge that enhances organisational learning and benefits the MNE as a whole in its current and future operations.

As part of the organisational learning process, developed-market MNEs typically acquire knowledge in, and about, foreign markets by progressively expanding abroad, internalising local knowledge, gaining confidence and absorptive capacity, and applying that knowledge to address KGs in new operating environments (Petersen, Pedersen, & Lyles, 2008). Managers – expatriate and local – are crucial in this learning process because they are on the frontline of individual and organisational knowledge acquisition. As Simon (1991, p. 17) put it, 'organisations learn in only two ways: (1) by the learning of its members, or (2) by ingesting new members who have knowledge the organisation didn't previously have.' Both are rooted in, and have important implications for, HRM. This is evident, for instance, in the role of expatriates as knowledge carriers between the head office and subsidiary (Chang, Gong, & Peng, 2012; Downes & Thomas, 2000; Lazarova & Tarique, 2005). Likewise, the use of specialised consultants, such as international project consultants (Welch & Welch, 2012; Welch, Welch, & Tahvanainen, 2008), brings knowledge that the firm does not possess.

Particularly over the past decade, there is a growing literature on the challenges of MNEs operating in hostile environments from both a HRM perspective (Bader & Berg, 2013, 2014; Bader & Schuster, 2015; Lee & Reade, 2015; Reade, 2009, 2015; Reade & Lee, 2012) and a strategic perspective (e.g. Czinkota, Knight, Liesch, & Steen, 2010; Suder, 2006). Further, whilst there has been a study by Suder, Birnik, Nielsen, and Riviere (2016) that investigated knowledge creation, acquisition, and leveraging in hostile environments for the benefit of the MNE, the supportive role of HRM in this context has not been addressed. In the current study, we investigate a case in which a developed market MNE learns in a hostile (or extreme) environment, with implications for leveraging this learning to other hostile environments particularly through expatriates to make that contribution. We propose that expatriate managers play a more important role in the organisational learning process than currently reflected in the literature because of the intensive experiential learning that takes place when located in hostile environments. The KGs experienced are likely to be wide and knowledge gained is 'rare' in these environments. By 'rare' knowledge we mean knowledge that is not ordinarily available to most organisations in the world, and is thus to a vast extent inimitable (Suder et al., 2016). Here, we conceptualise rare knowledge as the identification and addressing of KGs experienced by expatriates in a hostile environment, and supported by HR practices, that benefits the individual and the organisation. We hence expand the understanding of the role of expatriates, as well as the HR function in hostile environments, and posit that through creation, capturing and leveraging of rare knowledge the firm will be in a better position to apply context-appropriate business and HRM strategies compared to most competitors when entering a new market in a similarly hostile environment.

We expect to contribute to the literature in the following ways. First, we advance prior research on the perceptions of expatriate and local managers in hostile environments by examining the challenges they face (identification of KGs), as well as their solutions (addressing the KGs) through the lens of HRM and organisational learning. Most studies in the field of HR that involve managerial perceptions in hostile environments (e.g. Bader & Schuster, 2015; Reade & Lee, 2012) focus on attitudinal and behavioural phenomena such as commitment and performance rather than organisational learning. We concentrate specifically on HR supported rare knowledge acquisition and sharing as a key feature of the MNE's internationalisation path through compensational learning. This builds on the findings of Suder et al. (2016) which did not elaborate on HR support and interventions.

Second, as part of theory building, we propose a mechanism for capturing and leveraging on-site managerial learning of rare knowledge for subsequent use by MNEs in other hostile locations, thereby minimising its loss for the organisation. We focus on debriefing of experiential learning which has been used in the military for capturing and leveraging knowledge in hostile environments (Firing,

Johansen, & Moen, 2015; Firing, Moen, & Skarsvåg, 2015). To our knowledge it has not been used by MNEs in the service sector in such environments. This research has implications for international HRM as well as for building organisational resilience through acquisition and exploitation of knowledge. As such, our study is expected to contribute to the international HRM, organisational learning, and international business literature.

We utilize a qualitative, in-depth case study methodology, which is a valid approach for hostile environments since little is known about these contexts. In-depth, context-rich, behavioural scrutiny of firms has the potential to uncover the challenges, or KGs, perceived by managers, and how they respond to those challenges (Gligor, Esmark, & Gölgeci, 2016). This serves as a basis for considering appropriate HR practices and interventions for facilitating the creation, capturing and leveraging of managerial learning. The firm under study is a European joint venture in the Afghan telecommunications industry. Afghanistan represents a hostile operating environment due to a particularly challenging institutional and security profile (Quartz [QZ], 2014; World Bank, 2008a, 2012a), and is therefore an appropriate 'extreme' location for this study. The case selection was motivated by its representativeness as a non-commodity-sector MNE from a highly developed market doing business in hostile, extreme contexts.

The article now proceeds with the theoretical background and research questions, the methodology including the case study context and organisation, and findings of the research. Based on the findings we develop a theoretical framework for the supporting role of HR in rare knowledge creation, and a mechanism for capturing and leveraging such rare knowledge throughout the MNE. This is followed by a discussion of implications and the conclusion.

Organisational learning and the role of expatriates

Recent HRM and international business literature suggest that hostile business environments typically have a negative impact on the firm's employees and performance (Bader & Berg, 2013, 2014; Reade & Lee, 2016; Oh & Oetzel, 2011; Reade, 2009; Reade & Lee, 2012). Yet, in this era of advanced business internationalisation and increased terrorism threat, an increasing number of developed-market MNEs enter hostile environments to learn and to gain additional competitive edge (Birnik & Cormack, 2010; Suder, Bader, & Grosse, 2016). These firms challenge our understanding of internationalisation strategy (Barkema & Drogendijk, 2007; Hennart, 2009; Sanchez-Peinado & Pla-Barber, 2006), knowledge creation (Brouthers, Brouthers, & Werner, 2008; Brouthers & Hennart, 2007) and the management of people in hostile environments (e.g. Bader, 2015; Bader, Berg, & Holtbrügge, 2015; Lee & Reade, 2016; Reade, 2015; Reade & Lee, 2012).

In particular, there is a need for international HR strategies to be informed by on-site managerial perceptions of challenges and responses to hostile conditions. Such strategies are essential given that learning from experience becomes increasingly difficult the more turbulent the environment (March, 1991). We conceptualise individual, group and organisational learning as intimately linked in hostile operating contexts, since the contribution of learning to organisational knowledge is in part dependent on the turbulence in the environment (March, 1991). In these hostile, extreme environments, managers, particularly expatriates and their interactions with local conditions and local staff, may enable a firm to acquire a set of rare knowledge and capabilities. While the main task of expatriate managers is generally to deploy organisational capabilities abroad, it is important to recognise that acquiring knowledge at the local level is also critical for organisational learning. Organisational learning builds on individual and in-group learning in that experimentation and socialisation are building blocks. That is to say, knowledge is local and tacit, and forms the basis of organisational learning (Nonaka, 1994).

The MNE's learning process generally involves: the individual expatriate manager's identification of KGs at the local level, the closing of these gaps through innovative solutions, and the capturing and leveraging of local knowledge to enhance the organisational stock of knowledge. We describe this process in four steps, and delineate how these steps differ for MNEs operating in a hostile environment compared to MNEs operating in a stable environment. We will refer to Figure 1, which is shown in a later section.

The individual learning process begins, as a first step, with an assessment of KGs through intuition and interpretation (Crossan, Lane, & White, 1999). Managers identify KGs through perceived challenges that characterise an unfamiliar situation or environment. KGs exist when the host country operating environment is different or 'distant' from that of the MNE home country operating environment. In other words, an expatriate, particularly from a 'distant' country context, is more likely to perceive KGs than local managers and employees. Distance has been conceptualised as cultural, psychic, economic, political, institutional, and historical distance, among others (Slangen & van Tulder, 2009). Here, we highlight the level of security and development in the concept of distance. KGs are largest, we submit, when the host country is distant in terms of security threats, in addition to cultural, economic, and institutional distance. Security threats are particularly salient when their individual, group and organisational impact is directly linked to survival; thus, a willingness to find solutions becomes paramount. Managers must be willing to learn. We stipulate that such KGs represent the general challenges likely to be perceived specifically by expatriate managers in a hostile environment. Managerial perception of KGs, leading to individual search for solutions enabled by HR support, is the first step in the organisational learning process. This is shown in Figure 1.

Closing KGs is the second step required by the organisation (also represented in Figure 1). In the same way that it is important for managers to be willing to acquire new knowledge, it is critical for them to be willing to share it (Lazarova & Tarique, 2005; Minbaeva & Michailova, 2004) when knowledge on the local

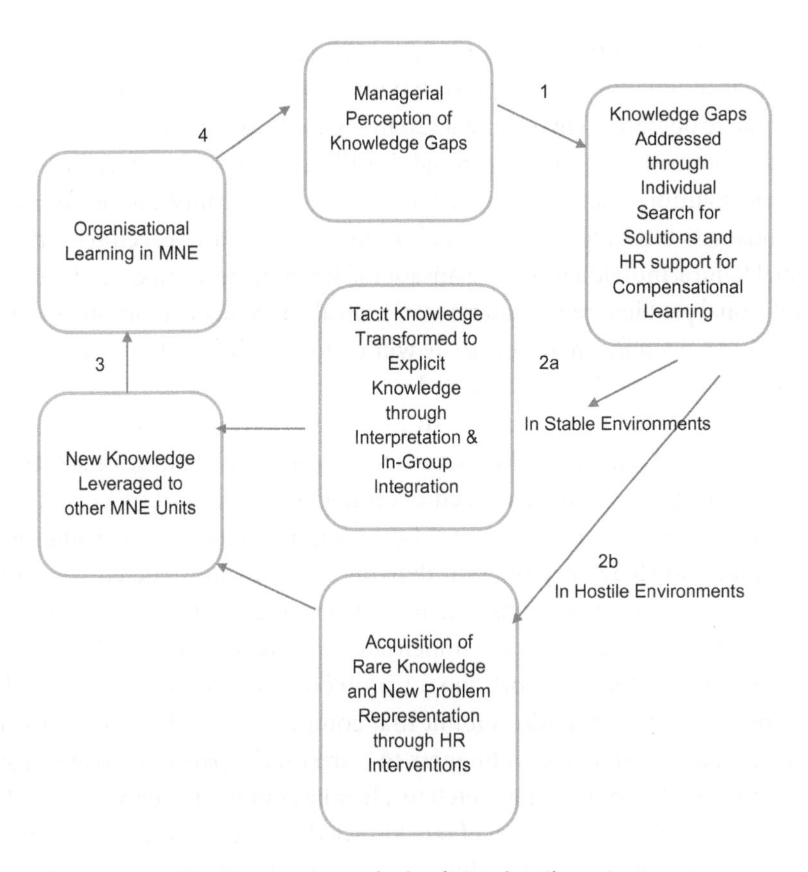

Figure 1. Organisational learning process and role of HR in hostile environments.

level is tacit and resides with a few individuals. At this point individual solutions are 'articulated' (Nonaka, 1991, p. 168) or shared with other members of the local group. In this way, tacit knowledge becomes explicit as members interpret various solutions and integrate (some of) them. Such in-group exercise of 'successive rounds of meaningful dialog' is also known as 'externalization' (Nonaka, 1994, pp. 19–20). A number of possible mechanisms have been suggested for capturing and sharing knowledge gained from international assignments. They include joint meetings of managers between different units of the organisation (Gerybadze, 2004) and participation in global teams (Holtbrügge & Berg, 2004).

At this stage, we posit that a divergence occurs in the organisational learning process for MNEs operating in a stable environment and those operating in a hostile environment. In stable environments (2a in Figure 1) the development of new problem representations does not need to take place as new members are usually presented with an 'appropriate problem representation' that they learn to use effectively (Simon, 1991, p. 132). This is the case when learning opportunities are infrequent and lack a disruptive element. Organisations tend to maintain routines and view problems through a familiar lens; otherwise stated, managers try to solve problems ' by searching selectively through a problem space defined by a particular problem representation' (Simon, 1991, p. 23). 'Learning myopia' (March, 1999) can lead to failures to adapt to changing conditions (Petersen et al., 2008).

In a hostile operating environment (2b in Figure 1), or developed environments in which circumstances change through hostile activity such as terrorist attacks, relying on solutions that do not match on-the-ground reality can result not only in lost business but in lost lives of staff in the extreme case. Faced with risk and potential failure, individual and organisational learning needs to extend into creating additional problem representations of radically new behaviours and solutions. This implies a need for managers to be willing to search for alternatives and new solutions (Madsen & Desai, 2010), and to act on them (Sitkin, 1992), in order to address the KGs that they perceive. To close large KGs requires *compensational learning* (Suder et al., 2016), that is, an active search for innovative solutions to unique challenges, or challenges seen as unique when without precedent for the individual or the organisation. It has been demonstrated that learning opportunities and knowledge exploitation dynamics can be constructed within high risk, weak government contexts (Birnik & Cormack, 2010; Suder et al., 2016). In such contexts, the capacity to compensate for KGs is not only critical but also enhances a firm's stock, or portfolio, of problem-solving approaches (problem representations). We therefore submit that compensational learning is twofold, as it necessitates a proactive willingness to learn on the part of managers (Suder et al., 2016), and HR practices adapted to a hostile context that enhance employee welfare and facilitate the creation of rare knowledge. The latter reflects the important extension of analysis and findings of Suder et al. (2016).

Consequently, organisational learning differs in stable and hostile environments. Stable environments comprise mainly evolved ways – following the ingestion of new members with diverse backgrounds – of solving current and future organisational problems. These evolved new ways result form a combination of the organisational memory (problem representations, or the way we do things here) and new members' ways to approach problems. In hostile environments organisational memory is missing or scarce, or at worst damaging; compensational learning is critical and problems are to be represented differently (from the home way). It is more than a matter of people with different backgrounds and past experiences (most of which from home) discussing how to solve a problem; it is a matter of how expatriates and local staff represent the problem and how they create local (organisational) memory from scratch by first unlearning assumptions and prior beliefs.

The third step, as represented in Figure 1, is the leveraging of knowledge that has been captured. Knowledge leverage is essential for the effective transfer of learning throughout the organisation. As Nonaka (1991, p. 165) suggests, 'making personal knowledge available to others is the central activity of the knowledge-creating company.' In the context of MNEs, expatriates have been used as knowledge transfer agents (Chang et al., 2012; Downes & Thomas, 2000) including international project consultants on a contractual basis in hostile environments

(Welch & Welch, 2015; Welch et al., 2008). As with knowledge capture, knowledge leverage depends on managerial sharing of new knowledge. Documentation of knowledge allows for the possibility of wide dissemination throughout the organisation. The suggested mechanisms for both capture and leverage of knowledge such as participation in global teams (Holtbrügge & Berg, 2004) do not take into consideration knowledge acquisition in a hostile environment, with weak infrastructures and institutional voids, nor the alternative forms of expatriate assignments that might be found in such an environment, including international project consultants (Welch & Welch, 2015). Given that knowledge is difficult to attain in hostile environments (Suder et al., 2016), and there is a high turnover among the expatriates accepting such missions, as we will show later, previously identified mechanisms may not be adequate.

The fourth and last step represents the internalisation of rare knowledge, or new problem representations, which has been leveraged and assimilated across various MNE units. This 'internalisation' step comprises the conversion of explicit knowledge from tacit knowledge (Nonaka, 1994, p. 19), a dynamic process of knowledge creation and organisational learning as proposed by Nonaka (1994) and subsequent related work.

It is important to mention here that our aim in presenting the figures was to illustrate the organisational learning process in MNEs and the role of HR particularly in hostile environments, and at what point and how organisational learning in hostile environments differs from organisational learning in stable environments. Our objective was not to discuss each step in detail, but rather to concentrate on hostile environments along with the opportunities and challenges they bring, in order to propose critical HR practices and interventions to harness the benefits and overcome the threats. Particularly, we propose that additional HR mechanisms need to be considered for capturing and leveraging knowledge in hostile environments, since new challenges require innovative approaches, and there is a paucity of studies dealing with this increasingly important matter.

Operating in hostile environments – an HRM perspective

Managerial perceptions: from negative to positive

It was stated above that managerial perceptions of challenges, or the gap between *what is known* and *what is needed* in a new situation or environment, constitutes the first step in the organisational learning process. Over the past decade, a growing body of research has examined the attitudes, feelings and behaviours of employees exposed to hostile conditions such as war and terrorism (e.g. Bader, 2015; Bader & Schuster, 2015; Lee & Reade, 2015; Reade, 2009; Reade & Lee, 2012; Suder et al., 2016).

Much of the literature points to negative effects on firms and individuals. Individuals have reported lower work motivation and productivity (Bader & Berg, 2013, 2014; Howie, 2007; Reade, 2009), lower job satisfaction and commitment

(Howie, 2007; Mainiero & Gibson, 2003; Reade, 2009; Reade & Lee, 2012), lower trust in, and perceived support from, colleagues and top management (Reade, 2009). In addition to these negative implications for the firm, individuals are negatively affected on a personal level by experiencing greater stress, anxiety and depression (Bader & Berg, 2014; Howie, 2007; Mainiero & Gibson, 2003). In the context of international business, such impact has been found for expatriates (e.g. Bader & Berg, 2013) and host country nationals (e.g. Reade & Lee, 2012) of foreign-invested firms located in conflict zones.

There is, however, anecdotal and empirical evidence to suggest that a hostile environment can present opportunities for learning and the creation of new knowledge (Reade, 2015; Reade & Lee, 2016; Suder et al., 2016). As an anecdotal example, social turmoil in the Middle East during the so-called Arab Spring was found to generate alternative solutions to problems and new strategies for the survival of small business owners (e.g. Wonacott, 2012). An empirical study by Reade and Lee (2016) found that employees who are exposed to violent political conflict are motivated to engage with colleagues to innovate products, services, and processes. Reade (2015) notes that employee innovation behaviour and the search for alternate ways of operating under adverse conditions is consistent with observations of anthropologists and others. Robben and Nordstrom (1996), for instance, highlight the existence of the *creative and hopeful* in conditions of violent conflict, and the importance of the human imagination in devising appropriate solutions. Indeed, there is evidence in the employee creativity and innovation literature to suggest that perceived environmental threat is positively related to creativity (Anderson, Potočnik, & Zhou, 2014; George & Zhou, 2007). This is consistent with the constructive side of conflict (e.g. Baron, 1991).

The above suggests that there are negative and positive manifestations of hostile environments with implications for HRM. In essence, the negative manifestations represent the first hand challenges (KGs) that managers perceive and organisations face, which might not have been addressed, or fully addressed, with HR practices that are either absent or not adapted to the 'distant' context. The positive manifestations represent effective managerial or organisational responses (to those challenges) that were enabled by HR practices adapted to the 'distant' context and capable of harnessing opportunities inherent in a hostile context.

HR intervention for capturing and leveraging rare knowledge

The acquisition of rare knowledge provides a basis for group and organisational learning if it is effectively captured from the individual and shared more broadly in the organisation. When KGs are identified and addressed locally in a hostile context, the knowledge thus acquired is at risk of remaining tacit at the local level, or even to be lost. Managerial perceptions of challenges at the local level and their innovative responses are likely to stay with few people at the local level or to 'walk out the door' at the conclusion of expatriate assignments if not captured. In this case, there may be an enhancement of managerial learning, but not necessarily organisational learning. This may be especially true with contracted international project consultants (Welch & Welch, 2012, 2015; Welch et al., 2008) and expatriates working under high levels of stress. Knowledge acquired by individuals in the field needs to be made explicit to enhance group learning at the subsidiary level and organisational learning more broadly within the MNE. For that, an organisation needs to process information efficiently in addition to creating information and knowledge (Nonaka, 1994).

A mechanism for capturing and leveraging knowledge in a hostile environment requires an HR intervention that takes into consideration the high security-related threat and associated stress that is experienced by expatriates.

Conceptual model and research questions

We strive to answer the following research question: Given challenges that managers in hostile contexts perceive as predominant (identification of KGs), how do managers respond to these challenges (address KGs); and how can the HR function support the creation, capturing and leveraging of 'rare' knowledge to benefit the MNE as a whole for current and future operations? Figure 1 presents a conceptual model that provides a roadmap for our study.

As shown at the top of Figure 1, the learning process begins with managerial perception of KGs in hostile environments; we use this as the basic assumption of our study. KGs are then addressed through individual search for solutions and HR support for compensational learning. This is followed by an HR intervention or mechanism for acquiring or capturing rare, tacit knowledge, which translates to group knowledge acquisition at the local level. Such knowledge is then leveraged across the organisation through an HR intervention or leveraging mechanism. Figure 1 shows the different process that occurs for learning in a hostile environment (the loop represented in 2b) compared with learning in a stable environment (the loop represented in 2a). The main difference, as noted earlier, is that, in hostile environments, the organisation develops new problem representations to deal with 'unusual' situations through compensational learning. Our data collection focuses on part of this conceptual model by uncovering managerial perceptions of challenges, or KGs, and how they are addressed. From this, we develop a set of HR practices for facilitating rare knowledge creation and a proposed HR mechanism for capturing and leveraging such rare knowledge to enhance group and organisational learning in the MNE.

Methodology

To address these research questions, we rely on an in-depth case study approach (Gligor et al., 2016) that we stipulate is crucial for examining the proposition that managerial perception and response to extreme conditions in a hostile environment creates rare knowledge that can be captured and leveraged with the support of HR practices and interventions. The following presents the case study context, company, and method of investigation.

Case study context and company

Afghanistan, the case study context, is least developed by world comparison on almost any measure. Suder et al. (2016) details the country's very low GDP per capita (at a rank of 219 of 229 surveyed countries), high unemployment, extreme poverty (Central Intelligence Agency [CIA], 2009), low literacy with less than 15% female literacy, spotty access to electricity, a very challenging business climate (ranked by World Bank at 160/183 countries, World Bank [2008b, 2012b]), and corruption at its highest (Transparency International, 2010).

The case study company, the mobile operator Roshan, was founded in 2003 during a period when Afghanistan had very little functioning infrastructure or infrastructure development, and most territory was controlled by the Taliban (The Economist, 2007). Only 'two telephones for every 1000 Afghans' were available in 2002, and Roshan was challenged by 'extremely limited institutional capacity and understanding of technical, commercial and regulatory issues in telecommunications' (Public Private Infrastructure Advisory Facility [PPIAF], 2006, p. 1). Roshan, a large investor in Afghanistan, was set up as an international joint venture (IJV), as the second Global System for Mobile Communications (GSM) operator in the country, behind a state-owned provider. The European Monaco–based MNE, Monaco Telecom Group (MTG, owner of MT International, MTI), is founder of the operator and is wholly foreign-owned: 51% by the Aga Khan Fund for Economic Development (AKFED), 36.75% by MTI, as managing stakeholder, 12.25% by TeliaSonera AB. The main operators in Afghanistan today include Etisalat, MTN Group, Roshan, and Afghan Wireless.

The success of Roshan, i.e. MTI's Afghanistan operation, and MTI's distinct international strategy is also reflected in its operations in Algeria, Kosovo and Tunisia and in six West African countries. As noted in Suder et al. (2016), the strategy to geographically diversify 'to locations where no-one else in the industry locates' (interview, Veran & Suder, 2010–2012) reveals the firm's aim to draw on its rare knowledge to maintain competitive advantage in a services and infrastructure sector that is 'particularly dense and competitive on a global scale' (Suder et al., 2016, p. 16). The IJV was subsequently successful in obtaining 41% market share by 2007, with 3.5 million active subscribers by 2010, and managers having lead over more than 1,114 employees in 2009, as the largest private employer. However, whilst Suder (2016) set the scene for a better of understanding of this success from an internationalisation perspective, the study did not reveal the HR support that shapes such success internally. The present case study will fill this gap.

Case study method of investigation

The selection of this case was made to be as representative as possible for a foreign developed-market IJV operating in an extreme or hostile location. Several sources acknowledge Roshan as a representative developed-market MNE operating in hostile environments (PPIAF, 2006; Suder et al., 2016). While the firm is representative of firms operating in this environment, the case study environment itself is 'extreme' or 'atypical' in accordance with case study methodology classifications. This classification suggests case study contexts are simultaneously extreme, critical, and paradigmatic for various disciplines and research lenses. Also, it is worth noting that our study does not compare business environments; rather we focus on the hostile business environment only and in depth.

We were given access to data over an extended period of time. This included ten semi-structured interviews, a diary providing insider views from one senior executive, and various company reports provided by the firm. This led to 'thick' qualitative research, with an 'inquiry from the inside' (Evered & Louis, 1981) that reveals knowledge acquisition methods within the managerial team. Direct observation, company reports, a diary and management interviews became available for this research – given that the above-mentioned senior executive made a decision to start documenting knowledge (cf of methodology see Suder et al. [2016]). Access to the full set of data provided supporting quotes, and evidence from the interviews, journals, and documentation. Eisenhardt and Graebner (2007) note the relevance of such evidence and case studies. Our case data methodology, focusing on the immediate post-entry phase from 2004 of operations of Roshan, is solidly embedded in the 'extreme' case method (Brown & Eisenhardt, 1997; Ghauri, 2004; Yin, 2003). In the present study, we focus on HR-related issues contained in the data-set of Suder et al. (2016), an important field that this previous article had not examined.

A written diary that had been kept for a period of three months by the executive, an expatriate, complements the other strands of our investigation. Several expatriates also underwent semi-structured managerial interviews, as well as three local Afghan managers in senior executive positions on site. The expatriate managers included the chief operating officer (French), communications director (Polish), corporate sales manager (Indian), general counsel (British), network director (Algerian/French), national dealer (Indian), and treasury manager (Kenyan). The Afghan managers were regional directors. The transcripts of these interviews were coded consistent with open, axial and selective coding clustered into open codes and axial coding and then into a central category in selective coding: Initial codes, very detailed, reflected respondents' comments 'in vivo,' then were clustered as 'open' codes into related categories, as in axial coding in grounded theory; finally, an emerging coding structure was identified through selective coding, which focused on 'challenges' requiring organisational and managerial responses (Suder et al., 2016). Codes made in the margins of the transcripts and diary, investigated through qualitative data processing software (NVivo, Version 7), helped ascertain and deepen the investigation.

In this paper, we reviewed the coding structure, which corresponds to our first order analysis closely grounded in the collected data. Yet, beyond this step, we extended the more theoretical second-order analysis aimed at identifying underlying strategies that might be relevant beyond this particular case (Gioia & Chittipeddi, 1991; Van Maanen, 1979), and concluded on the mechanisms observed that support sharing of knowledge, which could be identified as HR practices and interventions. Thus we reference Suder et al. (2016) as a basis for this work, and we provide a summary of this methodology and analysis in our text.

In summary, the initial research was based on a combination of four methods: direct observation, company reports, a diary and management interviews; the latter three methods were scrutinised through content analyses. The interview protocol was designed then double checked and revised. Each quote has been verified; they have respectively been made by different interviewees, which satisfied quality standards and depth in scale and scope. For this research, we selected and paid particular attention to the methods in which information were captured and shared, with the focus on expatriates.

Findings

Initial content analysis and coding revealed two prominent themes: security and development challenges and solutions, together with HR practices that were either available or lacking. These themes are outlined below and supported with selected quotes from the interviews and diary.

Security challenges and responses requiring HR support

The expatriate managers acknowledged the lack of security as the foremost category of perceived challenges (KGs), requiring the most immediate response. In this category, the personal danger factor presented the most salient issue. As an example of this concern, one respondent mentioned, 'you can have a brilliant morning and end up with a dead body in the afternoon.' This points to an extreme level of personal security threat; threat perception by expatriates is significant and leads to exit or coping mechanisms. As stated by one expatriate manager: 'I didn't know what kind of sub-conscious psychological damage I might be making to myself by working in a place like this.'

Besides personal danger, limited personal freedom to move around was salient. Content analysis revealed words and phrases such as, 'we are confined….' and 'heavily constrained.' The high security situation results in a management response of constrained living, in this case a highly guarded compound. The diarist noted, for instance, that 'we are confined to spend 98% of our lives on two premises,' referring to the office and the compound. Movements between locations (even between compound and office) are considered high risk, and one is accompanied by escorts and guards in vehicles with bullet-proof windows. Interviewees noted the importance of not becoming complacent about security given the frequency of terrorist attacks. The risk of complacency is summed up by one interviewee who notes that 'when you live in a state of constant threat, you adapt to it.'

Security measures were also set up as clear and simple rules that employees are expected to follow at all times, e.g. not traveling alone or after dark, not walking on the streets, avoiding crowded places. As noted by one interviewee, 'No westerners walk the streets.' Others mentioned that it is important to 'try to avoid being close to ISAF, UN, etc' since these agencies can be targets of terrorist attack. They caution that, when 'outside cities, don't use expensive vehicles like Land Cruiser etc. like the UN. We use an old Corolla.' If employees do not follow company rules, they are sacked. Complacency puts lives at risk.

Managers also highlighted the increased security risk outside Kabul, the capital city, because the government has less control than community leaders in outlying areas. One manager noted that Roshan 'had to shut off some sites because the Taliban wanted money' and it became dangerous to operate. Learning included new styles of negotiation and decisions about business continuity or closure. The general response to heightened security outside Kabul is to 'go local' for the company and for expatriates in order to learn to gain community support, trust and protection. Advice captured was to 'go to the communities to get them to protect you.' To gain protection, managers went into the community to build relationships and to strategize for investment in water pumps, bridges, schools, and other infrastructure needed by communities.

Managers acknowledge that it is difficult to recruit other expatriate staff and suppliers to Afghanistan. 'The average time it takes us to find an expat is 6 months; some takes up to 9 months or more.' Another manager notes, upon his decision to extend his contract: 'The flipside is that I became a misfit. Working here makes you a misfit. I cannot come back to a normal company.' This sometimes meant that the managers responsible for hiring expatriate staff had to learn about hardship incentives to match the context, such as higher salaries, or to accept suboptimal arrangements with those willing to come for a short time, and to adjust their managerial decision processes accordingly.

Respondents noted that expatriates working in Afghanistan are often pressured by their families to return home frequently or permanently because of the stress they face: 'After some time he couldn't stand the pressure from his family and had to resign.' Regular travel home and good communication facilities make it possible to keep in touch with family and friends and helps to reduce stress, yet are perceived as complications by local staff: 'since expatriates tend to be less on the ground than locals, the decision-making process is longer.'

Development challenges and responses requiring HR support

The lack of development had been identified as the second major category of perceived challenges (Suder et al., 2016), indicating KGs. The lack of knowledge and skills, directly linked by managers to the lack of institutional development, is one other concern for expatriates: there is 'no infrastructure, no schools.' There was a perceived need for HR support to fill this gap through training and development for employees, as well as organising education for government officials, customers and suppliers. Hiring for attitude – such as enthusiasm, determination, and willingness to learn – was considered an essential HR practice. HR support for training also supported knowledge creation and capture in regards to weak infrastructure: Telecommunications, roads, transport and schools were built up, security trained up to protect it, and the managers had to learn how to negotiate and strike deals within a weak rule of law. As stated by one manager: 'We will not pay a bribe but this slows everything down because people won't let you pass through them… they try to make your life harder… fraud is also an issue.'; 'You also can't expect stability. Example is taxes. Today there is no tax on this and – tomorrow there is. And it is applied 50 years back.'

Towards a theoretical framework: the role of HRM in creating, capturing and leveraging rare knowledge

The predominant challenges perceived by managers, security and development, were met by managerial and organisational responses. The expatriates themselves handled HR tasks, support and interventions, given that in such environment there was no distinct HR department. These responses involved the management of people and processes. The case study company developed HR practices on an ad hoc basis in response to challenges as they arose. Our findings include suggestions from managers on how the HR function could better support expatriates in a hostile environment. This includes recruitment adjustments ('HR needs [during the recruitment interviews] to dig down in their reasons for moving here. The life is tough and people should only come here if they are really ready. Select only people with this ability. Tests might also work in this regard.'), good communication channels with family, reinforced team building ('ensure a good team'), sports and socialisation ('people can work out their tensions'; positive note on existing 'pool room, watch movies'), support for mental health specifically for males ('You have to constantly talk to your family. Most males tend not to but you have to.'), space and time adjustments ('people live in confined spaces so they need to get out and feel free'), support with training and development adjustments ('Patience [when managing in this environment] is very important') and knowledge transfer ('where people interact and learn from each other'; 'Recruit ... expats that are able to deliver knowledge downwards'). One respondent mentioned that in seeking expatriates that are a good fit in that regard, 'we act almost … as an uncle….'; 'I look for those who (are…) ready to transfer knowledge.' Also, the HR function needs to be prepared for staff change.

On the basis of our findings, we propose a formalised set of HR practices to address the challenges (KGs) identified by respondents in our case study. We posited that such practices support the creation of rare knowledge. We now expand this by adding that capture and transfer of knowledge is crucial, as it otherwise remains on the individual managerial level at risk of loss. An informal capturing and leveraging of knowledge took place in the form of a diary. The diary was used to capture knowledge by an expatriate manager, who subsequently used that knowledge in another post located in a hostile environment. Also, interviewees note that trainings were developed and processes emerged ('training people in-house – build our own training program'). Building on this informal practice, we propose a formalised HR mechanism for capturing and leveraging rare knowledge for the benefit of the MNE.

HR support for rare knowledge creation

The findings illustrate managerial perception of challenges, or KGs, in a hostile environment, the learning created and ways in which managers sought to address these KGs. We have proposed earlier that identifying KGs in a hostile environment and addressing them through innovative solutions constitutes managerial learning and rare knowledge. Referring to our conceptual model in Figure 1, and based on our findings, we now consider the role of HR in supporting the creation of rare knowledge. The findings reveal that the primary KGs requiring solutions revolved around security and development. The use of HR tools remained relatively rudimentary as managers rather than HR experts developed them. However, they reveal the significance of HR support for knowledge creation, capture and leverage, with no specific distinction as to the agent. Also, motivations to share knowledge may differ, as contingent to the motivation of expatriates in their roles. One interviewee stated:

> The expat staff can be roughly divided into two groups in terms of what motivates them to come here: those who are in for the money, and those who are here because they like being able to help improving other people's lives, develop the world, etc.

While we did not focus on this distinction, it highlights the potential need to capture their experiential knowledge before exit.

The KGs, their solutions, and HR support are presented in Table 1. As shown, the perceived KGs around security include personal danger, high security costs, weak government outside of Kabul, limited freedom to move around, and difficulty to recruit expatriates. Various solutions were found to address these KGs, which have implications for the type of HR support needed. For instance, HR support would include the creation of systems for ensuring that all security measures are in place, and to provide expatriates and their families with a handbook of precautionary measures and emergency contact information. Security measures also include strict provisions for following security guidelines, and guarding expatriates when traveling in rural areas, such as pairing the expatriate with trusted local staff. Because of limited movement, HR support includes providing expatriates

Table 1. Knowledge gaps, solutions and HR support*.

Knowledge gaps	Solutions	HR Support
Security issues		
Personal danger	Ensure adequate security measures	Ensure that all security measures are in place Create handbook of security precautionary measures and provide to all staff and families
High security costs	Follow security rules	Ensure that staff and family follow the rules Do not allow for complacency
Government weak outside Kabul	Go local	Ensure that all staff – expatriates and locals – are well guarded especially in rural areas
Limited freedom to move around	Adopt the right mindset	Provide gyms and entertainment facilities
Difficult to recruit expats and find suppliers	Relax despite circumstances	Be prepared to pay more for recruits and supplier services Ensure that all staff have time to relax and access to communication networks to talk with family and friends
Development issues		
Lack of skills	Hire for attitude	Provide education and training to close skill gaps
Weak infrastructure	Build infrastructure	Be prepared to have staff become involved not only with business activities but with necessary infrastructure development
Weak rule of law	Build powerful relationships	Encourage staff to expand networking; support hosting of business and community events
Corruption and fraud	Allow buffers	Instruct staff to build extra time into all projects Do not allow for bribes; create a strong code of ethics
Unpredictable government	Work to raise standards	Instil in managers the importance of setting a leadership example by being consistent in management approach and not succumbing to bribery

*Adapted from Suder et al. (2016).

with space and equipment for relaxation and exercise, such as a gym, as well as quality modes of communication to keep in touch with family. Further, HR support includes monetary and other incentives to attract expatriate managers to a hostile location, with appropriate security measures in place, as they hence become potential kidnapping targets ('they will know you have good salary, and you are a good target').

The KGs around development included lack of skills of local staff, and dealing with weak infrastructure and rule of law, corruption and fraud, as well as an unstable and unpredictable government. HR support in the area of lack of skills includes providing training for local staff, suppliers and even government officials. This means hiring expatriate managers who are willing to share knowledge. HR support for dealing with a weak infrastructure means being prepared to have staff become involved in building required infrastructure, including that which is ordinarily provided by the government such as roads (Suder et al., 2016). According to interviewees, a weak rule of law requires building a network of relationships with those who can get things done. The HR function can support network building by hosting networking events in the business and wider community. Regarding corruption, fraud, and unpredictability, the HR function can create and enforce a code of ethics that forbids bribery. Additionally, it is important that managers be instilled with the importance of setting a positive leadership example by displaying consistency and good personal ethics.

HR interventions for capturing and leveraging rare knowledge

In addition, we extract from our data the need for HR interventions to capture and leverage such rare knowledge. Importantly, our data suggests that debriefing, exit interviews, and documentation as HR interventions would be a valuable mechanism to capture and leverage rare knowledge for organisational learning. This case study allows us to elaborate on the relevance of these tools as a means to extract and leverage learning. Expatriates undergo significant stress. The documentation and leverage of their learning to others particularly through debriefing provides expatriates with an opportunity to 'unload' their stress while at the same building a stock of rare knowledge in the MNE. On basis of the case company's profile, we stipulate that this knowledge is transferable to other MNE units in similar contexts.

Debriefing is commonly used in the military following extreme events such as a rescue mission during a terror attack (e.g. Firing, Johansen, et al., 2015; Firing, Moen, et al., 2015). Debriefing is thought to enhance learning from stressful events because it provides an opportunity to discuss and reflect on the experience. Recall that firms increase their knowledge base through experiential learning (Petersen et al., 2008; Pitelis, 2007; Verbeke, 2003). Debriefing creates the space for learning from experience. Similar to Nonaka's (1994) conceptualisation of 'externalization,' that is, the conversion of tacit knowledge into explicit knowledge through 'successive rounds of meaningful dialogue' (p. 20), debriefing facilitates the creation of a 'common perspective' (p. 24) that helps teams to build the necessary trust and helps the organisation to learn. Firing, Johansen, and Moen (2015) found that a holistic debriefing of events, that allowed participants to express emotions as well as thoughts, contributed to enhanced social support and trust, which in turn gave participants greater scope for reflection and the construction of meaning from their experiences that enhanced their learning. This was found to contribute to development of a common meaning shared by participants.

Transposed to the MNE operating in a hostile environment, we propose that debriefing can facilitate learning that can be documented and codified for subsequent use; the interviews held for this research have provided evidence for this. Indeed it can be considered the central prong of a proposed three-pronged leveraging tool. A second prong is journaling, as done by the participant observer in this case. By keeping a diary, the individual and the organisation acquired rare learning. Such journaling exercise could be used in conjunction with debriefing. Individuals can be encouraged to reflect, write, and share their thoughts and emotions with the group that can then be codified for future use in management. A third prong is exit interviews of people who move to a different post or leave the organisation altogether. People come and go in organisations. If rare learning is not sufficiently documented in the organisation, it can be lost. As an HR intervention, debriefings can be scheduled regularly and learning outcomes documented for use in managing people. This can become an important potential security management feature in hostile or high-risk contexts. Together with debriefing, journaling and exit interviews serve to embed rare knowledge in the MNE through organisational learning, contributing to competitive advantage.

Managerial willingness to learn and share

We posit that HR support and interventions, on the one hand, and managerial willingness to learn and share new knowledge, on the other hand, are not only critical for organisational survival but reinforce each other. This occurs at the individual and in-group levels at the subsidiary. That is, HR support is likely to reinforce individual managerial willingness to learn new knowledge and behaviours, thus creating rare knowledge. It does this through enabling compensational learning. This is an individual learning phenomenon. Managers must then be willing to share this new knowledge with others in the group. Managerial willingness to share and document such knowledge will be facilitated by HR interventions such as debriefing, journaling and exit interviews, thus capturing rare knowledge for its subsequent leveraging to other MNE units. This is an in-group learning phenomenon. In this way, individual and in-group learning co-evolve with the support of HR practices. The co-evolving nature of the relationship between HR practices and managerial willingness to learn and share is depicted in Figure 2.

Implications for organisational learning in the MNE operating in hostile environments

Creating, capturing and leveraging rare knowledge to increase its scale and scope throughout the MNE completes the organisational learning loop as shown in

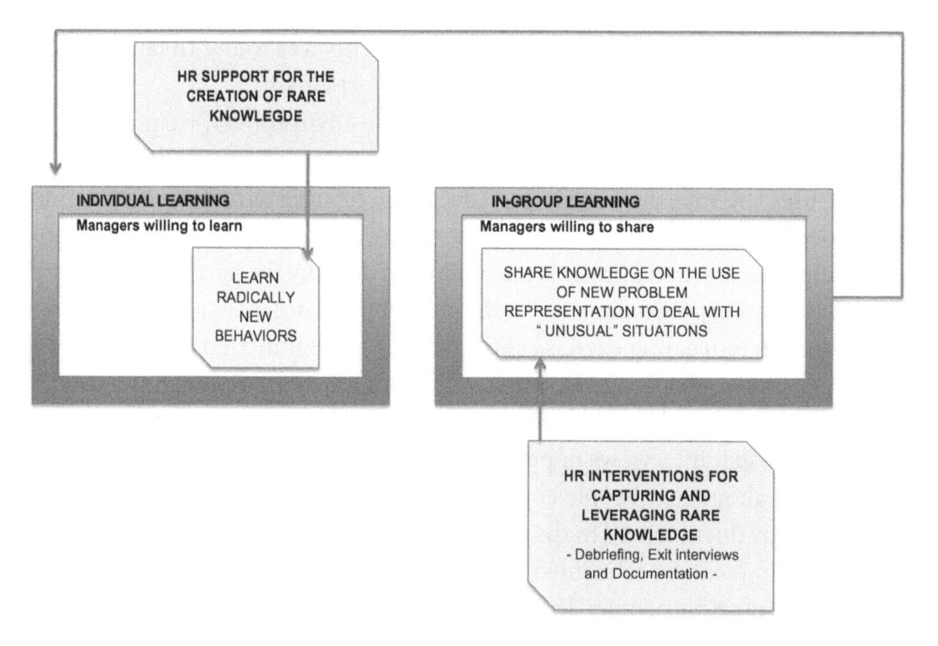

Figure 2. The co-evolving relationship between HR practices and managerial willingness.

Figure 1. Figure 3 further unpacks the MNE organisational learning process presented earlier in Figure 1, by indicating the implications for organisational learning that depend on the willingness of expatriate managers to engage in experiential learning and to share their learning. As shown, we state that organisational learning is maximised through the leveraging of new problem representations, made possible by managerial willingness to learn experientially and to share knowledge gained, supported by HR practices. Conversely, organisational learning in the MNE suffers when expatriate managers are either not willing to learn or share, since any experiential learning risks being lost, and the organisation does not gain a valuable new set of problem representations with which to use strategically in other hostile environments. Figure 3 further illustrates the critical role of HRM to support managers' willingness to learn and share rare knowledge, as well as to harness new problem representations across the organisation. This figure helps visualize how both expatriate willingness and HR support are complementary, and how one cannot function as effectively without the other. This complementary relationship may indeed appear intuitive or simple, yet the high rate of expatriate turnover and number of firms exiting hostile environments suggest that this complementarity has not always been accomplished in practice. A visualization of implications might enhance awareness of this simple yet sometimes overlooked relationship by companies operating in hostile markets.

Discussion

MNEs are increasingly moving into hostile environments, yet research on the HRM dimension of knowledge acquisition and transfer in such contexts to enhance organisational learning and competitiveness is lacking. In this study we examined the role of HRM in supporting the creation, capturing and leveraging of rare knowledge, particularly by expatriate managers. Utilizing an in-depth qualitative case study, the findings allowed us to develop a framework for understanding the relationships between HRM and these critical aspects of managerial and organisational learning that we argue differ in hostile environments. In this way, we contribute to building theory on the relationship between HRM and organisational learning in MNEs.

Firstly, we have conceptualised the difference between organisational learning and the role of HRM in hostile environments compared to stable operating environments. As in Figure 1, the key difference is the need for the MNE to address KGs and learn new problem representations that are radically different from the firm's current stock of knowledge. This is what we refer to as rare knowledge. MNEs, including non-commodity, service firms, are increasingly shifting operations to parts of the world that are 'distant' in terms of institutional and security conditions. We have argued that this requires a broadening of HRM practices and interventions to support addressing these KGs and to capture and leverage rare

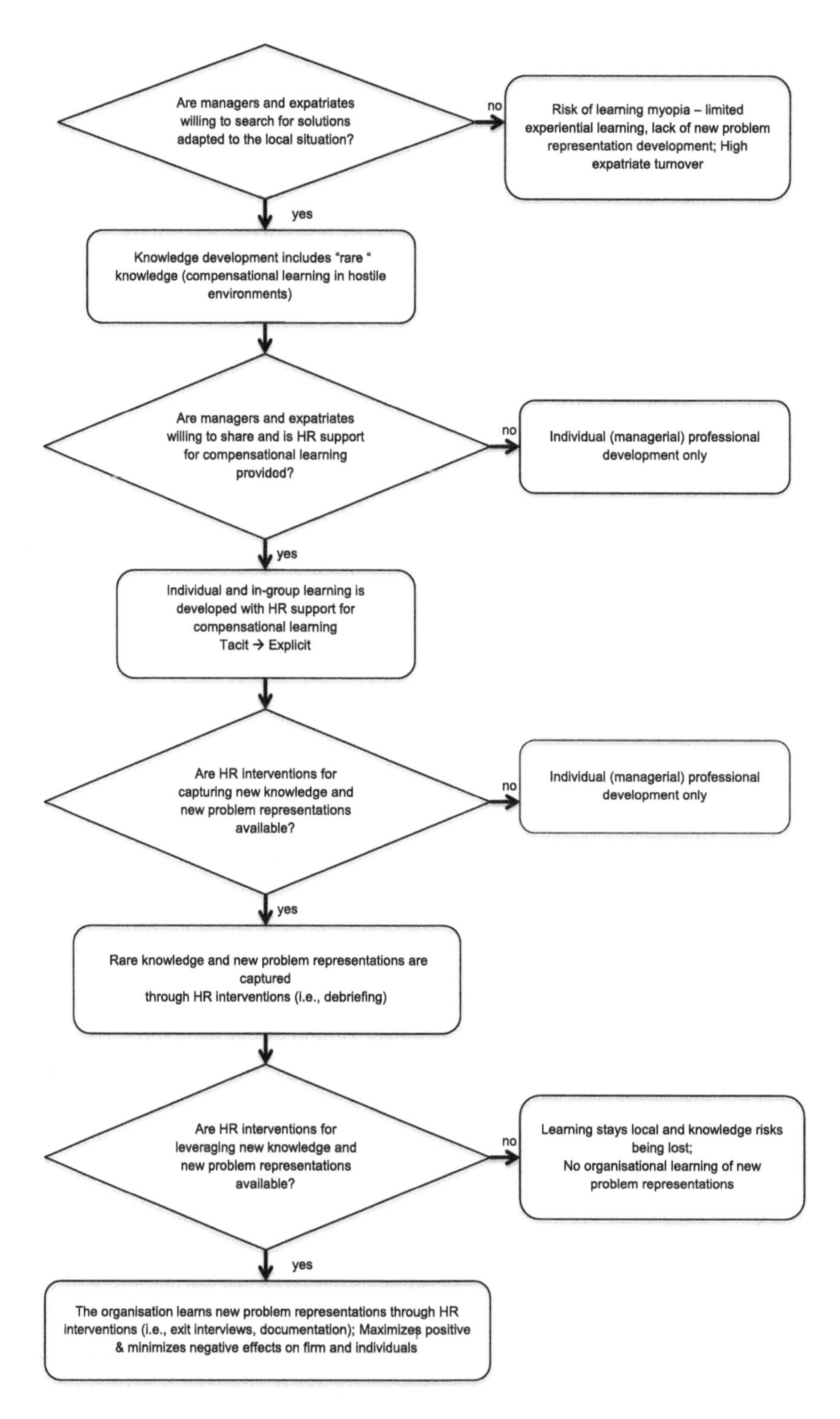

Figure 3. Implications for organisational learning that depend on the (1) willingness of expatriate managers to engage in experiential learning and to share their learning and (2) the existence of HR support and interventions.

knowledge gained by expatriate managers through experiential, compensational learning, for the benefit of the MNE.

Secondly, we have proposed a formalised set of HR practices to support rare knowledge creation, shown in Table 1, that is based on the findings of substantial KGs around security and the lack of development. On the security side, expatriate managers felt that they were in danger, had limited freedom, and in general were exposed to stressful conditions. This mirrors recent findings in the terrorism and HR literature (Bader, 2015; Reade, 2009; Suder, 2006). We have suggested a number of HR practices to address these issues including, for instance, ensuring that security measures are in place and followed by expatriates and their families. On the development side, expatriate managers stated the need to create everything required for the success of the firm, including building infrastructure that is usually provided by the government. Managers identified the need to build local relationships as a way to get things done in the absence of rule of law, as well as for support and protection, consistent with prior research (e.g. Reade, 2015). We have suggested, for instance, HR support in the form of hosting business and community events to expand networking opportunities.

Thirdly, we have proposed an HR mechanism for capturing and leveraging on-site managerial learning for subsequent use in other locations that we believe is crucial to preserve and utilise tacit knowledge at the local level that resides with individual managers, and risks being lost altogether with staff turnover. We extracted debriefing of experiential learning, journaling and exit interviews as part of our conceptualisation of a critical HRM intervention in hostile contexts. Since MNEs have few HR tools to date for knowledge acquisition in such environments, we have turned to organisations that are used to operating in hostile environments, military organisations. We have proposed a technique used in the military – debriefing – as a mechanism to acquire and disseminate new problem representations of rare knowledge.

Specifically, we have proposed holistic debriefing, which goes beyond the traditional debriefing of enquiring about tactics and logistics into the realm of emotions (Firing, Johansen, et al., 2015; Firing, Moen, et al., 2015). Debriefing involves reflection of events, and thus the addition of journaling as an added feature to aid in documentation is thought to be valuable for individual and organisational learning. Exit interviews are a way to capture knowledge from managers who are leaving the post or organisation and can yield additional knowledge of benefit to the firm. In sum, debriefing supported by journaling and exit interviews have implications for the way human resources are managed and the way knowledge is acquired, used and disseminated. In order for such HR and knowledge management tools to be successful, however, MNEs will need to ensure that there are staff trained to conduct debriefings (Kinchin, 2007), including, perhaps, the training of expatriates in such methods during pre-departure training programs before they are posted to a hostile environment.

Finally, we have proposed that there needs to be a managerial willingness to learn and share. HR support practices that facilitate rare knowledge creation if managers are willing to learn, and capturing and leveraging if managers are willing to share. Figure 2 showed the co-evolving relationship between HR practices and the creation, capturing and leveraging of rare knowledge. This supports the findings of Reade and Lee (2016) in a conflict environment, and the findings of anthropologists and others that indicate a positive relationship between an adverse environment and human creativity and innovation (e.g. Anderson et al., 2014; George & Zhou, 2007; Robben & Nordstrom, 1996). Figure 3 indicates the positive returns to the organisation when expatriate managers are willing to both learn and share and, conversely, the limitations to the MNE if not.

Our research has practical implications for organisations contemplating a move to a hostile environment. Firms today are required to operate in an increasingly uncertain global context, with more internationally driven yet shorter assignment structures. To benefit from knowledge creation, MNEs can utilize debriefing and other HR methods to capture and leverage this knowledge. These tools hold a key to facilitating organisational learning and value-creation in other hostile environments that can increase the firm's competitiveness and success of its further internationalisation efforts.

Conclusions, limitations and implications for further research

We used a hostile operating environment context to uncover findings that could not have been investigated as well through other research methods. The findings allowed us to propose HR practices and interventions adapted to hostile environments yet potentially transferable. The findings, while inspiring and significantly expanding the work of Suder et al. (2016), should be viewed as a basis for further conceptualisation and theory building in the international HRM, organisational learning, and international business literature streams. While our method was appropriate for our research objectives, there are limitations as in every study. Our study is based on only a single though highly relevant case. We based this contribution on an existing data-set and expanded its analysis. This study has encompassed a broader scope of fieldwork that holds much potential for testing and extending future theory development. In particular, theory-building purposes will become feasible if this case becomes part of a wider study on HR practices and interventions, either in similar extreme business contexts (constituting multiple case studies) or as part of a 'polar' case study, in which two contrasting environments are compared (e.g. one context with extreme institutional void, and the other with well-developed institutions) (Eisenhardt & Graebner, 2007).

Future research could also examine in-company contextual factors and individual-level factors and that might be determinants or mediators of knowledge acquisition in hostile environments that were raised in the findings but not the focus of this analysis. For instance, the length of contractual arrangements may have a bearing on commitment and extra-role behaviour, or engagement outside one's scope of work (e.g. Vandaele & Gemmel, 2006). The propensity to engage in extra-role behaviours could influence managerial willingness to search for innovative solutions, and to engage in other organisational citizenship behaviours outside of the in-role behaviours associated with one's scope of work (Podsakoff, Ahearne, & MacKenzie, 1997). However, challenges identified by managers in this study suggest that individual survival was also at stake, hence in-role and extra-role behaviours are likely to become blurred in such extreme circumstances.

A further line of inquiry would be to consider the prior experience of expatriate managers in a hostile environment (e.g. Bader, Reade, & Froese, 2016) and how that might affect the extent of KGs in a particular hostile environment location. Research is needed to delve into this aspect of knowledge acquisition in hostile environments, and the associated time factor. In other words, is the learning of 'rare' knowledge time-limited for an individual? Also, would such knowledge be beneficial to firms in developed country contexts (e.g. home country) during and after terrorist attacks?

While learning improves the effectiveness of current operations and/or creates potential alternatives or options (Forsgren, 2002; Huber, 1991), the capability of learning, and documenting the learning creates the managerial basis for a broader scale of locations in which the learning can be deployed. Expatriates are instrumental to the success of the MNE in this regard. Organisational learning is made possible through informed management and HR practices that maximise the positive and reduce the negative manifestations of hostilities. Adequate knowledge acquisition and transfer from hostile environments holds the potential for strategic internationalisation innovation (Cantwell & Narula, 2001) and resilience in the current era of terrorism and globalised threats.

Disclosure statement

No potential conflict of interest was reported by the authors.

References

Anderson, N., Potočnik, K., & Zhou, J. (2014). Innovation and creativity in organisations: A state-of-the-science review, prospective commentary, and guiding framework. *Journal of Management, 40*, 1297–1333.

Bader, A. K., Reade, C., & Froese, F. (2016). *Terrorism and expatriates' withdrawal cognitions: Differential role in the work and non-work domains* Academy of International Business, 2016 Annual Conference Proceedings, New Orleans, LA.

Bader, B. (2015). The power of support in high-risk countries: Compensation and social support as antecedents of expatriate work attitudes. *The International Journal of Human Resource Management, 26*, 1712–1736.

Bader, B., & Berg, N. (2013). An empirical investigation of terrorism-induced stress on expatriate attitudes and performance. *Journal of International Management, 19*, 163–175.

Bader, B., & Berg, N. (2014). The influence of terrorism on expatriate performance: A conceptual approach. *The International Journal of Human Resource Management, 25*, 539–557.

Bader, B., Berg, N., & Holtbrügge, D. (2015). Expatriate performance in terrorism-endangered countries: The role of family and organizational support. *International Business Review, 24*, 849–860.

Bader, B., & Schuster, T. (2015). Expatriate social networks in terrorism-endangered countries: An empirical analysis in Afghanistan, India, Pakistan, and Saudi Arabia. *Journal of International Management, 21*, 63–77.

Barkema, H., & Drogendijk, R. (2007). Internationalising in small, incremental or larger steps? *Journal of International Business Studies, 38*, 1132–1148.

Baron, R. (1991). Positive effects of conflict: A cognitive perspective. *Employee Responsibilities and Rights Journal, 4*, 25–36.

Birnik, A., & Cormack, R. (2010). Managing market entry in Oman: The case of Nawras. *Thunderbird International Business Review, 52*, 403–418.

Brouthers, K. D., Brouthers, L. E., & Werner, S. (2008). Real options, international entry mode choice and performance. *Journal of Management Studies, 45*, 936–960.

Brouthers, K., & Hennart, J. (2007). Boundaries of the firm: Insights from international entry mode research. *Journal of Management, 33*, 395–425.

Brown, S., & Eisenhardt, K. (1997). The art of continuous change: Linking complexity theory and time-paced evolution in relentlessly shifting organizations. *Administrative Science Quarterly, 42*, 1–34.

Cantwell, J., & Narula, R. (2001). The eclectic paradigm in the global economy. *International Journal of the Economics of Business, 8*, 155–172.

Central Intelligence Agency. (2009). The world factbook: Afghanistan. March 15, 2009, https://www.cia.gov/library/publications/the-world-factbook/geos/af.html

Chang, Y. Y., Gong, Y., & Peng, M. W. (2012). Expatriate knowledge transfer, subsidiary absorptive capacity, and subsidiary performance. *Academy of Management Journal, 55*, 927–948.

Crossan, M. M., Lane, H. W., & White, R. E. (1999). An organisational learning framework: From intuition to institution. *Academy of Management Review, 24*, 522–537.

Czinkota, M., Knight, G., Liesch, P., & Steen, J. (2010). Terrorism and international business: A research agenda. *Journal of International Business Studies, 41*, 826–843.

Dewhurst, M., Harris, J., & Heywood, S. (2012, June 2012). The global company's challenge. *McKinsey Quarterly*. Retrieved from http://www.mckinsey.com/insights/organisation/the_global_companys_challenge

Downes, M., & Thomas, A. S. (2000). Knowledge transfer through expatriation: The U-curve approach to overseas staffing. *Journal of Managerial Issues, 12*, 141–149.

Economist. (2007). Shining a light – Face value. *The Economist*, p. 10. London.

Eisenhardt, K. M., & Graebner, M. E. (2007). Theory building from cases: Opportunities and challenges. *Academy of Management Journal, 50*, 25–32.

Evered, R., & Louis, M. R. (1981). Alternative perspectives in the organizational sciences: "Inquiry from the inside" and "Inquiry from the outside". *The Academy of Management Review, 6*, 385–395.

Firing, K., Johansen, L. T., & Moen, F. (2015). Debriefing a rescue mission during a terror attack. *Leadership & Organization Development Journal, 36*, 778–789.

Firing, K., Moen, A., & Skarsvåg, K. (2015). Debriefing to learn from extreme events: The case of Utøya. *International Journal of Training and Development, 19*, 301–309.

Forsgren, M. (2002). The concept of learning in the Uppsala internationalization process model: A critical review. *International Business Review, 11*, 257–277.

George, J., & Zhou, J. (2007). Dual tuning in a supportive context: Joint contributions of positive mood, negative mood, and supervisory behaviors to employee creativity. *Academy of Management Journal, 50*, 605–622.

Gerybadze, A. (2004). Knowledge management, cognitive coherence and equivocality in distributed innovation processes in MNCs. *Management International Review, 44*, 103–128.

Ghauri, P. (2004). Designing and conducting case studies in international business research. In R. Marchan-Piekkari & C. Welch (Eds.), *Handbook of qualitative research methods for international business* (pp. 109–204). Cheltenham: Edward Elgar.

Gioia, D., & Chittipeddi, K. (1991). Sensemaking and sensegiving in strategic change initiation. *Strategic Management Journal, 12*, 433–448.

Gligor, D., Esmark, C., & Gölgeci, I. (2016). Building international business theory: A grounded theory approach. *Journal of International Business Studies, 47*, 93–111.

Heidelberg Institute for International Conflict Research. (2015). *Conflict Barometer 2014*. Heidelberg: Department of Political Science, University of Heidelberg Press.

Hennart, J. (2009). Down with MNE-centric theories! Market entry and expansion as the bundling of MNE and local assets. *Journal of International Business Studies, 40*, 1432–1454.

Holtbrügge, D., & Berg, N. (2004). Knowledge transfer in multinational corporations: Evidence from German firms. *Management International Review, 44*, 129–146.

Howie, L. (2007). The terrorism threat and managing workplaces. *Disaster Prevention and Management: An International Journal, 16*, 70–78.

Huber, G. P. (1991). Organizational learning: The contributing processes and the literatures. *Organization Science, 2*, 88–115.

Kinchin, D. (2007). *A guide to psychological debriefing: Managing emotional decompression and posttraumatic stress disorder*. London: Jessica Kingsley.

Lazarova, M., & Tarique, I. (2005). Knowledge transfer upon repatriation. *Journal of World Business, 40*, 361–373.

Lee, H.-J., & Reade, C. (2015). Ethnic homophily perceptions as an emergent IHRM challenge: Evidence from firms operating in Sri Lanka during the ethnic conflict. *The International Journal of Human Resource Management, 26*, 1645–1664.

Madsen, P. M., & Desai, V. (2010). Failing to learn? The effects of failure and success on organizational learning in the global orbital launch vehicle industry. *Academy of Management Journal, 53*, 451–476.

Mainiero, L., & Gibson, D. (2003). Managing employee trauma: Dealing with the emotional fallout from 9-11. *Academy of Management Executive, 17*, 130–143.

March, J. (1991). Exploration and exploitation in organizational learning. *Organization Science, 2*, 71–87.

March, J. G. (1999). *The pursuit of organisational intelligence*. Malden, MA: Blackwell.

Minbaeva, D. B., & Michailova, S. (2004). Knowledge transfer and expatriation in multinational corporations: The role of disseminative capacity. *Employee Relations, 26*, 63–679.

Nonaka, I. (1991, July–August). The knowledge-creating company. *Harvard Business Review, 2007*, 162–171.

Nonaka, I. (1994). A dynamic theory of organizational knowledge creation. *Organization Science, 5*, 14–37.

Oh, C. H., & Oetzel, J. (2011). Multinationals' response to major disasters: How does subsidiary investment vary in response to the type of disaster and the quality of country governance? *Strategic Management Journal, 32*, 658–681.

Petersen, B., Pedersen, T., & Lyles, M. (2008). Closing knowledge gaps in foreign markets. *Journal of International Business Studies, 39*, 1097–1113.

Pitelis, C. (2007). Edith Penrose and a learning-based perspective on the MNE and OLI. *Management International Review, 47*, 207–219.

Podsakoff, P. M., Ahearne, M., & MacKenzie, S. B. (1997). Organizational citizenship behavior and the quantity and quality of work group performance. *Journal of Applied Psychology, 82*, 262–270.

Public Private Infrastructure Advisory Facility (2006, April). *Gridlines*. Transforming telecoms in Afghanistan, 1.

Quartz. (2014). And there was light: Afghanistan just spawned a multinational that's taking on global giants in Africa. Retrieved July 7, 2016, from http://qz.com/192010/afghanistan-just-spawned-a-multinational-thats-taking-on-global-giants-in-africa/

Reade, C. (2009). Human resource management implications of terrorist threats to firms in the supply chain. *International Journal of Physical Distribution and Logistics Management, 39*, 469–485.

Reade, C. (2015). Firms as peaceful oases conceptualising the role of conflict-sensitive human resource management. *Business, Peace and Sustainable Development, 5*, 7–28.

Reade, C., & Lee, H.-J. (2012). Organizational commitment in time of war: Assessing the impact and attenuation of employee sensitivity to ethnopolitical conflict. *Journal of International Management, 18*, 85–101.

Reade, C., & Lee, H.-J. (2016). Does ethnic conflict impede or enable employee innovation behavior?. *International Journal of Conflict Management, 27*, 199–224.

Robben, A. C. G. M., & Nordstrom, C. (1996). The anthropology and ethnography of violence and sociopolitical conflict. In C. Nordstrom & A. C. G. M. Robben (Eds.), *Fieldwork under fire: Contemporary studies of violence and survival* (pp. 1–23). Berkeley: University of California Press.

Sanchez-Peinado, E., & Pla-Barber, J. (2006). A multidimensional concept of uncertainty and its influence on the entry mode choice: An empirical analysis in the service sector. *International Business Review, 15*, 215–232.

Simon, H. A. (1991). Bounded rationality and organizational learning. *Organization Science, 2*, 125–134.

Sitkin, S. B. (1992). Learning through failure: The strategy of small losses. *Research in Organisational Behaviour, 14*, 231–266.

Slangen, A., & van Tulder, R. (2009). Cultural distance, political risk, or governance quality? Towards a more accurate conceptualization and measurement of external uncertainty in foreign entry mode research. *International Business Review, 18*, 276–291.

Suder, G. (2006). Location decisions, or: Modelling operational risk management under international terrorism. In G. Suder (Ed.), *Corporate strategies under international terrorism and adversity* (pp. 111–127). Cheltenham: Edward Elgar.

Suder, G., Bader, B., & Grosse, R. (2016). *The legacy of 09/11 in international business research: A 15 year review and an outlook*. Academy of International Business, Annual Conference, 29 June 2016 Proceedings, New Orleans LA.

Suder, G., Birnik, A., Nielsen, N., & Riviere, M. (2016). Extreme case learning: The manager perspective on rare knowledge and capabilities development. *Knowledge Management Research & Practice*, (First online 28 June 2016. http://link.springer.com/article/10.1057/s41275-016-0001-2?wt_mc=Internal.Event.1.SEM.ArticleAuthorOnlineFirst). doi:10.1057/s41275-016-0001-2

Transparency International. (2010, December 20). *Corruptions perceptions index (CPI)*.

Van Maanen, J. (1979). The fact of fiction in organizational ethnography. *Administrative Science Quarterly, 24*, 539–550.

Vandaele, D., & Gemmel, P. (2006). *Performance implications of in-role and extra-role behaviour of frontline service employees, No. 06/411*. Ghent: Ghent University, Faculty of Economics and Business Administration.

Veran, A., & Suder, G. (2010–2012). *Personal interviews of Monaco Telecom's Director General by G. Suder*. Working paper notes, SKEMA Business School, Sophia Antipolis. Unpublished.

Verbeke, A. (2003). The evolutionary view of the MNE and the future of internalization theory. *Journal of International Business Studies, 34*, 498–504.

Welch, C. L., & Welch, D. E. (2012). What do HR managers really do? HR roles on international projects. *Management International Review, 52*, 597–617.

Welch, C. L., Welch, D. E., & Tahvanainen, M. (2008). Managing the HR dimension of international project operations. *International Journal of Human Resource Management, 19*, 208–222.

Welch, D., & Welch, C. (2015). How global careers unfold in practice: Evidence from international project work. *International Business Review, 24*, 1072–1081.

World Investment Report. (2015). *Reforming international investment governance*. New York, NY: United Nations.

Wirtz, B., Mathieu, A., & Schilke, O. (2007). Strategy in high-velocity environments. *Long Range Planning, 40*, 295–313.

Wonacott, P. (2012, January 17). An entrepreneur weathers a tumultuous Arab Spring. *Wall Street Journal*. Retrieved from https://www.wsj.com/articles/SB10001424052970203436904577150690233235850

World Bank. (2008a, February 14). Doing business. Retrieved from http://www.doingbusiness.org/ExploreEconomies/?economyid=2

World Bank. (2008b, February 14). Worldwide governance indicators. Retrieved from http://info.worldbank.org/governance/wgi2007/sc_chart.asp

World Bank. (2012a, September 16). Doing business. Retrieved from http://www.doingbusiness.org/data/exploreeconomies/afghanistan/

World Bank. (2012b, September 1). Afghanistan country overview 2012. Retrieved from http://www.worldbank.org.af/WBSITE/EXTERNAL/COUNTRIES/SOUTHASIAEXT/AFGHANISTANEXTN/0,contentMDK:20154015~menuPK:305992~pagePK:141137~piPK:141127~theSitePK:305985,00.html

Yin, R. K. (2003). *Case study research: Design and methods*. London: Sage.

A risk management model for research on expatriates in hostile work environments

Richard A. Posthuma, Jase R. Ramsey, Gabriela L. Flores, Carl Maertz and Rawia O. Ahmed

ABSTRACT
Although much has been written about the causes of expat riate adjustment, more research is needed on managing the fear and anxiety experienced when expatriates work in hostile environments. The perceived risks of terrorism, kidnapping, crime, and civil unrest can have negative effects on the performance of expatriates and the organizations that employ them. While research has begun to examine expatriates' stress in hostile environments, there is comparatively little research on the effectiveness of management practices that can reduce such stress. We integrate the expatriate adjustment, psychological contract, and risk management literature to develop a model that can guide efforts to reduce environmental stress and its negative effect on expatriate adjustment. Specifically, we build on recent work by Bader and colleagues to develop propositions to guide future research with the aim of improving the conditions of expatriates working in hostile environments.

Introduction

Risk management for expatriates working in hostile environments is important because, as multinational corporations (MNCs) seek out new opportunities for growth, they are increasingly entering locations where there is a risk of harm to expatriates (Bader & Berg, 2014). Those risks can include terrorism, kidnapping, home invasion, disease, street crime, and a myriad of other perils. While some risks may involve foreign governments or groups opposed to governments, it is more common that the targets are businesses and their employees (Harvey, 1993). Previously, it may have been more common for expatriates to face these risks in just a few developing countries (e.g. Chile, Indonesia, and Brazil). However, as MNCs have expanded operations to include more dangerous countries (e.g. Nigeria, Columbia, and South Africa), terrorism and other crimes have posed significant threats to expatriates and their organizations (Bader & Berg, 2013; Czinkota, Knight, Liesch, & Steen, 2010).

Additionally, in recent years there has been a perception of increased risks for expatriates even in developed countries such as Germany and France (Caligiuri & Bonache, 2016; OECD, 2010, 2015). As such perceived risks for expatriates increase, fewer may bring their family members to the foreign work location (GMAC, 2015; Wagner & Westaby, 2009). This separation could cause further strain between family members and make the expatriates' adjustment to the foreign assignment even more difficult. Interestingly, even for those not directly harmed by these dangers to personal safety, indirect effects such as stress affecting both expatriates and their families can be much more common and pervasive (Bader & Berg, 2014). Thus, the importance of risk mitigation for expatriates is growing, as expatriates sojourn into a greater number of hostile, risky places around the world.

While we know much about domestic hostile environments (e.g. sexual harassment), relatively less is known about an expatriate's hostile environment. The environments are different because the hostile environment that expatriates face is often outside of the workplace. It includes risks to expatriates while at their residence in the foreign country, traveling to and from work, shopping, at their children's school, etc. Thus, the work environment for expatriates extends beyond what is typically thought to be the traditional work domain in domestic settings. The domain of the work environment for expatriates includes not only the actual workplace where they engage in their core job (e.g. tasks, duties, and responsibilities), but also any place in the foreign country where they and their family members spend time. They are living and working in the foreign country because of their employer, and for that reason, things that happen outside of the workplace are more likely to be associated with work (Haslberger & Brewster, 2009). Not surprisingly, expatriates expect that their employers go beyond taking care of their core work-related obligations (Gregersen & Black, 1992), but that they engage in a broader social exchange which incorporates non-work issues as well (Bader, 2015). They perceive that employers need to engage in a broader social exchange that incorporates non-work issues as well (Bader, 2015). This means that the relationship between the expatriate and employer extends into issues and topics that are not traditionally considered part of the work domain. This makes focused, systematic study and management response more complex. We argue that the conception of the psychological contract between the employee and employer needs to be expanded in order to account for the unique issues faced in a hostile environment.

Specifically, MNCs need to be concerned with managing both the direct and indirect effects of environmental risks to expatriates if they want to take advantage of the opportunities of conducting business in such environments (Czinkota et al., 2010). Multinational corporations will need to counter-balance the benefits of operating in these environments with effective methods of managing the risks. Multinational corporations can take great strides to keep expatriates from being directly involved in or injured by these dangers (Cameron, 2007) or adversely impacted by associated stress, but they need guidance from research. Researchers need guidance on the most important constructs and relationships on which to focus. Unfortunately, there has been limited research on how best to manage these risks (Bader, Schuster, & Dickmann, 2015). To address this need, we have developed this expatriate risk management (ERM) framework using a psychological contracts approach with the purpose of exploring how certain HRM practices (e.g. expatriate risk management practices) can contribute to expatriates' adjustment in hostile environments.

This article extends important work on hostile environments by Bader and Berg (2013, 2014), and Bader, Berg, and Holtbrügge (2015) in three ways. First, instead of looking at performance as the dependent variable, we propose expatriate adjustment to be a more proximally related outcome leading to role performance (Maertz et al., 2016). Many factors can impact work performance (e.g. skills, knowledge, traits, abilities), but we focus here on the established effects through expatriate adjustment. Additionally, focusing on the more proximal outcome of adjustment level allows a more precise understanding of moderators of risky environment-performance relationships. Second, we propose that the stress-adjustment relationship is moderated by the key construct of expatriate psychological resilience. Resilience has recently emerged as a critically important psychological construct necessary for success across occupations, which incorporates trait, capacity, and process aspects (Kossek & Perrigino, 2016). Third, we discuss how organizational-level ERM practices can reduce the individual-level stress inherent in a hostile environment. In so doing, we extend ERM literature by arguing that psychological contracts help in understanding the negative effects of stress from a hostile environment and ways to reduce them.

Literature review

Prior research has explored the causes and effects of expatriates' adjustment to foreign assignments (Black et al., 1992; Hechanova et al., 2003; Tung, 1998). This line of research has tended to focus on cognitive and attitudinal issues for the expatriates and their spouses (Bhaskar-Shrinivas et al., 2005; Froese et al., 2013; Takeuchi et al., 2002). For example, research has shown that expatriates are generally better adjusted when they have foreign language ability, higher self-efficacy, interpersonal relationship skills, and when their spouses are better adjusted to the foreign work location (Bhaskar-Shrinivas et al., 2005).

We argue that working in a hostile environment can itself have a significant impact on several expatriate perceptions and attitudes, which in turn can influence their performance (Bader & Berg, 2013). Some effects may even be positive. In hostile environments, research has shown that traumatic events at work can have a few positive effects such as an increase in group cohesiveness (Drabek & McEntire, 2003) and improvement in extra-role performance such as having better organizational citizenship behaviors (Karam, 2011).

Yet, traumatic events in hostile environments are more likely to have negative consequences. Such events should increase the likelihood that expatriates will experience a lower sense of well-being (Bader & Schuster, 2015). This can include feeling more fear, stress, anxiety, depression, and irritability, and having greater difficulty concentrating and sleeping (Reade & Lee, 2012). Expatriates who experience hostile work conditions also have poorer attitudes toward their job, team, and organization (Reade, 2009). This can result in feeling disconnected from their organization, which leads to withdrawal from work, reduced motivation, and reduced productivity (Alexander, 2004; Mainiero & Gibson, 2003), followed by reduced efficiency and effectiveness (Howie, 2007). These conditions can also result in premature departure from the expatriate assignment and in negative attitudes towards host country nationals (Bader & Berg, 2013).

Recent research has provided some foundation for understanding the cognitive and attitudinal factors affecting expatriates in hostile environments (Bader & Berg, 2014). Hypotheses about these factors have been tested and explanations offered (Bader & Berg, 2013), answering questions about why some expatriates working in hostile environments perform better than others. For example, we know that terrorism can increase stress levels in expatriates, which ultimately has negative effects on job commitment and satisfaction (Bader & Berg, 2013). Additionally, large and diverse social networks and social support from co-workers and employers help expatriates in hostile environments to have improved psychological well-being (Bader, 2015; Bader & Schuster, 2015). While we believe that understanding how working in a hostile environment affects attitudes through the mechanism of stress is a prudent start to understanding this unique working context, more outcomes should be studied. For instance, Bader and Berg (2013) added performance as a dependent variable from the effects of work attitudes. Extending prior research, we propose here that expatriate adjustment should be examined as the most proximal outcome construct of the stress caused by a hostile environment.

Many existing studies in this stream include discussion – in a somewhat abbreviated manner – of possible managerial implications of their findings. For example, Bader and Berg (2013), Bader (2015), Bader and Schuster (2015) suggested that organizations should help expatriates: (1) use social support to reduce stress, (2) seek more interactions with host country nationals, (3) get in touch with expatriate groups and other groups and associations in the foreign country, (4) include family members in pre-departure training, and (5) emphasize the importance of safety measures. However, such suggested practices are not guided by an overall conceptual model that integrates prior research into a model that can guide future research. In this article, we extend this work and the growing stream of research on managerial practices regarding how they can successfully aid expatriates and their employers in hostile environments.

Our model is also based on the risk management literature (Miller, 1992; Posthuma et al., 2011). This literature focuses on the identification, analysis, and implementation of practices that enable organizations to manage the risks they face (Tan & Enderwick, 2006; Ting, 1988). A risk management approach for expatriates can include factors such an analysis of the degree of risk, a decision about whether or not to avoid the risk, methods to manage the risk, and ways of transferring risks to others (e.g. through subcontracting, etc.; Czinkota et al., 2010).

The prior literature tended to apply a risk management approach to political risk involving state actors or natural disasters such as floods (Czinkota et al., 2010). Risks faced by expatriates in hostile environments certainly include political risk and natural disasters but also include violence, kidnapping, and other more salient dangers. To a large degree these risks are unpredictable and uncontrollable (Bader & Berg, 2014). In fact, some risks (e.g. terrorism) are, by their very nature, intended by their perpetrators to be unpredictable and uncontrollable. For this reason, those risks can cause higher stress levels and other negative individual outcomes (Harrison et al., 2004; Kraimer et al., 2001).

Thus, a risk management approach moves the expatriate literature in a different direction by explicitly dealing with direct danger faced by expatriates. We propose a risk management model based on the perspective of identifying successful HRM practices that have been shown to improve organizational performance. Risk management methods provide a useful overarching framework to guide the coordinated and logical development of insights about successful management of expatriates working in hostile environments. Although this research focuses on HRM practices, it is also a useful complement to the research stream that focuses on cognitive and attitudinal factors in adjustment.

Proposition & model development

We next propose a model that will integrate multiple streams of research into an overarching framework to help understand individual and organization policy effects within a hostile environment and to guide future research. See Figure 1.

To briefly overview this model, risks of working in hostile environments will reduce the expatriates' ability to adjust. The risks of hostile environments will cause expatriates to experience stress (e.g. anxiety, fear, increased blood pressure). This stress is the mechanism through which working in a hostile environment primarily affects adjustment. However, when organizations help expatriates manage risk, the negative hostile environment – stress – adjustment relationships are each weakened, while the psychological contract is strengthened. Finally, psychological resilience should help mitigate the negative effects of stress on adjustment during the vexing context of a hostile environment.

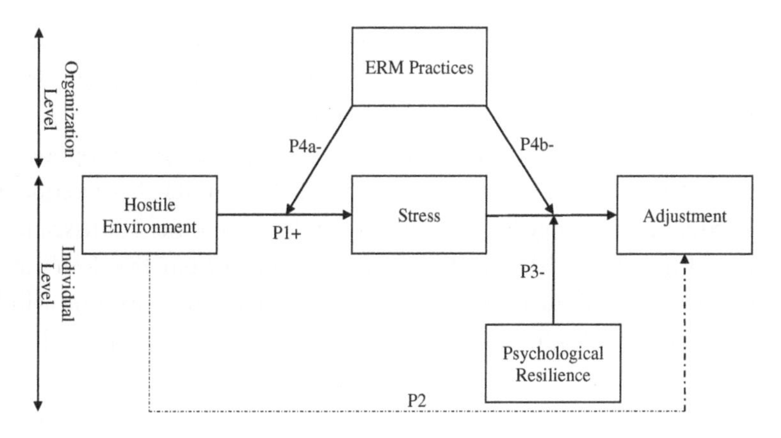

Figure 1. Conceptual model.

Expatriates in hostile environments

In an effort to remain competitive, many MNCs are expanding their operations to higher risk places because of the growth opportunities they provide (Bader et al., 2015). Some of the most enticing places for growth and profits also happen to be considered high-risk because they suffer from political, economic, and/or other social instabilities. These instabilities can result in a hostile environment for employees, including the threats of terrorism and other perils (Bader & Berg, 2014). Terrorism is defined as premeditated violence used by subnational groups against non-combatant targets in order to achieve a political, religious, or ideological objective through intimidation and fear (Czinkota et al., 2010). Nations and governments are typically the primary targets of terrorists. However, as the security of governmental buildings, embassies, and military facilities increases, so does the vulnerability of less-guarded targets, such as crowded city streets, public markets, and businesses (Bader & Berg, 2014; Czinkota et al., 2004, 2005). In order to attract attention, terrorists plan and carry out random acts of violence intended to kill and destroy, instilling a sense of fear (Jain & Grosse, 2009). These acts take place without warning and can occur anywhere at any time (Bader & Berg, 2013). Further, accepting a foreign assignment can entail uprooting one's life and often the lives of family members. The higher levels of interdependence and uncertainty involved in expatriate assignments make the employer-employee relationship for expatriates even more important than for domestic employment. International managers are generally more involved in expatriates' lives professionally and personally. This increased influence over various aspects of the expatriates' lives results in expanded employer obligations as perceived by the employee (Guzzo et al., 1994), particularly in a risky hostile environment.

These perceived obligations make up the psychological contract (Robinson et al., 1994). Unlike a purely transactional exchange, which includes features like compensation, job responsibilities, and length of assignment, the psychological contract is made up of relational elements (Rousseau & McLean Parks, 1993).

These relational elements can be personal, socio-emotional, or value-based expectations that expatriates await from their employers (Guzzo et al., 1994). For instance, these unwritten expectations might be based on intangible considerations, such as interpersonal relationships, well-being, and growth opportunities (Guzzo et al., 1994). They are made when expatriates voluntarily surrender some of their freedom in exchange for a similar surrender by another (Rousseau, 1995). In the case of hostile environments, 'surrender some of our freedom' can have dire consequences, and thus 'a similar surrender' by the organization will likely be expected to be very high. This is an extra aspect for the psychological contract in a potentially hostile environment.

Three dimensions of the psychological contract are relevant to the hostile environment context. First, the dimension of 'scope' refers to the extent to which the boundary between one's employment relationship and other elements of an expatriate's life seems permeable (Sels et al., 2004). A narrow scope is a strict division between work and personal life. A broader scope expresses an employers' concern for an employee's family situation and extra role behavior. In a hostile environment context, we suggest that HRM practices focus on a broader scope of the psychological contract due to the expanded nature of the situation. Second, the dimension of 'stability' refers to static vs. flexible psychological contracts (Sels et al., 2004). Static means a rigid application of rules and practices, along with a low tolerance level of uncertainty. Flexible reflects a high tolerance for uncertainty, change, and interpretation of the rules. In the context of this study, HRM practices should match the highly uncertain situation with a flexible stability psychological contract dimension. Finally, regarding the 'time frame'; long vs. short, because expatriates are, by definition, mobile employees, HRM practices should focus on the relative short term (Sels et al., 2004), which recognizes that most expatriate assignments are limited, and the form of the psychological contract will change considerably upon repatriation.

Stress

Not only do expatriate employees face greater physical dangers than their counterparts in safer countries, but they also experience increased psychological stress due to the pervasive threat of violence in such contexts (Czinkota et al., 2004). International assignments can entail many stressors because they not only bring new job responsibilities, but they also bring a new culture, possible language barriers, and sometimes new types of food and weather to which expatriates need to become accustomed (Hechanova et al., 2003).

Prior research has shown that while most employees do not frequently suffer direct consequences (e.g. death, physical injury) from the risks of working in a hostile environment, they do experience significant indirect effects including a sense of distress, fear, or vulnerability (Bader & Berg, 2014; Czinkota et al., 2005; Reade, 2009). This occurs because expatriate assignments uproot lives and those of family members, causing all to feel more vulnerable (Haslberger & Brewster, 2009). Exacerbating these natural feelings of vulnerability is the fact that in hostile environments people have higher fear of risks that are unfamiliar and outside of their control (Czinkota et al., 2005, 2010; Leventhal, 1970; Slovic, 2000; Sunstein, 2003; Tversky & Kahneman, 1974). There are other stressors endemic to working in a hostile environment including safety concerns and intra-family tension (Bader et al., 2015). Therefore, in line with prior literature on hostile environments:

Proposition 1: *Hostile environments increase expatriate stress.*

Expatriate adjustment

Research has convincingly shown that expatriate adjustment is positively related to higher levels of performance (Bhaskar-Shrinivas et al., 2005). While the effects on expatriate performance of a hostile environment is certainly relevant (Bader & Berg, 2013), we argue that stress from this environment first influences the expatriate's adjustment levels, which are conceptually closer to environmental stressors than the work performance behavior (e.g. Maertz et al., 2016). Hence, the effects of hostile environment that we focus on involve (indirect effects on performance through) stress the expatriate experiences directly impacting adjustment criteria levels.

Specifically, Maertz et al. (2016) recently theorized that reaching a better level of adjustment processing is largely dependent on acculturative stress reduction through learning and identity management processes. This model proposes that stress would slow the adjustment process in three ways: by creating a disruptive stress reduction motive at the beginning of interactions, by making learning and identity management processes less functional, and by inhibiting memory storage of any lessons learned. Thus, additional stressors, beyond normal acculturative stressors of encountering novelty, from external threats from a hostile environment could relegate expatriates to remaining at lower levels of adjustment for a longer period than those not in such an environment. Together, these arguments imply:

Proposition 2: *The negative relationship between a hostile environment and expatriate adjustment is mediated by stress.*

Psychological resilience

Research has shown that some expatriates are more sensitive than others to the indirect negative effects of working in hostile environments (Reade, 2009). Expatriates who are more sensitive to hostile environments will suffer greater consequences when events like terrorism or ethno-political conflict occur (Reade & Lee, 2012). Prior research suggests that these negative effects can be reduced through screening out highly sensitive employees from consideration for the assignment and by organizations providing higher levels of social support to expatriates (Reade & Lee, 2012). However, in addition to alleviating the negative effects of sensitivity, organizations can enhance expatriates' ability to avoid negative stress effects by selecting for positive factors.

One such factor is psychological resilience (Block & Kremen, 1996). As one review summarized,

> Resilience has become increasingly important to personal and job effectiveness, as individuals must be "resilient" in all life aspects. These range from major events like natural disasters and terrorism to everyday occurrences such as dealing with a difficult work colleague. (Kossek & Perrigino, 2016, p. 730).

Employees who have higher levels of resilience are better able to respond positively to adversity and have more flexibility to adapt to the changing demands of situations outside of their control (Block & Kremen, 1996). Recent research has shown that employees with higher levels of psychological resilience also had higher levels of commitment and lower levels of turnover in response to organizational change (Shin et al., 2012). We recognize that psychological resilience is only one of several individual factors that can enhance expatriate success (e.g. Bhaskar-Shrinivas et al., 2005), but an important one.

Prior research has shown that psychological resilience increases employee willingness to change (Shin et al., 2012). This willingness to change will benefit expatriates in hostile environments who need to adapt to the unpredictable and sometimes changing threats they face. In fact, Kossek and Perrigino (2016) claim that resilience is of greater importance today than ever with the erosion of the psychological contract. Thus, it is a most appropriate moderator of our relationships here, which are based on the psychological contract obligations of the organization within such hostile environments, discussed in the next section.

Expatriates may enhance their relevant psychological resilience by receiving training on how to deal with terrorist events (Liou & Lin, 2008). The confidence that expatriates gain from training should increase their self-efficacy to persist once on assignment. In turn, increased self-efficacy could induce expatriates to believe they are able to manage the risks, and therefore, they should be more likely to engage in emergency planning and preparedness exercises (Czinkota et al., 2010). Through these mechanisms psychological resilience will positively impact expatriates' perceived ability to cope, and thereby, weaken the hostile environment's stress effects that can inhibit adjustment progress.

Proposition 3: *The negative relationship between stress and expatriate adjustment is moderated by psychological resilience, such that the negative relationship will become weaker.*

ERM practices

While the unit of analysis for our model is the individual expatriate, the inclusion of organizational factors calls for a cross-level analysis (Rousseau, 1995). Aycan (1997, p. 435) put forth a conceptual model of how organizational practices (e.g.

planning and support) affected expatriate adjustment, 'which is commonly the case in organizational cross-level analysis'. She separated the organizational characteristics that would affect expatriate adjustment into pre- and post-departure periods. For example, strategic planning that involves consulting with the local host unit to anticipate potential problems before departure should reduce the uncertainty about the assignment. Further, HR managers should maintain continuous communication and assistance with their expatriates, post-arrival. We extend her model by proposing that organizational-level ERM practices can reduce individual-level negative impacts of working in hostile environments. We chose ERM practices (e.g. kidnap and ransom insurance, or a comprehensive international security plan) because they embody the most relevant HRM practices to this special issue: managing people in hostile environments.

These practices help alleviate factors such as threat perceptions and fear that expatriates could experience. For example, an expatriate working for a large German firm told us that he adjusted well during his assignment in Iraq just after the Gulf War because his company 'took good care' of him. After further questioning, it became apparent that his firm understood that if he (and his family) were stressed, he would not adjust (and could return to Germany before his goals were accomplished). The HR department found him a nice home in a heavily guarded compound, arranged a full time (armed) driver, frequently sent him and his wife to 'safer' countries to vacation, and enrolled his children in a school within the same compound. All of these services limited some risks and 'helped reduce the stress I felt while in recent war zone'. These ERM practices are in line with a broad scope, flexible stability, and short-term understanding of the expatriate's psychological contract.

Risk can be defined as the exposure to the possibility of losing something of value, whether financial wealth, physical or emotional well-being, or status (Kungwani, 2014). Organizations have much to gain from a successful expatriate assignment. However, when expatriate assignments fail, organizations suffer financially as well as from loss of information, reduced confidence, and broken relationships (Bader & Berg, 2014). Risk evaluation is a process that organizations can engage in to better manage the risks of expatriates working in hostile environments. It includes two elements: risk identification and risk analysis. Risk identification is the process of collecting information about the environment and all the threats and dangers that could impact expatriate performance. Because of the obvious effects of traumatic events possible in hostile environments, the indirect psychological effects may often be overlooked. In this step, the risk management team would need to identify dangers that would result in a loss to expatriates' physical safety (e.g. assault, kidnapping, car-jacking, theft, home invasion) as well as their psychological safety (e.g. perceived threat of physical dangers, stress, fear, anger). Also, they need to identify indirect effects such as loss of trust in the employer – effects that prior research has proven to be important. Organizations that thoroughly identify direct and indirect risks to expatriates will be better able to choose the appropriate methods to manage those risks, thereby, leading to improved adjustment for those experiencing stress.

Risk analysis includes estimating the probability of a loss occurring, as well as the severity of the loss. There are existing published country and city-level risk reports (Cameron, 2007). These reports are sometimes based on analysts' qualitative judgments based on secondary sources. In addition to qualitatively analyzing the probability and severity for each risk, organizations can perform their own quantitative estimates for each, in the environments where they operate. Following the risk management perspective, one scorer could rate the probability that the risk will occur. The second could rate the severity of consequences if the risk does occur. These scores could be derived from subject matter experts who, based on prior experience or knowledge, analyze the risks (Boyacigiller, 1990). Although many multinational employers may use very informal methods for assessing risks, risk measurement can be substantially improved with such structured measurement techniques (McNulty et al., 2009). The combination of empirical assessments usually results in more accurate predictions (Meehl, 1954). For example, to gauge risks, clear descriptions of a behaviorally-anchored Likert-type scale with ratings from 1 to 10 (with lower scores indicating lower risk), can be used to enhance measurement (Shin et al., 2007). This analysis should include both the direct and indirect effects of working in hostile environments. Once analysis is completed, the organization would have a prioritized list of the risks that threaten expatriate adjustment. This would allow the risk management team to focus their efforts strategically to fit the risks of particular locations (Shin et al., 2007). However, beyond simply evaluating risks, we propose that organizations can better manage their risks by aligning their ERM practices to these.

Risk management has been suggested as a helpful approach in addressing issues related to political risks and terrorism for MNEs (Czinkota et al., 2010; Miller, 1992). Risk management techniques include identifying and analyzing risks, deciding whether or not the identified risks are acceptable, choosing the best practices to reduce the likelihood of losses, minimizing the harm that could be caused, and then measuring the results (Czinkota et al., 2010; Hopkin, 2014; MacDonald, 1966; Mehr & Hedges, 1974; Pmi, 2013; Ting, 1988).

A more formal risk analysis would identify all the risks (e.g. the types of perils or dangers that could be involved) and then analyze each in terms of the likelihood or frequency with which they might occur and the severity of harm (MacDonald, 1966; Mehr & Hedges, 1974). For example, an employer could identify several risks (e.g. that the expatriate or their family might be kidnapped and held for ransom, succumb to an illness, have their home invaded by robbers, etc.). For each of these perils an assessment of the likelihood and severity of harm would be conducted, and a determination would be made about whether the benefits obtained from employing expatriates in that environment outweigh these risks, taking into account the application of risk management techniques (e.g. loss prevention, harm mitigation). Depending on the threats faced in a particular country, safety measures could include providing expatriates housing within a protected campus, armored vehicles, or body guards (Bader & Berg, 2014). Other steps could include registering with an international travel hot line to facilitate the receipt of warnings about changing risks, safer driving practices to avoid kidnapping, better security precautions to avoid computer hacking, and so forth. Even organizations that believe they are not a target, or that take strong precautions to prevent such disasters, can educate their employees on what measures to take in such an event. Not only could such crisis planning prove useful in response to various disasters and emergencies, but expatriate families feeling equipped to deal with unforeseen disasters could have the additional benefit of enhancing the psychological contract between employees and the organization (Liou & Lin, 2008).

According to this contract, expatriates are likely to respond to the risks of working in a hostile environment with a heightened expectation that their employer will provide them added workplace security (e.g. access controls, armored vehicles, body guards). Moreover, they have expectations that their employers will provide guidance and assistance in handling their sense of fear and vulnerability (Alexander, 2004; Bader & Berg, 2014; Reade, 2009). When organizations fail to meet these expectations, expatriates will have lower evaluations of their employers, will trust them less, and will perceive them as being unsympathetic (Mainiero & Gibson, 2003; Reade, 2009; Ryan et al., 2003). This can result in the negative affective state of psychological contract violation (Morrison & Robinson, 1997), which would increase overall stress effects.

Organizations can enhance positive outcomes during work in hostile environments by meeting expatriate expectations (i.e. psychological contract fulfillment) and providing them with resources that are outside of typical work related factors (e.g. flexible scope). For example, when employers provide additional social support to expatriates, this may engender increased levels of employee affective commitment and improved organizational citizenship behaviors (Bader & Berg, 2013, 2014; Liu, 2009). Also, employers can help to increase expatriates' sense of well-being by helping enhance their social network both at the pre-departure phase and during their expatriate assignments (Bader & Schuster, 2015).

Finally, employers could help reduce stress from intra-family conflicts that might result from the hostile environment by including the expatriate's family in pre-departure training and ongoing counseling during the expatriate assignment (Bader & Berg, 2013). This could include providing the expatriate, spouse, and family with information about the evacuation process that the company will use should emergencies occur or violence escalate in the foreign country (Bader et al., 2015). In this way, they will have a greater sense that the employer is fulfilling its tacit obligations to care for them (e.g. broad scope). Involving the expatriate's spouse and family in the pre-departure phase and encouraging them to participate in the decision to go on the assignment, can also reduce the likelihood of intra-family tension while in the foreign country (Bader et al., 2015). These are examples of HRM practices that provide the expatriate and his/her family with additional coping resources, thereby enhancing their perceptions that the employer has met its heightened obligations under the psychological contract.

In summary, employers using these types of practices should reduce the negative individual-level effects of (i) a hostile environment on stress through reducing expatriates' perceptions of threat from the environment, and (ii) stress on expatriate adjustment level through providing expatriates and their families with coping resources (e.g. Lazarus & Folkman, 1984).

Proposition 4a: *Organizational expatriate risk management practices moderate the hostile environment – stress relationship, such that a higher degree of ERM practice reduces the negative environment – stress relationship.*

Proposition 4b: *Organizational expatriate risk management practices moderate the stress – adjustment relationship, such that a higher degree of ERM practice reduces the negative stress – adjustment relationship.*

These moderating effects of organizational ERM practices can each increase the expatriate's perceived psychological contract quality with the organization.

Discussion and conclusion

The purpose of this article was to build on recent work by Bader and his colleagues in developing propositions to guide future research with the aim of improving the adjustment and performance of expatriates working in hostile environments. The risks expatriates face in those environments (e.g. terrorism, crime, health, and safety) can be evaluated by identifying the risks and analyzing their likelihood and severity. We propose that ERM practices can facilitate a reduction in threat associated with hostile environments, and increase the psychological coping capacity of expatriates and their families. Future research could study the extent to which attitudinal stressors, individual differences, and ERM practices interact to reduce the negative effects of the risks of working in hostile environments on expatriate adjustment.

There are several contributions in this research framework. We build on the foundation of prior research examining the cognitive and attitudinal factors affecting expatriates in hostile environments. We integrate psychological contract research with the expatriate adjustment and stress literatures to examine how ERM practices can alter the relationship between these variables. Using risk management literature as well, we built our framework to facilitate future research in identifying the connections between research and managerial practices useful for organizations operating in hostile environments. This not only connects different research streams, but also will help to close the gap between research and practice on ERM.

Finally, while we went into detail on how companies should measure risk, we said less about measuring other constructs in our model. We purposely included broad constructs and propositions to make them potentially applicable across settings and research variables. Some environmental risks clearly have inherently higher effects on stress than others. Working in a place such as Caracas, Venezuela, which has the highest homicide rate in the world would likely increase an expatriate's stress more than being in a place like Santo Domingo, Dominican Republic, which is known more for hurricanes that are much less frequent. Finally, adjustment should probably be measured as three components per Black and Gregersen (1991) or with the newer scale recently published in this journal by Hippler et al. (2014). We did not want to limit future researcher's operationalization of the constructs, and encourage a variety of designs and methodologies to examine proposed relationships.

If successful, this research should yield knowledge of what ERM and other HR practices work best to reduce stress and promote adjustment under different environmental risks. Beyond providing contingency recommendations, this would greatly aid management's ability to determine whether using expatriates is superior to an ethnocentric staffing strategy. In conclusion, we hope that this broad framework will help guide research studies on ERM, and on ways to lower expatriate stress and facilitate adjustment more generally.

Disclosure statement

No potential conflict of interest was reported by the authors.

References

Alexander, D. C. (2004). *Business confronts terrorism: Risks and responses*. Madison, WI: Terrace Books.

Aycan, Z. (1997). Expatriate adjustment as a multifaceted phenomenon: Individual and organizational level predictors. *The International Journal of Human Resource Management, 8*, 434–456.

Bader, B. (2015). The power of support in high-risk countries: Compensation and social support as antecedents of expatriate work attitudes. *The International Journal of Human Resource Management, 26*, 1712–1736.

Bader, B., & Berg, N. (2013). An empirical investigation of terrorism-induced stress on expatriate attitudes and performance. *Journal of International Management, 19*, 163–175.

Bader, B., & Berg, N. (2014). The influence of terrorism on expatriate performance: A conceptual approach. *The International Journal of Human Resource Management, 25*, 539–557.

Bader, B., Berg, N., & Holtbrügge, D. (2015). Expatriate performance in terrorism-endangered countries: The role of family and organizational support. *International Business Review, 24*, 849–860.

Bader, B., & Schuster, T. (2015). Expatriate social networks in terrorism-endangered countries: An empirical analysis in Afghanistan, India, Pakistan, and Saudi Arabia. *Journal of International Management, 21*, 63–77.

Bader, B., Schuster, T., & Dickmann, M. (2015). Special issue of international journal of human resource management: Danger and risk as challenges for HRM: How to manage people in hostile environments. *The International Journal of Human Resource Management, 26*, 2015–2017.

Bhaskar-Shrinivas, P., Harrison, D. A., Shaffer, M. A., & Luk, D. M. (2005). Input-based and time-based models of international adjustment: Meta-analytic evidence and theoretical extensions. *Academy of Management Journal, 48*, 257–281.

Black, J. S., & Gregersen, H. B. (1991). Antecedents to cross-cultural adjustment for expatriates in Pacific Rim assignments. *Human Relations, 44*, 497–515.

Black, S., Gregersen, H. B., & Mendenhall, M. E. (1992). *Global assignments: Successfully expatriating and repatriating international managers*. San Francisco, CA: Jossey-Bass.

Block, J., & Kremen, A. M. (1996). IQ and ego-resiliency: Conceptual and empirical connections and separateness. *Journal of Personality and Social Psychology, 70*, 349–361.

Boyacigiller, N. (1990). The role of expatriates in the management of interdependence complexity and risk in multinational corporations. *Journal of International Business Studies, 21*, 357–381.

Caligiuri, P., & Bonache, J. (2016). Evolving and enduring challenges in global mobility. *Journal of World Business, 51*, 127–141.

Cameron, D. (2007). Managing travel risk: A duty of care toolkit. *Journal of Business Continuity & Emergency Planning, 1*, 158–166.

Czinkota, M., Knight, G. A., & Liesch, P. W. (2004). Terrorism and international business: Conceptual foundations. In G. G. S. Suder (Ed.), *Terrorism and the International Business Environment: The Security-business Nexus* (pp. 43–57). Cheltenham: Edward Elgar.

Czinkota, M. R., Knight, G. A., Liesch, P. W., & Steen, J. (2005). Positioning terrorism in management and marketing: Research propositions. *Journal of International Management, 11*, 581–604.

Czinkota, M. R., Knight, G., Liesch, P. W., & Steen, J. (2010). Terrorism and international business: A research agenda. *Journal of International Business Studies, 41*, 826–843.

Drabek, T. E., & McEntire, D. A. (2003). Emergent phenomena and the sociology of disaster: Lessons, trends and opportunities from the research literature. *Disaster Prevention and Management: An International Journal, 12*, 97–112.

Froese, F. J., Jommersbach, S., & Klautzsch, E. (2013). Cosmopolitan career choices: A cross-cultural study of job candidates' expatriation willingness. *The International Journal of Human Resource Management, 24*, 3247–3261.

GMAC. (2015). *Global relocation trends. 2015 survey report*. Expatica Retrieved from: https://www.expatica.com/hr. Accessed 2016.

Gregersen, H. B., & Black, J. S. (1992). Antecedents to commitment to a parent company and a foreign operation. *Academy of Management Journal, 35*, 65–90.

Guzzo, R. A., Noonan, K. A., & Elron, E. (1994). Expatriate managers and the psychological contract. *Journal of Applied Psychology, 79*, 617.

Harrison, D. A., Shaffer, M. A., & Bhaskar-Shrinivas, P. (2004). Going places: Roads more and less travelled in research on expatriate experiences. *Research in Personnel and Human Resources Management, 23*, 199–248.

Harvey, M. G. (1993). A survey of corporate programs for managing terrorist threats. *Journal of International Business Studies, 24*, 465–478.

Haslberger, A., & Brewster, C. (2009). Capital gains: Expatriate adjustment and the psychological contract in international careers. *Human Resource Management, 48*, 379–397.

Hechanova, R., Beehr, T. A., & Christiansen, N. D. (2003). Antecedents and consequences of employees' adjustment to overseas assignment: A meta-analytic review. *Applied Psychology, 52*, 213–236.

Hippler, T., Caligiuri, P. M., Johnson, J. E., & Baytalskaya, N. (2014). The development and validation of a theory-based expatriate adjustment scale. *The International Journal of Human Resource Management, 25*, 1938–1959.

Hopkin, P. (2014). *Fundamentals of risk management: Understanding, evaluating and implementing effective risk management*. London: Kogan Page Publishers.

Howie, L. (2007). The terrorism threat and managing workplaces. *Disaster Prevention and Management: An International Journal, 16*, 70–78.

Jain, S. C., & Grosse, R. (2009). Impact of terrorism and security measures on global business transactions: Some international business guidelines. *Journal of Transnational Management, 14*, 42–73.

Karam, C. M. (2011). Good organizational soldiers: Conflict-related stress predicts citizenship behavior. *International Journal of Conflict Management, 22*, 300–319.

Kossek, E. E., & Perrigino, M. B. (2016). Resilience: A review using a grounded integrated occupational approach. *The Academy of Management Annals, 10*, 729–797.

Kraimer, M. L., Wayne, S. J., & Jaworski, R. (2001). Sources of support and expatriate performance: The mediating role of expatriate adjustment. *Personnel Psychology, 54*, 71–99.

Kungwani, P. (2014). Risk management – An analytical study. *IOSR Journal of Business and Management, 16*, 83–89.

Lazarus, R. S., & Folkman, S. (1984). *Stress, appraisal, and coping*. New York, NY: Springer.

Leventhal, H. (1970). Findings and theory in the study of fear communications. *Advances in Experimental Social Psychology, 5*, 119–186.

Liou, D. Y., & Lin, C. H. (2008). Human resources planning on terrorism and crises in the Asia Pacific region: Cross-national challenge, reconsideration, and proposition from western experiences. *Human Resource Management, 47*, 49–72.

Liu, Y. (2009). Perceived organizational support and expatriate organizational citizenship behavior: The mediating role of affective commitment towards the parent company. *Personnel Review, 38*, 307–319.

MacDonald, D. L. (1966). *Corporate risk control*. Hoboken, NJ: Wiley.

Maertz, C. P., Takeuchi, R., & Chen, J. (2016). An episodic framework of outgroup interaction processing: Integration and redirection for the expatriate adjustment research. *Psychological Bulletin, 142*, 623–654.

Mainiero, L. A., & Gibson, D. E. (2003). Managing employee trauma: Dealing with the emotional fallout from 9-11. *Academy of Management Executive, 17*, 130–143.

McNulty, Y., De Cieri, H., & Hutchings, K. (2009). Do global firms measure expatriate return on investment? An empirical examination of measures, barriers and variables influencing global staffing practices. *The International Journal of Human Resource Management, 20*, 1309–1326.

Meehl, P. E. (1954). *Clinical versus statistical prediction: A theoretical analysis and a review of the evidence*. Washington, DC: American Psychological Association.

Mehr, R. I., & Hedges, B. A. (1974). *Risk management: Concepts and applications*. New York, NY: McGraw-Hill/Irwin.

Miller, K. D. (1992). A framework for integrated risk management in international business. *Journal of International Business Studies, 23*, 311–331.

Morrison, E. W., & Robinson, S. L. (1997). When employees feel betrayed: A model of how psychological contract violation develops. *Academy of Management Review, 22*, 226–256.

OECD. (2010). *International mobility: Measuring innovation: A new perspective*. Paris: Author.

OECD. (2015). *International migration outlook 2015*. Paris: Author.

Pmi, A. (2013). *Guide to the project management body of knowledge (PMBOK® Guide)* (5th ed.). Newton Square, PA: Project Management Institute.

Posthuma, R. A., Roehling, M. V., & Campion, M. A. (2011). Employment discrimination law exposures for international employers: A risk assessment model. *International Journal of Law and Management, 53*, 281–298.

Reade, C. (2009). Human resource management implications of terrorist threats to firms in the supply chain. *International Journal of Physical Distribution & Logistics Management, 39*, 469–485.

Reade, C., & Lee, H.-J. (2012). Organizational commitment in time of war: Assessing the impact and attenuation of employee sensitivity to ethnopolitical conflict. *Journal of International Management, 18*, 85–101.

Robinson, S. L., Kraatz, M. S., & Rousseau, D. M. (1994). Changing obligations and the psychological contract: A longitudinal study. *Academy of Management Journal, 37*, 137–152.

Rousseau, D. (1995). *Psychological contracts in organizations: Understanding written and unwritten agreements*. London: Sage Publications.

Rousseau, D. M., & McLean Parks, J. (1993). The contracts of individuals and organizations. *Research in Organizational Behavior, 15*, 1–1.

Ryan, A. M., West, B. J., & Carr, J. Z. (2003). Effects of the terrorist attacks of 9/11/01 on employee attitudes. *Journal of Applied Psychology, 88*, 647.

Sels, L., Janssens, M., & Van Den Brande, I. (2004). Assessing the nature of psychological contracts: A validation of six dimensions. *Journal of Organizational Behavior, 25*, 461–488.

Shin, S. J., Morgeson, F. P., & Campion, M. A. (2007). What you do depends on where you are: Understanding how domestic and expatriate work requirements depend upon the cultural context. *Journal of International Business Studies, 38*, 64–83.

Shin, J., Taylor, M. S., & Seo, M.-G. (2012). Resources for change: The relationships of organizational inducements and psychological resilience to employees' attitudes and behaviors toward organizational change. *Academy of Management Journal, 55*, 727–748.

Slovic, P. (2000). *The perception of risk London*. London, UK: Earthscan.

Sunstein, C. R. (2003). Terrorism and probability neglect. *Journal of Risk and Uncertainty, 26*, 121–136.

Takeuchi, R., Yun, S., & Tesluk, P. E. (2002). An examination of crossover and spillover effects of spousal and expatriate cross-cultural adjustment on expatriate outcomes. *Journal of Applied Psychology, 87*, 655–666.

Tan, W. J., & Enderwick, P. (2006). Managing threats in the global era: The impact and response to SARS. *Thunderbird International Business Review, 48*, 515–536.

Ting, W. (1988). Multinational risk assessment and management: Strategies for investment and marketing decisions. *The International Executive, 30*, 31–33.

Tung, R. L. (1998). A contingency framework of selection and training of expatriates revisited. *Human Resource Management Review, 8*, 23–37.

Tversky, A., & Kahneman, D. (1974). Judgment under uncertainty: Heuristics and biases. *Science, 185*, 1124–1131.

Wagner, M. R., & Westaby, J. D. (2009). The willingness to relocate to another country: The impact of cultural similarity, destination safety, and financial incentive. *International Journal of Psychology, 44*, 257–265.

Localization of staff in a hostile context: an exploratory investigation in Afghanistan

Michael Dickmann, Emma Parry and Nadia Keshavjee

ABSTRACT
Hostile environments pose a distinct threat to international organizations and their staff and yet they are under researched within the literature on IHRM. Localization of staff may present a means to manage some of the risks and also to provide the resources needed to achieve competitive advantage. Drawing on the resource-based view and institutional theory, we explored resource- and capability-based and institutional influences in relation to the decision of whether to localize professional staff in a hostile environment (Afghanistan). Using in-depth semi-structured interviews with representatives from four organizations in Afghanistan, our investigation identified new influences on localization at the societal and organizational level. These include ongoing security issues as well as influences on localization such as corruption, impartiality and the need for outside experiences as well as perspectives not identified in previous work. In addition, we emphasize the importance of both picking appropriate valuable local human resources and using appropriate internal capabilities to develop and deploy them in such a way to build firm-specific assets which are also rare, inimitable and non-substitutable, thus leading to sustainable competitive advantage.

This paper focuses on the factors influencing localization of staff in multinational corporations (MNCs) in hostile environments. Previous research on localization (Al-Lamki, 1998; Forstenlechner, 2010; Fryxell, Butler, & Choi, 2004; Wong & Law, 1999) has focused almost exclusively on stable and non-hostile contexts. Given that a highly dynamic, insecure and idiosyncratic context is likely to have a particularly strong effect on organizational practices, studying localization drivers and constraints in hostile environments is overdue. We therefore address this weakness in the literature via an exploratory study set in Afghanistan.

Afghanistan is unique given its many violent conflicts, the historically long-term presence of the international community and armed forces and the high level of insecurity in the country. Studying 'deviant' cases such as this can give novel insights as the characteristics predicted through extant work may not occur (Emigh, 1997; Piekkari, Welch, & Paavilainen, 2009). First, we will expand on the existing literature, uncovering the factors that influence localization. Our first contribution is therefore that we have developed a new set of factors affecting localization based on these novel insights. Second, we use the resource-based view (RBV) and institutional theory in explaining these influences, therefore embedding our discussion of localization within a sound theoretical framework, addressing this criticism of the localization literature (Law, Song, Wong, & Chen, 2009). Third, we make a practical contribution, providing guidance to practitioners who are looking to localize their staff in Afghanistan or other similar country contexts. In essence, we explore different resource and capability-based and institutional influences within a context that can be described as unusual due to the high risks, insecurity and corruption alongside the unusual tribal structures in Afghanistan.

Staff localization is the degree to which expatriate managers are replaced by competent local staff (Law et al., 2009; Potter, 1989). We adopt the more comprehensive definition provided by Bhanugopan and Fish (2007, p. 366), which states, 'localization is a process in which local officers increase their competencies, and consequently improve their performance, the main objective being to train and develop locals to enable them to replace expatriates with competency and efficiency'. In this paper we will examine the factors that influence the decision to localize staff, rather than examining organizational localization in the sense of building local supply chains or a local customer base. In the first instance we turn to the RBV and institutional theory as well as the extant literature on staff localization in order to develop a framework for our research.

Resource-based influences on localization

According to the RBV, sustainable competitive advantage for organizations can be achieved via firm heterogeneity created by the acquisition of resources which are valuable, rare, difficult to imitate and non-substitutable (VRIN) (Barney, 1991; Wernerfelt, 1984). Wernerfelt (1984, p. 172) describes a resource as 'anything which could be thought of as a strength or weakness of a given firm'. Much of the literature on the RBV suggests that the acquisition of superior resources is the main mechanism for the creation of economic rents (e.g. Barney, 1986, 1997; Peteraf, 1993; Wernerfelt, 1984).

It has long been accepted that these resources can include human resources (Wright, McMahan, & McWilliams, 1994). Indeed, previous work on the RBV has emphasized the role of human resources as the sources of above normal returns for organizations as opposed to physical assets (Bowman & Toms, 2010). The knowledge, skills and activities of the workforce can therefore be viewed as core resources that contribute to the firm's competitive advantage (Wright, Dunford, & Snell, 2001; Wright et al., 1994). In addition to the value of a (human) resource, sustainable competitive advantage requires that resources are also rare, inimitable and non-substitutable. Based upon the work of Wright et al. (1994), we can presume that individuals with high levels of particular abilities are rare, that these abilities are difficult to imitate due to social ambiguity and complexity and that they cannot easily be substituted by other types of resources (e.g. technology). In relation to the focus of this paper, the decision to localize staff should therefore be based upon the belief that this will allow the organization to create valuable, rare, inimitable and non-substitutable (VRIN) resources.

The literature has focused on the resource-based influences that might encourage an organization to choose a strategy of expatriation rather than localization. For example, the use of expatriates within the subsidiary of an MNC might allow an organization to import knowledge, skills and activities that are seen as VRIN within the local context. It has long been known that when an organization believes that it has insufficient local human resource quality, it is more likely to resort to expatriation (Edström & Galbraith, 1977). For instance, as German dual vocational training provides a broader and more in-depth vocational education compared to the UK system (Müller, 1998), German MNCs in the UK are often tempted to expatriate German staff or to implement a German-style dual vocational training system in other countries (Dickmann, 2003). Thus, lower skills, knowledge and experience within labour markets may discourage staff localization if the organization cannot compensate for perceived competency gaps. This may be particularly important where the competency gaps are substantial, the ability or willingness to create substitution mechanisms are low or where labour turnover is high, so the organizational investment is risky (Dickmann, 2003; Edwards, Colling, & Ferner, 2007).

In addition, the strategic configurations literature has argued that organizations have a choice with respect to their international strategies, structures, policies and processes (Bartlett & Ghoshal, 1999). Organizations that aim to have a high level of worldwide integration are more likely to resort to intensive cross-border expatriation flows as this is seen as instrumental to global competitive advantage (Dickmann & Müller-Camen, 2006). Furthermore, organizations with ethnocentric global talent management approaches also stifle localization as they are more likely to encourage head office staff to gain international experience and more likely to create a 'glass ceiling' for local talent (Scullion & Collings, 2006, 2011). These factors constitute resource-based drivers for expatriation rather than for localization. In essence, depending on the organization's view on how competitive advantage is being created, these factors could either be drivers of or constraints to localization.

On the other hand, managers in MNCs often complain about a lack of global talent or candidates to work abroad (Fayol-Song, 2011; RES Forum, 2016). Expatriation candidates may be weary of the potential negative career consequences (Doherty & Dickmann, 2012; Richardson & Mallon, 2005), or may have local obligations including care responsibilities or a partner's diverging interests (Dowling, Festing, & Engle, 2008; McNulty & Inkson, 2013) that prevent them from working abroad. In this case, organizations might be encouraged to adopt a localization strategy in order to be able to access the resources they need.

On top of this, the literature suggests that a primary advantage for many organizations to localize is to reduce costs as expatriate packages are typically higher than those for local staff (Selmer, 2004a; Wong & Law, 1999). However, while this does not always have to be the case as the low pay and general plight of South Asian construction workers in the United Arab Emirates demonstrates (Keane & McGeehan, 2008), some research shows that expatriates often come from high pay countries and typically experience a substantial pay uplift (Brookfield, 2015; Doherty & Dickmann, 2012). Related to this is mitigating the risk of expatriate failure and the costs associated with expatriates prematurely returning to their home country before the end of the planned assignment period (Harzing, 1995; Harzing & Christensen, 2004; Wong & Law, 1999).

Based on these arguments, localization can be viewed simplistically as a means of obtaining appropriate human resources easily and at a lower cost. However, this argument, while undoubtedly influential in the choice of a localization strategy, presumes that the skills of an expatriate are not rare and are easily substitutable. However, we argue that local employees also bring additional context specific value, particularly in a hostile context. Previous work on the RBV emphasizes the importance of the environment and the opportunities and threats within it in determining how valuable a particular resource is (Priem & Butler, 2001). Indeed, the value of a resource is dependent on its fit with both the internal and external context. An expatriate might therefore have good fit with the internal organizational context but not with the external context of the host country.

In line with this, the literature on localization has suggested that organizations with multi-domestic and international HR configurations (Bartlett & Ghoshal, 1999; Dickmann, Müller-Camen, & Kelliher, 2008) are often committed to employee localization due to the idea that using local staff can provide local responsiveness and that this will provide competitive advantage and deliver value for their (often service-oriented) operations. In addition, local staff have a better command of the local language and it is normally easier for them to do business (Dickmann & Baruch, 2011).

Building on Oliver's (1997) suggestion that resource selection is influenced by the institutional context of resource decisions and Priem and Butler's (2001) call for further consideration of context when using the RBV, we argue that localization can be an appropriate strategy when the firm is operating in hostile environments. In line with Barney's (1991, p. 105) definition of a resource as valuable if it 'exploits opportunities and/or neutralises threats in a firm's environment', in hostile contexts the use of 'locals' might provide superior benefits in relation to VRIN resources to using foreign staff. Locals may be less of a target for terrorist activities (Krueger & Laitin, 2008), have knowledge of the local culture, can inspire the wider local staff base and can therefore provide a critical competitive advantage to organizations (Law et al., 2009; Selmer, 2004a). Different strands of literature clearly outline the impact of insecure environments either specifically commenting on Afghanistan (Murray, 2007; Rubin & Rashid, 2008) or in more general terms analysing terrorism from a variety of perspectives including its impact on tourism (Bianchi, 2006; Hall, Timothy, & Duval, 2012), security arrangements or public administration (Carter, 2002; Wood & Dupont, 2006) its treatment in the media (Norris, Kern, & Just, 2003) or its effects on business and employees (Czinkota, Knight, Liesch, & Steen, 2010; Howie, 2007; Reade & Lee, 2012). Many of the sources clearly outline the high degree of risk that both locals and foreigners face in hostile environments such as those in Afganistan, Pakistan, Democratic Republic of Congo, Nigeria or Iraq. Surprisingly however, security implications of working in hostile environments have been neglected in localization research so far and there is an obvious need to explore this.

Capability-based influences

Literature on the RBV has distinguished between resources, as defined above, and 'capabilities' (Amit & Schoemaker, 1993; Makadok, 2001). Capabilities are defined as 'a firm's capacity to deploy resources, usually in combination, using organizational processes, to effect a desired end' (Amit & Schoemaker, 1993, p. 35). Indeed, value creation from the use of resources depends on the way that these resources are developed and deployed within the firm (Lockett, 2005; Penrose, 1959). A capability can be distinguished from a basic resource in that its primary purpose is to optimize the productivity of the firm's resources (Makadok, 2001). In line with this distinction, the success of a localization strategy is dependent on the use of appropriate HR practices at the organizational level, particularly to develop firm-specific skills and understanding and therefore build inimitable and non-substitutable resources (Dierickx & Cool, 1989). Within the framework of the RBV, HRM practices can be viewed as capabilities designed to facilitate the development and deployment of VRIN human resources – in this case by allowing the organization to benefit from the use of local human resources as described above.

Usefully, for our study, Makadok (2001) distinguishes between two mechanisms within organizations for creating economic rents and therefore competitive advantage. First, a resource-picking mechanism when the firm acquires resources that create rents, and second, a capability-building mechanism, when the firm achieves competitive advantage by becoming more effective than their rivals at developing and deploying resources. In line with Makadok's arguments, in this paper, we suggest that these mechanisms are not mutually exclusive and that, in relation to localization of human resources, organizations must both effectively acquire and deploy VRIN human resources in order to achieve competitive advantage. We therefore also focus on the HRM practices needed for the successful development and deployment of local staff.

For example, the localization literature suggests that a career system that gives support, responsibility and managerial experience to locals as well as one that selects, trains, rewards and repatriates expatriate managers in relation to their localization activities, can be a strong facilitator for localization (Law et al., 2009). Selmer (2004a) argues that the ability and willingness of expatriate managers to train their own replacement is also a determining factor in localization success. HR practices to motivate expatriates to work towards localization include developing refined selection criteria, providing expatriates with training to be coaches/mentors, implementing regular performance monitoring, introducing incentives for localization, as well as having good repatriation practices (Rees, Mamman, & Bin Braik, 2007; Selmer, 2004a, 2004b; Wong & Law, 1999). In addition, in the Gulf countries, improving recruitment standards, creating dedicated training programmes and developing career paths to encourage staff retention are key HR processes that could help to successfully localize and better integrate nationals into the workforce (Forstenlechner, 2010).

Poor HR practices can act as barriers to localization. In Papua New Guinea for example, significant obstacles to localization were found including the 'performance of local staff; and inappropriate training and development programmes offered to local staff' (Bhanugopan & Fish, 2007, p. 372). In addition, Fryxell et al. (2004) argued that top management support and confidence by the expatriate in local managers are important aspects of successful localization. A lack of confidence by the expatriate in the effective decision-making capabilities and communication skills of the local could act as an influence on localization.

Institutional influences of staff localization

We also consider the influence of external institutional pressures on the decision to localize (or otherwise). Organizational decisions are not only driven by the desire to create value but are also influenced by pressures from the context in which an organization is operating. Institutional theory and neo-institutionalism (DiMaggio & Powell, 1983) suggest that organizational practices are directly shaped by the rules and structures built into their larger environments (Powell, 1998). Organizations, including MNCs, feel the need to develop practices that fit with local institutions in order to provide them with the legitimacy to operate within that context.

Indeed, the country or region specific influences on localization can be compelling from a political, economic and/or social perspective (Petison & Johri, 2008). For example, in the Gulf Cooperation Council countries, government regulation has been the key driver behind localization via quotas and other techniques to restrict expatriate hiring in favour of local recruitment (Al-Lamki, 1998; Williams, Bhanugopan, & Fish, 2011). This means, even if VRIN human capital might be more easily obtained via expatriates, the legislative and political context renders using an expatriation strategy difficult.

In addition, cultural distance – differences in communication styles and values that are linked to national cultures – should be taken into account

(Shenkar, 2001). Cultural distance studies show substantial differences between national cultures with important effects on internal business structures and processes as well as the cooperation of staff from different cultural areas (Morosini, Shane, & Singh, 1998; Slangen, 2006). With high cultural distance the difficulties of working together are likely to increase (Moran, Abramson, & Moran, 2014). Wong and Law (1999: 28) state that 'many Chinese employees find it easier to interact with Chinese managers, both because they share a language and a common cultural background'. Where organizations do not see expatriation as a primary control and coordination mechanism (for a Japanese example see Gaur, Delios, & Singh, 2007), highly culturally distinct contexts may support employee localization due the need to increase legitimacy and ease of working.

Organizational legitimacy is the acceptance of the organization by its environment and is essential for organizational survival (Kostova & Zaheer, 1999). Legitimacy in relation to national or regional institutions is a complex construct and can be analysed for the whole or parts of the organization (Kostova & Zaheer, 1999). External legitimacy can suffer when the host government or the wider, local public perceive that local employees are disadvantaged with respect to their career progression (Forstenlechner & Mellahi, 2011). Where locals perceive a 'glass ceiling' to their careers it is usually more difficult for an organization to attract the best talent (Dickmann & Baruch, 2011). National organizational legitimacy considerations can therefore be an institutional driver of localization.

The legitimacy of firms abroad is one element that influences their success (Czinkota et al., 2010). In unstable contexts, companies seen as 'moral' (or legitimate) might have a lower risk of attack from terrorists (Henisz & Zelner, 2005) – a further reason to localize. In the same vein, companies might reduce the risk of violence against foreign staff by adopting HR policies and practices that help to minimize tensions, such as employing locals (Oetzel & Getz, 2012).

Based on the above discussion, the factors affecting the decision to localize can be divided into those related to resource- or capability-based influences at the national or organizational level, and institutional influences on localization. This gives rise to three research questions:

(1) What resource-based factors influence the use of staff localization in Afghanistan?
(2) What organizational-level capabilities facilitate an effective localization strategy?
(3) What institutional factors influence the decision to localize in Afghanistan?

Afghanistan context

Afghanistan serves as a good example of a hostile environment because of its history of military and terrorist conflict. Afghanistan's location has made the country a source of significant geopolitical interest and tension and decades of civil war have left the country devastated (Leonard & Dhanani, 2009). The recent conflicts following the terrorist attacks in September 2001 and the ensuring neo-Taliban insurgency has created a highly fragile and insecure environment with manifold threats to locals and expatriates – including an acute danger to their lives (Giustozzi, 2008). Despite the gradual progress that has been made in increasing the stability of the central government and expanding democratic freedoms, lack of security continues to remain a serious challenge for the Afghanistan government and a primary impediment to development and stability in the country (Leonard & Dhanani, 2009; Murtazashvili, 2016). As in other developing countries, development assistance funds are needed to help build capacity where there is a severe shortage of adequately trained personnel (Bhanugopan & Fish, 2007).

In 2002, thc lack of qualified staff at all levels within organizations was a major problem affecting the speed, scale, quality and costs of the reconstruction and development effort in Afghanistan (Leonard & Dhanani, 2009). Therefore, expatriate support was critical as Afghanistan started to develop its economy, political and judicial systems alongside health and education sectors (UNDP, 2013). Ongoing insecurity makes it increasingly difficult to attract and retain expatriate staff and hostile environments have been shown to negatively impact performance and work attitudes of international assignees (Bader & Berg, 2013, 2014). Threats to personal lives can be a strong deterrent to working in hostile environments but do not have to be, depending on individuals and their risk assessment (Dickmann & Cerdin, 2016). In times of high insecurity many expatriates evacuate the country, leaving locals to maintain business continuity and ongoing operations in that country (Leonard & Dhanani, 2009). Therefore, localization is critical to the sustainability and stability of organizations in Afghanistan and might diminish some of the implicit barriers to the careers of local staff.

Methodology

While previous studies used quantitative methods, this research is exploratory as so little research on localization in Afghanistan or other hostile environments has been undertaken. Semi-structured interviews therefore allowed us to obtain richer information, capture people's perspectives and experiences and provide a greater degree of flexibility to gather additional insights during the interviews, whilst probing for further comments if required (Yin, 2003).

Interview design and tools

An interview protocol was designed based on key thematic areas identified in the literature, including the drivers behind localization (Fryxell et al., 2004; Petison & Johri, 2008; Williams et al., 2011; Wong & Law, 1999); key conditions or HR practices leading to successful localization (Forstenlechner, 2010; Fryxell et al.,

2004; Law et al., 2009; Law, Wong, & Wang, 2004; Selmer, 2004a, 2004b); and the constraints associated with localization (Al-Lamki, 1998; Bhanugopan & Fish, 2007; Williams et al., 2011). Questions focused on: interviewees' length of time in the country, with the organization and their role in the localization process (as an expatriate, local or management); the perceived drivers, challenges and facilitators of localization; the key practices used to facilitate localization; and organizational awareness of localization. With HR staff, background questions were also related to the number of positions that have been localized to date and key targets and timeframes.

To ensure the quality and appropriateness of the research questions, the interview was piloted in Summer 2013 with three individuals who had all previously worked in Afghanistan (and had been involved in the localization process) as expatriates, locals and/or as management.

Sampling

Due to the hostile nature of the context, it was necessary to focus on a limited number of organizations in collecting data. Purposive sampling was used to select each organization and consideration was given to key criteria such as the type of institution, the size of the organization, the availability of expatriate and local managers and the stage of localization in order to promote as much variability as possible within the data. Data were collected from four organizations: two non-profit humanitarian organizations and two for-profit organizations in telecommunications and business consulting. One for-profit organization was a medium sized enterprise (195 employees) while the others were all larger organizations (between 650 and 1700 employees). These organizations were selected because they operate across the country in a number of provinces, which varied in the level of potential safety. The organizations were all pursuing a localization strategy at the time of data collection.

Across the four organizations, 18 in-depth interviews were conducted with the CEO and/or HR manager, local managers and expatriate managers currently working in Afghanistan. In total, three expatriate CEOs/Lead Partners, one local CEO, two expatriate HR managers, one local HR manager, five local senior managers, three expatriate senior managers, one expatriate middle manager and one expatriate project director were interviewed. To gain an additional perspective, an interview was also conducted with a consultant who was providing support to one of the organizations in its localization process. Purposive sampling was used to ensure the seniority of interviewees within the organization, functional background and experience of localization. The criteria for selecting interviewees were: a minimum of two years in country (in the case of expatriates) and a minimum of one year working with the organization. These criteria ensured that the interviewees had sufficient knowledge of the country and experience within the organization to speak effectively about localization and HR practices.

Data collection

Due to the ongoing security situation in Afghanistan, all interviews were conducted by telephone rather than face-to-face between June and September 2013. Interviews lasted approximately 60 min each and were recorded and transcribed. Transcripts were entered into 'NViVo' software for structured analysis. Broad codes were identified based on sub-questions that are being addressed in the research, such as driving factors, HR practices and challenges, combined with themes that had arisen in previous research. The codes were checked by a second researcher and emerging classification gaps discussed. Themes were used as a basis to code the discussions with interviewees and the remaining codes were developed based on common keywords or phrases used by interviewees such as trust, insecurity, impartiality, etc.

As with all qualitative research, there was a degree of interpretation in how to order, analyse and present the data (Yin, 2003). Oliver (1997) has outlined the overlaps and interrelationships when combining institutional and RBVs. In the findings below we discuss those factors that could be viewed as relating primarily to organizational legitimacy as institutional. Where factors primarily seemed to be related to the need to obtain VRIN resources or to develop and deploy those resources in order to achieve competitive advantage, we present those as resource- or capability-based influences.

Findings and discussion

Resource-based and institutional influences on localization

A number of both resource and capability-based and institutional influences on staff localization were elicited from the qualitative data. We will first present data on resource-based influences below.

Resource-based influences

The resource-based influences discussed by interviewees were: availability of local and expatriate resources; cost and freedom and familiarity with the context.

Availability of local resources

The majority of interviewees (13) argued that one of the biggest barriers to localization is the incapability of Afghans to take on certain expatriate positions. While external labour market conditions are also part of the institutional context, as these primarily had an effect on the ability to access the required resources in order to create competitive advantage, we treat this factor as a resource-based influence.

> It's not always easy to find resources, local resources, with the right level of skills which are available on the market, willing to change job, etc., etc. There is not an over abundant supply of highly qualified staff in the market. It's quite the opposite in fact; highly

> qualified individuals are a very, very, very scarce resource. (Expatriate, Lead Partner, for-profit)

With 15 interviewees the vast majority of respondents recognized that the competencies and skills of local staff had increased and a growing number of local staff had the capacity to be promoted into mid and senior management positions in the organizations. However, the need for particular perspectives, skills and experience was seen as a key driver for using expatriates by the majority of interviewees. There was a feeling from existing Afghan staff themselves that they needed outside experiences and perspectives to be able to step into certain roles and/or that expatriates' external perspectives and insights would still be needed.

> ... if we don't have expatriates, then we will be kind of isolated in this world. Of course we need other thoughts, we need other people to come and give new ideas, what's happening in other countries... if they are more localized then I would believe we will be more isolated. (Local, for-profit)

This need for outside perspectives has created a barrier to localizing certain positions in the minds of Afghans. While this was linked to internal innovation and value creation, there is a relationship to the external Afghan labour market that lacks people who possess the leading-edge skills, knowledge and experience to be successful in global MNCs. While similar conditions also exist in countries that have poor (vocational) education systems, this constraint was worsened due to the hostile environment.

Availability of expatriates

Most interviewees in the for-profit organizations (5) outlined the fact that, due to the hostile environment and restriction of personal liberties, it was difficult to find enough high-quality expatriates willing to live in Afghanistan.

> In terms of expat recruitment, 2014 has had its own challenges... People don't want to relocate to our Afghanistan. If they want to relocate to Afghanistan they are asking for a huge compensation. (Local, HR, for-profit)

This supports previous findings that MNCs often complain about not having enough suitable expatriation candidates (Harris & Brewster, 1999; RES Forum, 2016; Selmer, 2004a). In hostile environments this perceived shortage may be especially acute due to both a lack of employees who are willing to move to these locations and limitations on the legitimacy of importing expatriates due to concerns about safety.

Half of the interviewees (9) outlined external factors such as insecurity in the country and the uncertainty of post-2014 which acted as constraints on the decision to use expatriates. Therefore, this drove the decision to localize for all the organizations participating in the study (Nojumi, Mazurana, & Stites, 2010). While the authors distinguish between city and rural conditions, the particular location within a country can be highly important for staff's willingness to work/move there (Dickmann, 2012). In hostile environments security is likely to weigh substantially on the minds of staff (Bader & Berg, 2013). These factors placed significant pressure on organizations to localize due to issues such as the potentially severe business implications of an expatriate evacuation. One interviewee explained:

> ... all these kinds of uncertainties in the future that raise some questions in the management ... the biggest question was that are we ready to lead or continue with the Afghan team in case we are forced to evacuate all of our expatriate staff? (Local staff, non-profit)

The implied death risk to foreigners and Afghans means that security is likely to be a major concern for foreign staff. Given that security in host location has been rated as an important factor for individuals when deciding whether and where to work abroad (Dickmann & Cerdin, 2016; Doherty, Dickmann, & Mills, 2011), it is surprising that localization models have hitherto neglected security as a factor.

Costs

Internal cost factors were highlighted by a few interviewees (7) as being moderately important in the decision to localize. While both non-profit and for-profit staff recognized the cost implications of employing expatriate staff and the need to reduce these costs over time, cost appeared to be more of a driving factor for the for-profit organizations than the non-profits. Furthermore, the reduction of costs was more of an outcome of localization than a true driver. Interviewees from only one organization suggested that it needed to focus on optimizing its resources via investing in localizing part of its staff base in order to operate effectively.

> ... from the business perspective it will make sense for us to use as much as possible, the local resources rather than international resources which tend to be much harder to obtain and much more expensive, etc. So we thought that, from a business perspective, it will make sense for us to invest in capacity building and training our teams to make sure that they reach the right level of competency to be able to deliver to our clients. (Expatriate, for-profit)

The cost of being in a hostile environment per se was clear as a few interviewees (6) discussed the need to make contingency plans in case an expatriate leaves.

> ... it could be creating more shadows – shadow positions, but that means increasing our cost. For example, if you have a Director then you create a shadow position of Deputy Director though you don't need that position 100% but you create this position so that if something happens and the Director, who's an expatriate, leaves, so the Deputy Director can take over and continue. (Local, non-profit)

It became clear that not only the potential long-term cost advantages of localization have to be taken into account. In addition, transition costs are important factors in staff localization decisions.

The above findings support the idea that localization can be viewed in terms of simplistic substitution of labour. However, there was also some evidence that using local human resources can also provide value because of their context-specific experience.

Freedom and familiarity with local context

A dozen interviewees suggested that because locals may be less of a target for terrorists (Krueger & Laitin, 2008), can speak the language(s) better and have enhanced networks, they may be able to move more freely. For example, one interviewee explained:

> from a business perspective, Afghanistan … if you see that it's very difficult for an expatriate to travel outside of Kabul, but when you have a local Director, the local Director can go anywhere. (Local, HR, for-profit)

Given that the insecure context restricts the travel patterns of foreign staff more than that of locals (in many countries), expatriates would be more restricted and would have a lower reach in their activities, especially in societies where meeting face to face is important (Trompenaars & Hampden-Turner, 2011). Expatriates would have a business disadvantage. A hostile environment, therefore, can be a key driver for localization.

Developing an understanding of the distinct local context and culture was seen as being important by a few interviewees (5).

> I mean, if you can find the right people that do the work, you always want to have a local. Frankly, I mean, it just makes your job a lot easier. [Afghan] people can speak the language and they understand local context (Expatriate, for-profit)

The links to local networks (and tribes) were mentioned by only a few interviewees as a driver of localization. This was generally seen as allowing staff to operate appropriately, to avoid high-risk situations and to build business. In this, it represents a strong value proposition.

Capability-based influences

The interviewees also suggested a number of organizational strategies, policies and practices that could be described as capabilities related to the development and deployment of local human resources.

HR localization planning

The majority of interviewees (10) felt that *planning* was important for localization in two ways. The first related to understanding their strategy, the types of investments and other resources needed. The second involved succession planning within the organization, looking at potential candidates for specified current or future roles.

> Some people went from [career conversations] and implemented a different way of working, so that started a shift … We have worked with them to look at potential for current role and future roles. That's the first time, I think, that a more formal approach to planning has taken place and at the same time or earlier, HR also started a skills and needs analysis. (External Consultant)

Whilst almost all interviewees in this study recognized the importance of planning in terms of identifying priorities, selecting appropriate action and monitoring efforts, some (10) felt it was often difficult given the uncertainty in Afghanistan. Two interviewees, whilst recognizing the importance of planning, felt that for the most part this was being done at an individual level rather than taking a more systematic approach.

Interviewees discussed two specific aspects of planning and preparation. First, a large majority of interviewees (15) referred to conducting *training needs analyses* for staff and looked at providing a wide range of approaches aimed at improving the capacity of staff at all levels, including on the job training, online learning, classroom training, higher education programmes (e.g. Masters degrees – in house and abroad), succession and career planning and both formal and informal mechanisms of mentoring and coaching. All of these approaches can be described in terms of developing firm-specific assets, which are more likely to be VRIN due to the combination of firm and context specific competencies (Dierickx & Cool, 1989).

> So, always, we continue to put a lot of emphasis on the capacity building of staff. We try and link it with our annual performance appraisal process and training needs assessments. (Expatriate, CEO, non-profit)

Second, in addition to capacity building initiatives, interviewees in all of the organizations commented on some type of *restructuring* or *creation of new roles* that supported their localization process. In one organization, it involved spinning off its field research team, into a completely localized unit.

> First of all, what we have done is, we have employed our local staff and we have created a company that is called [Subsidiary] that is owned by our local staff… The goal behind this is, first of all, we wanted them to be more responsible for their future because it can always happen that the security in Afghanistan or anything else prevents [Parent Company] one day from working there… We wanted a company to be structured in a way that should we have to leave the place, at least there will be a functioning body like this entity, [Subsidiary], able to work for other clients than [Parent Company]. (Expatriate, for-profit)

Organizations were creating new positions, either deputy positions (for Afghans) shadowing expatriates to give them exposure and/or advisory positions (for expatriates) that allow Afghans to take the lead and have advisors supporting them. These initiatives could be described as capability-building (Makadok, 2001).

Many of the interviewees (10), expatriates and locals, felt that putting Afghans 'in the front line' was critical. However, there were some important aspects raised by interviewees. The first was the risk of putting Afghans into the front line too soon.

> … the organization would suffer if people are put into roles or local staff put into expatriate roles where they didn't have the capacity to deliver these roles and he [the CEO] definitely didn't want just anyone to be given the roles. (External consultant)

Second, both deputy and advisory positions require creating mirror or duplicate positions within the organization that can be quite costly. Naturally, the uncertainty of post-2014 developments and the continued hostilities make planning for staff localization highly difficult. Good HR localization planning has been seen as essential to localization success (Law et al., 2009) but rarely have authors developed in-depth exploration of planning in highly dynamic and hostile environments.

A large majority of interviewees (15) felt that there was strong management support behind localization initiatives. This could involve establishing a formal localization committee or individuals in leadership positions championing localization initiatives and is in tune with Fryxell et al.'s (2004) recommendations.

Attraction, development, reward and retention of local employees

A small majority of interviewees (10) felt that their investments in staff and identifying career paths were also mechanisms to resource, develop, reward and retain them in the organization.

> People stay at our company because it's a learning environment. They see their career growth – that is the environment. Those are the factors that are keeping people with our company and Afghanisation [it] is one of the main factors that help us to attract and retain our talent. (Local, HR, for-profit)

The retention mechanisms by these organizations seem to be working in the sense that none of the respondents raised staff loss to competitors as a substantial challenge. However, four interviewees talked about previous experiences of staff leaving the country.

> Not only in terms of keeping expatriates in the country, it's keeping locals in the country, which is the bigger challenge right now. It's kind of a brain drain situation and locals are trying to get out of the country. The people we have spent years to train them… (Local, HR, for-profit)

It is, therefore, abundantly clear that successful localization programmes need to avoid low quality, misguided training and development programmes (Bhanugopan & Fish, 2007) and need to draw up sophisticated talent management approaches (Forstenlechner, 2010). In addition, talent retention – including drawing up successful reward initiatives – is a key consideration (Dickmann & Baruch, 2011).

Selecting and incentivizing expatriates to foster local staff

A small majority of respondents (10) suggested that the unwillingness or inability of expatriates to support the localization of their position can be a significant challenge.

> Obviously in some situations then they have seen that the local national is coming up and then will be taking over and the expatriate doesn't want to leave the job… because they want to extend their contracts. (Local, HR, for-profit)

While the high interest of some expatriates to work in a hostile environment has been neglected in the localization literature it is now emerging in the global careers literature (Dickmann & Cerdin, 2016).

Within the localization process, the willingness and expatriates' ability to provide mentoring and to transfer knowledge was seen as critical.

> The person should have the willingness for this. The person should find the time for this responsibility and this mentor or the supervisor has to be capable for mentoring that person in the required field or subjects. (Local, for-profit)

Most organizations tried to ensure that expatriates are clearly informed of their role to provide capacity building support to their local counterparts in the country.

> In fact we have been quite lucky, I think, in the people we have brought on board over the last decade. Many of those people actually really fell in love with the country and spend four, five, six, eight years in the country and have gone a long way in training people. (Expatriate, for-profit)

However, the measuring of *expatriates' performance* on these aspects and the incentives provided to support their efforts were less developed. Performance appraisals usually included some measurement related to capacity building or knowledge transfer. In some cases, it was felt that whilst there were some assessments related to capacity building or knowledge transfer, more specific key performance indicators were needed. A substantial majority of interviewees (12) felt that there were little to no incentives, financial or non-financial, for the expatriates to support staff localization.

> You have to allocate some weightage to this mentoring, coaching and things like that so that habitually it becomes a part of your job because you know at the end of the day, you'll be assessed like that. And it must link to incentive. Now... somebody performs at 100 level, he also gets a $2,500 or $3,000 bonus. And if somebody doesn't work the whole year, he also gets $3,000 bonus. It's a flat, so there's no reward incentive systems. (Expatriate, non-profit)

Building confidence in local staff

Half of the interviewees (9) argued that the notion of confidence was important in terms of expatriates having confidence in Afghans.

> It's only if you give them the opportunity and if you show them that you're confident that they will be able to do it, that they will do it. (Expatriate, for-profit)

While expatriates' opinions regarding the capabilities of their host teams are important (Fryxell et al., 2004), another facet of confidence emerged in the interviews that was important for the localization process and has not been sufficiently explored in the literature so far.

Creating self-confidence amongst local staff

One of the softer aspects of localization (for some of the interviewees) was creating self-confidence amongst the local staff and providing opportunities for decision-making. Most Afghans and expatriates (10) spoke about the importance of supportive environments as well as opportunities for Afghans to demonstrate their capability.

> Our organization had built, or maybe provided, that conducive environment for Afghans to gain self-confidence by doing and seeing the success of their work. (Local, non-profit)

Ten interviewees mentioned examples of how their organization was working to increase the confidence and/or decision-making capability of Afghans. One expatriate spoke about how their organization decided to have only Afghans present at operational reviews (where expatriates often presented in the past). He explained:

> ... not a single expatriate will present during the operational review and we did it. It was the best operations review we ever had. The guys were just phenomenal. (Expatriate, for-profit)

The importance of instilling confidence in and of local staff, as well as providing opportunities for increased decision-making was evident in the discussions held with interviewees. Finding ways to build confidence in local staff is critical to successful localization and whilst some used this as an opportunity to support localization efforts, others felt that this was still a challenge that needed to be addressed. Building the confidence of local staff to ensure they are capable of rising to the organization's challenges as a facilitator has not been suggested in localization literature.

Institutional influences

The interviews also demonstrated institutional influences on the decision to localize.

Government regulations

Government regulations, often a driver for localization in other countries (Al-Lamki, 1998; Forstenlechner, 2010), were an important but not a critical influence on the decision to localize, with only five interviewees raising this. There are a number of regulations from the Afghan government in place which are designed to ensure that there are clear reasons for bringing expatriates into the country, and to:

> ... document why an organization would need an expatriate staff for a particular position rather than that position being taken by a national staff. (Expatriate, non-profit)

It should be noted that all of the organizations participating in the study had a staff base that was more than 90% local and therefore were probably not under intense localization pressure from the Afghani government at that time.

Legitimacy via top management commitment to localization

The majority of interviewees (13) emphasized that, notwithstanding the current security climate, they have been committed to localization in Afghanistan and the long-term development of the country from early on.

> Our company is a long term player in the country. (Expatriate, HR, for-profit)

In addition, the commitment of senior management to staff localization within the four organizations was not challenged by any of the interviewees. However, unlike previous literature, this was not seen as a means of developing competitive advantage but as a way of increasing legitimacy for the organization. This is in contrast to the intention of top management to achieve a high degree of global integration discussed in the extant literature (Dickmann et al., 2008).

Five interviewees described how commitment to the development of the country and the corresponding investments in education and training over recent years were seen to have created increased legitimacy for the organizations (Henisz & Zelner, 2005). In addition, this was seen as having created an opportunity for localization processes to be put in place and for competent local Afghans to move into senior leadership positions.

> We're almost a decade through this [localization] and at this point, we've come up to a level where we're able to capture local staff and many people who have been working with us since 2002. With the passage of time, these human resources have developed and as a result of their capacity building and training, they can be in a position to hold on to these management positions or what we can call decision making positions. (Expatriate, non-profit)

In addition, to those predicted by the literature, there were additional institutional influences that emerged from the interviews.

Business governance – external pressures and impartiality

Four interviewees (all of these expatriates) explained that localizing certain positions was difficult because of concerns around external pressures and the lack of impartiality of Afghans in leadership positions.

> But the position with accountability, where there will be some friction between them, you know, there are positions that need a really impartial decision making process and free from pressure, both internal and external. These positions will be difficult to localize. (Expatriate, HR, non-profit)

These concerns may come from Afghanistan's history of strong tribal and ethnic affiliation and the ability of Afghans to remain neutral when it comes to key decisions that may affect their communities or being impartial to certain ethnic groups over others.

Business governance – corruption

Four interviewees discussed corruption issues in the wider society and in dealings with organizational outsiders. Corruption and bribery were also raised as important by both Afghans and expatriates.

> The other thing of course is Afghanistan's history, culture and you know, a country with so many problems, this bribing, all those kinds of things. So it's questionable whether to put a local national head in charge of procurement for example. (Local, HR, for-profit)

A high degree of corruption can reduce regime legitimacy and interpersonal trust (Seligson, 2002). While it may not always be possible to escape institutional corruption – with the exception of withdrawing operations to avoid these – using trusted expatriates (Dowling et al., 2008; Edström & Galbraith, 1977) may reduce corrupt acts. If MNCs believe that local actors may be more likely to engage in corrupt acts, a high degree of institutionalized corruption represents an institutional constraint to localization. This has not been sufficiently factored into the localization literature so far.

Trust in local staff

The vast majority of interviewees (13) argued that low levels of trust in Afghans (due to the factors discussed above) are a strong factor in the resistance to localization for certain positions.

> I know for our organization there will be those positions that would be the last to be transferred to a local person, loyalty, trust, reasons like that. You will not for example, have a [Afghan] Chief Financial Officer in our organization for a long period of time. (Expatriate, for-profit)

Most interviewees felt that the issue of trust was important and played a large part in the resistance to localization. Low levels of trust can be a barrier to the localization process, or as Fryxell et al. (2004, p. 279) suggested, it 'probably also moderates many of the relationships between localization strategies and localization success'.

External perception of localized organization

In a few instances, four interviewees suggested that it was more a concern of external perception.

> So how will the organization look to its external stakeholders... there is plenty of examples of organizations that have, over time, become wholly Afghanised or localized, where trust has not been extended in the same way. So, whereas internally people may trust individuals absolutely and rightly, there is that external perception question. (External consultant)

Hitherto, this factor has not been outlined in the localization literature. In so far as the two not-for-profit case organizations were concerned, they were more highly resource dependent on the perception – and financial support – of other charities, international governmental and non-governmental organizations. It is important to factor the external perception of the local organization into the institutional factors that influence localization decisions.

Discussion

The results of this study extend our understanding of localization in the context of hostile environments such as Afghanistan. Understanding the context is critical as it can help organizations to adopt and implement an appropriate localization strategy (Petison & Johri, 2008). Building on existing literature on localization in non-hostile contexts, as well as the RBV and institutional theory, we have used our interview data to answer three research questions.

Our first research question asked what resource-based factors influence staff localization in Afghanistan. Our findings support the existing literature (Fayol-Song, 2011; Fryxell et al., 2004) in non-hostile countries that identifies the availability of resources and cost as influences of the decision to localize. However, whereas prior literature has identified the substantial long-term cost implications of expatriation as a driver of localization (Doherty & Dickmann, 2012; Dowling et al., 2008), the transition costs – for instance, the need to create shadow positions – have been neglected (Bhanugopan & Fish, 2007; Fayol-Song, 2011). Distinguishing transitionary and long-term costs might be important in order to understand the value-added through staff localization.

While substituting expatiate resources for local resources might be easier and cheaper this alone would suggest that these resources are easily substituted and imitated, thus not leading to sustainable competitive advantage. Effective 'resource-picking' (Makadok, 2001) also requires recognition of the additional, context-specific value that local resources can bring to an organization. While this might be the case in many contexts, within a hostile environment, the familiarity of local staff with the context and their freedom to move around without significant risk to their safety was seen as a key advantage of employing local resources (Dickmann & Cerdin, 2016). This might be seen as providing competitive advantage resources to the organization, at least in relation to those who are the first to adopt this strategy, in that they can operate more effectively within the country and therefore obtain competitive advantage over organizations using expatriates.

Our research led to some new insights in relation to the effect of insecurity on expatriation unwillingness or the higher freedom of movement of local staff into major influences that have been hitherto neglected by the localization literature. This is in stark contrast to existing literature from other countries such as China and the UAE, respectively (Fryxell et al., 2004; Williams et al., 2011; Wong & Law, 1999), which have concentrated on external institutional drivers such as government regulation.

Developments in the RBV suggest that resource-picking alone might not be sufficient to achieve sustainable competitive advantage (Makadok, 2001). The inimitability and non-substitutability of resources might be dependent on their effective development and deployment through internal capabilities. Internal capabilities, in this case appropriate organizational policies and practices, can be used to optimize the productivity of resources and to develop VRIN firm-specific assets (Dierickx & Cool, 1989), which can lead to sustainable competitive advantage.

In line with this argument, our second research question examined the organizational-level capabilities that influence staff localization. In line with previous research a number of HRM-related facilitators were identified. For example, intensive HR planning and strong management support were shown as necessary for the localization process, confirming extant findings (Fryxell et al., 2004; Law et al., 2009; Wong & Law, 1999) outside of hostile contexts. Our findings go beyond this research in adding particular attributes that the selection of local staff was based on within the hostile environment: individuals who had the confidence to speak their mind on important issues as well as a sense of loyalty to the organization. In terms of developing staff (Forstenlechner, 2010), all of the organizations in this study had implemented dedicated training programmes such as career planning, succession planning, formal degrees and mentoring/coaching programmes which helped local staff to take on positions of increasing responsibility.

Organizations in developing countries are struggling with the willingness and ability of expatriates to localize (Wong & Law, 1999). In Afghanistan we found that certain expatriates were unwilling to support localization as they had their own agendas. Selmer (2004b) suggests that making the objective of rearing a local successor part of regular performance assessment would help to reinforce localization as an official policy. Some organizations in Afghanistan have introduced performance management as a means of encouraging expatriates to play this role by implementing tracking mechanisms and incentives.

We extend the argument of Fryxell et al. (2004) that expatriates need to trust and have confidence in locals by arguing that it is also the confidence of local staff in themselves that needs to be developed and nurtured. Therefore, while HR strategies need to address trust issues at a relationship level between expatriates and local staff, they also need to identify strategies at an organizational level that will provide the opportunities for local staff to build their confidence, such as increasing local participation at meetings, providing opportunities to speak and voice opinions and providing the encouragement and recognition needed. Hitherto, these organizational recommendations are severely neglected in the literature.

Our third research question looked at the institutional influences on localization and confirmed much of the extant research outside of hostile contexts in relation to government regulations (Al-Lamki, 1998; Williams et al., 2011), culture (Nolan, 2011; Shenkar, 2001; Wang, 2007), organizational legitimacy (Forstenlechner & Mellahi, 2011; Henisz & Zelner, 2005) and issues of governance.

We go beyond the existing literature by identifying a number of institutional influences, which might be specific to hostile contexts. Examples include corruption, impartiality and external perceptions of organizations. While localization considerations such as attributions of trust and corruption in the sense of local business patterns and governments' investment decisions have been discussed in the literature (Bhanugopan & Fish, 2007; Fryxell et al., 2004; Gurgur & Shah, 2005), corruption and impartiality as barriers to staff localization are new additions. In addition, if organizations are committed to complete localization at the most senior levels, they need to prevent a potential loss of credibility from key stakeholders. An important contribution of our research therefore is to add further nuances to our understanding of institutional influences on localization, in particular within a hostile context.

Conclusion

This study utilized the RBV and institutional theory to examine the influences on the decision to localize staff within the highly insecure and fragile Afghan environment. Our research has supported Oliver's (1997) assertion that organizations' decisions are based upon a combination of institutional pressures and a desire to develop VRIN human resources in order to achieve competitive advantage (Barney, 1991). The data suggest that local staff resources were seen from an RBV perspective as valuable, rare (they had to be built), inimitable and non-substitutable in a hostile, terrorist environment. In particular, a combination of a resource-picking strategy focused on local resources and a capability-building strategy (Makadok, 2001) that develops and deploys these resources in a way that allows the development of firm (and context) specific assets that are VRIN (Dierickx & Cool, 1989) could lead to competitive advantage.

It is clear that the unusual nature of a hostile environment, including the fact that organizations were operating under conditions of terrorist activity, conflict and Afghan traditions, led to a set of influences on localization that differs from those identified in non-hostile environments. Because of this, the context specific capabilities of local human resources (e.g. language, higher freedom to move around, networks and cultural insights) are particularly valuable and set locals clearly aside from expatriates. The adjustment literature points out that some of these local advantages – language capabilities, cultural insights – are useful also in non-hostile environments (Black, Mendenhall, & Oddou, 1991). However, at the same time it describes the effects in terms of emotional well-being and adequacy of behaviour (Haslberger, Brewster, & Hippler, 2013) – in hostile environments the effects are likely to be much more pronounced and can make the difference in terms of death or survival. The combination of local capabilities with the development of firm-specific knowledge and experience (via the HR related capabilities) might result in resources which are not only valuable but are also rare, inimitable and non-substitutable, thus leading to competitive advantage.

Our empirical contributions lie in the identification of new influences on localization (e.g. insecurity, uncertainty associated with the withdrawal of NATO troops and organizational continuity, potentially high transition costs of having shadow positions for locals, the high degree of corruption and associated trust shortages, external perceptions of the organization or the confidence of locals to undertake hitherto expatriate functions) and the use of the RBV and institutional theory to explain our findings.

Theoretically, our contribution is in the impact of context on the decision to localize and the development of VRIN human resources via localization strategies. While several of the localization motivations within organizations are similar to non-hostile contexts – cost, superior local knowledge, trust – we have shown that within hostile environments local insights and networks can be more valuable and that within corrupt contexts trust elements are likely to have more weight for organizations. We have also suggested that the creation of VRIN human resources within a hostile context is both subject to institutional influences, which must be addressed, and dependent on the use of internal capabilities to effectively develop and deploy these resources. We suggest that, in Afghanistan at least, organizations are achieving competitive advantage via staff localization strategies. Within hostile environments we hold that organizations go beyond an evaluation of competitors and customers to assess contextual risks and the context-specific value of resources. They are willing to bear more substantial costs (such as transition costs) to mitigate the chances of terrorist attacks and other effects such as reputational damage. Local resources, therefore, hold value for organizations beyond business considerations due to their local knowledge, local experience and network support that allows them to cope with the institutional demands of a hostile environment. Specifically, we suggest that the higher the insecurity in a country, the stronger the drive to develop HR policies and practices that develop VRIN human resources via localization.

There are however variations with respect to the intensity of institutional barriers to localization. In a highly corrupt society, control and coordination reasons for expatriation (Edström & Galbraith, 1977) are likely to increase. While it may be important for actors to understand institutional idiosyncrasies and dualities (Kostova & Roth, 2002), organizations may want them not to act as locals or to identify too strongly to particular group interests such as those connected to tribal affiliations and agendas. Organizations will be forced to balance these local influences with the manifold drivers to localize. While the localization literature has identified some conflicting institutional pressures, our study suggests that governance and corruption has been insufficiently incorporated in the discussion. Therefore, we also propose that the higher the degree of corruption, the less strong the drive to develop HR policies and practices that encourage the development of human resources via localization.

While the study predominantly used societal and organizational perspectives, we also found evidence of psychological barriers that would hinder locals' career progress and ultimately, the organization's localization agenda. Modern career theory distinguishes between physical and psychological career boundaries (Sullivan & Arthur, 2006). A low confidence and self-esteem is seen to restrict an individual's career and organizational value (Gunz & Peiperl, 2007). A range of human resource and developmental interventions are suggested to help individuals to overcome career boundaries (Forrier, Sels, & Stynen, 2009). Thus we also suggest that the lower the local's confidence in his/her own abilities, the less willing the local will be to take on more important responsibilities. The lower the local's confidence, the more (or more intensive) localization support policies and practices are needed.

Practical implications

Organizational value is impacted by firms' localization paths and activities geared towards their resources. It seems clear to us that the above insights point to key factors that organizations need to take into account when designing their international HR strategies, policies and practices.

Practically, organizations can, first, encourage localization through a variety of activities, including a systematic analysis of their external environment, an assessment of expatriates' willingness to work towards finding a local successor and the systematic selection, development, performance management, rewarding and repatriation of international assignees (Selmer, 2004b; Wong & Law, 1999). Second, the assessment, coaching, delegation activities and development of locals to encourage their acquisition of necessary skills, abilities, knowledge and motivation to take on their new roles can foster localization. While these developmental activities are not unique to localization in hostile environments, organizations often seem to have a stronger impetus to localization in these contexts in order to reduce risk and/or increase local effectivity. In addition to the existing literature we have identified an element of trust – trust in oneself – that impacts on staff localization. Thus, organizations could attempt to assess the level of 'task-related self-confidence' their local talent possesses. If needed, they could draw up measures to build sufficient trust levels in their local talent. Our case companies have done this through what could be termed 'exposure' to challenging tasks. Pairing this with support and developmental activities is likely to improve this trust deficiency and prepare locals to take on more challenging responsibilities. Third, the expectation of management in the organization's work with external stakeholders (such as donors in the case of non-profit organizations) will be important. These newly identified external localization drivers and barriers have an impact on the extent and speed of localization, the HR policies and practices and also on the effectiveness of the organization in developing VRIN human resources via a localization strategy.

Limitations and further research

Our study has a number of limitations. The small number of organizations, the sample size of 18 interviewees as well as the purposive sampling of the interviewees presented a limitation in terms of wider applicability. While key themes of localization were taken from quantitative studies and models in previous research, the lack of qualitative studies on localization made it difficult to build on previous methodology. Therefore, we urge the reader to be careful in respect to applying these results to other countries, especially when these do not experience similar levels of insecurity, corruption or tribal structures.

Further research might include a similar study in other countries with hostile environments to see if aspects of localization are generalizable. In addition, given the changing context of Afghanistan, a longitudinal study looking at localization would provide interesting insights on what impact the security context, as well as the availability of resources, is having on the localization process. Other research – for instance from the perspectives of tourism, government policy, military, police and not-for-profit operations in hostile environments – has explicitly factored in the terrorism danger to human lives. Localization research would be well advised to strengthen its focus on the inherent risks of working in hostile environments. Finally, further exploration on the role of trust and how to build trust in the localization process, both external and internal, would provide additional practical insights.

This research has provided a novel perspective on localization efforts in Afghanistan by drawing on both the RBV and institutional theory. The changing landscape in Afghanistan after the withdrawal of NATO forces continues to be fraught with uncertainty. It is hoped that this research will help to strengthen localization efforts, to build on existing programmes and to build a strong culture of localization in Afghanistan.

Acknowledgements

This manuscript is based on data gathered for the Masters Thesis of Ms Nadia Keshavjee at Cranfield University. We would also like to thank Professor Cliff Bowman for his expert advice in relation to the incorporation of the RBV in this paper.

Disclosure statement

No potential conflict of interest was reported by the authors.

References

Al-Lamki, S. M. (1998). Barriers to Omanization in the private sector: The perceptions of Omani graduates. *The International Journal of Human Resource Management, 9*, 377–400.

Amit, R., & Schoemaker, P. J. H. (1993). Strategic assets and organizational rent. *Strategic Management Journal, 14*, 33–46.

Bader, B., & Berg, N. (2013). An empirical investigation of terrorism-induced stress on expatriate attitudes and performance. *Journal of International Management, 19*, 163–175.

Bader, B., & Berg, N. (2014). The influence of terrorism on expatriate performance: A conceptual approach. *The International Journal of Human Resource Management, 25*, 539–557.

Barney, J. (1986). Strategic factor markets: Expectations, luck and business strategy. *Management Science, 32*, 1231–1241.

Barney, J. (1991). Firm resources and sustained competitive advantage. *Journal of Management, 17*, 99–120.

Barney, J. (1997). *Gaining and sustaining competitive advantage*. Reading, MA: Addison-Wesley.

Bartlett, C. A., & Ghoshal, S. (1999). *Managing across borders: The transnational solution* (Vol. 2). Boston, MA: Harvard Business School Press.

Bhanugopan, R., & Fish, A. (2007). Replacing expatriates with local managers: An exploratory investigation into obstacles to localization in a developing country. *Human Resource Development International, 10*, 365–381.

Bianchi, R. (2006). Tourism and the globalisation of fear: Analysing the politics of risk and (in)security in global travel. *Tourism and Hospitality Research, 7*, 64–74.

Black, J. S., Mendenhall, M., & Oddou, G. (1991). Toward a comprehensive model of international adjustment: An integration of multiple theoretical perspectives. *Academy of Management Review, 16*, 291–317.

Bowman, C., & Toms, S. (2010). Accounting for competitive advantage: The resource-based view of the firm and the labour theory of value. *Critical Perspectives on Accounting, 21*, 183–194.

Brookfield (2015). *Global mobility trends survey*. New York, NY: Brookfield Global Relocation Trends.

Carter, A. (2002). The architecture of government in the face of terrorism. *International Security, 26*, 5–23.

Czinkota, M. R., Knight, G., Liesch, P. W., & Steen, J. (2010). Terrorism and international business: A research agenda. *Journal of International Business Studies, 41*, 826–843.

Dickmann, M. (2003). Implementing German HRM abroad: Desired, feasible, successful? *The International Journal of Human Resource Management, 14*, 265–283.

Dickmann, M. (2012). Why do they come to London? Exploring the motivations of expatriates to work in the British capital. *Journal of Management Development, 31*, 783–800.

Dickmann, M., & Baruch, Y. (2011). *Global careers*. London: Routledge.

Dickmann, M., & Cerdin, J.-L. (2016). Exploring the development and transfer of career capital in an international governmental organization. *The International Journal of Human Resource Management, 27*, 1–31. Published online 5. October 2016.

Dickmann, M., & Müller-Camen, M. (2006). A typology of international human resource management strategies and processes. *The International Journal of Human Resource Management, 17*, 580–601.

Dickmann, M., Müller-Camen, M., & Kelliher, C. (2008). Exploring standardisation and knowledge networking processes in transnational human resource management. *Personnel Review, 38*, 5–25.

Dierickx, I., & Cool, K. (1989). Asset stock accumulation and sustainability of competitive advantage. *Management Science, 35*, 1504–1511.

DiMaggio, P. J., & Powell, W. W. (1983). The iron cage revisited: Institutional isomorphism and collective rationality in organizational fields. *American Sociological Review, 48*, 147–169.

Doherty, N., & Dickmann, M. (2012). Measuring the return on investment in international assignments: An action research approach. *The International Journal of Human Resource Management, 23*, 3434–3454.

Doherty, N., Dickmann, M., & Mills, T. (2011). Exploring the motives of company-backed and self-initiated expatriates. *The International Journal of Human Resource Management, 22*, 595–611.

Dowling, P., Festing, M., & Engle, A. (2008). *International human resource management: Managing people in a multinational context* (5th ed.). London: Thomson.

Edström, A., & Galbraith, J. R. (1977). Transfer of managers as a coordination and control strategy in multinational organizations. *Administrative Science Quarterly, 22*, 248–263.

Edwards, T., Colling, T., & Ferner, A. (2007). Conceptual approaches to the transfer of employment practices in multinational companies: An integrated approach. *Human Resource Management Journal, 17*, 201–217.

Emigh, R. (1997). The power of negative thinking: The use of negative case methodology in the development of sociological theory. *Theory and Society, 26*, 649–684.

Fayol-Song, L. (2011). Reasons behind management localization in MNCs in China. *Asia Pacific Business Review, 17*, 455–471.

Forrier, A., Sels, L., & Stynen, D. (2009). Career mobility at the intersection between agent and structure: A conceptual model. *Journal of Occupational and Organizational Psychology, 82*, 739–759.

Forstenlechner, I. (2010). Workforce localization in emerging Gulf economies: The need to fine-tune HRM. *Personnel Review, 39*, 135–152.

Forstenlechner, I., & Mellahi, K. (2011). Gaining legitimacy through hiring local workforce at a premium: The case of MNEs in the United Arab Emirates. *Journal of World Business, 46*, 455–461.

Fryxell, G. E., Butler, J., & Choi, A. (2004). Successful localization programs in China: An important element in strategy implementation. *Journal of World Business, 39*, 268–282.

Gaur, A. S., Delios, A., & Singh, K. (2007). Institutional environments, staffing strategies, and subsidiary performance. *Journal of Management, 33*, 611–636.

Giustozzi, A. (2008). *Koran, Kalashnikov, and Laptop: The neo-Taliban insurgency in Afghanistan*. New York, NY: Columbia University Press.

Gunz, H. P., & Peiperl, M. (2007). *Handbook of career studies*. London: Sage.

Gurgur, T., & Shah, A. (2005). *Localization and corruption: Panacea or pandora's box?* (Vol. 3486). Washington, DC: World Bank.

Hall, C. M., Timothy, D. J., & Duval, D. T. (2012). *Safety and security in tourism: Relationships, management, and marketing*. London: Routledge.

Harris, H., & Brewster, C. (1999). The coffee-machine system: How international selection really works. *The International Journal of Human Resource Management, 10*, 488–500.

Harzing, A. (1995). *The persistent myth of high expatriate failure rates*. Retrieved November 25, 2013, from http://www.harzing.com/download/failurerates.pdf

Harzing, A., & Christensen, C. (2004). Expatriate failure: Time to abandon the concept? *Career Development International, 9*, 616–626.

Haslberger, A., Brewster, C., & Hippler, T. (2013). The dimensions of expatriate adjustment. *Human Resource Management, 52*, 333–351.

Henisz, W., & Zelner, B. (2005). Legitimacy, interest group pressures, and change in emergent institutions: The case of foreign investors and host country governments. *Academy of Management Review, 30*, 361–382.

Howie, L. (2007). The terrorism threat and managing workplaces. *Disaster Prevention and Management: An International Journal, 16*, 70–78.

Keane, D., & McGeehan, N. (2008). Enforcing migrant workers' rights in the United Arab Emirates. *International Journal on Minority and Group Rights, 15*, 81–115.

Kostova, T., & Roth, K. (2002). Adoption of an organizational practice by subsidiaries of multinational corporations: Institutional and relational effects. *Academy of Management Journal, 45*, 215–233.

Kostova, T., & Zaheer, S. (1999). Organizational legitimacy under conditions of complexity: The case of the multinational enterprise. *Academy of Management Review, 24*, 64–81.

Krueger, A. B., & Laitin, D. D. (2008). Kto kogo?: A cross-country study of the origins and targets of terrorism. In P. Keefer & N. Loayza (Eds.), *Terrorism, economic development, and political openness* (pp. 148–173). Cambridge: Cambridge University Press.

Law, K. S., Song, L. J., Wong, C., & Chen, D. (2009). The antecedents and consequences of successful localization. *Journal of International Business Studies, 40*, 1359–1373.

Law, K. S., Wong, C., & Wang, K. D. (2004). An empirical test of the model on managing the localization of human resources in the People's Republic of China. *The International Journal of Human Resource Management, 15*, 635–648.

Leonard, H., & Dhanani, Q. (2009). *Roshan: Light at the end of the tunnel in Afghanistan* (Report Number N1-310-041). Boston, MA: President and Fellows of Harvard College.

Lockett, A. (2005). Edith Penrose's legacy to the resource-based view. *Managerial and Decision Economics, 26*, 83–98.

Makadok, R. (2001). Toward a synthesis of the resource-based and dynamic-capability views of rent creation. *Strategic Management Journal, 22*, 387–401.

McNulty, Y., & Inkson, K. (2013). *Managing expatriates: A return on investment approach*. New York, NY: Business Expert Press.

Moran, R. T., Abramson, N. R., & Moran, S. V. (2014). *Managing cultural differences*. London: Routledge.

Morosini, P., Shane, S., & Singh, H. (1998). National cultural distance and cross-border acquisition performance. *Journal of International Business Studies, 29*, 137–158.

Müller, M. (1998). Human resource and industrial relations practices of UK and US multinationals in Germany. *The International Journal of Human Resource Management, 9*, 732–749.

Murray, T. (2007). Police-building in Afghanistan: A case study of civil security reform. *International Peacekeeping, 14*, 108–126.

Murtazashvili, J. B. (2016). *Informal order and the state in Afghanistan*. New York, NY: Cambridge University Press.

Nojumi, N., Mazurana, D., & Stites, E. (2010). *Life and security in rural Afghanistan*. Lanham, MD: Rowman & Littlefield.

Nolan, J. (2011). Good guanxi and bad guanxi: Western bankers and the role of network practices in institutional change in China. *The International Journal of Human Resource Management, 22*, 3357–3372.

Norris, P., Kern, M., & Just, M. R. (2003). *Framing terrorism: The news media, the government, and the public*. Hove: Psychology Press.

Oetzel, J., & Getz, K. (2012). Why and how might firms respond strategically to violent conflict? *Journal of International Business Studies, 43*, 166–186.

Oliver, C. (1997). Sustainable competitive advantage: Combining institutional and resource-based views. *Strategic Management Journal, 18*, 697–713.

Penrose, E. T. (1959). *The theory of growth of the firm*. Oxford: Blackwell.

Peteraf, M. A. (1993). The cornerstones of competitive advantage: A resource-based view. *Strategic Management Journal, 14*, 179–191.

Petison, P., & Johri, L. (2008). Localization drivers in an emerging market: Case studies from Thailand. *Management Decision, 46*, 1399–1412.

Piekkari, R., Welch, C., & Paavilainen, E. (2009). The case study as disciplinary convention: Evidence from international business journals. *Organizational Research Methods, 12*, 567–589.

Potter, C. (1989). Effective localization of the workforce: Transferring technology in developing countries. *Journal of European Industrial Training, 13*, 25–30.

Powell, W. W. (1998). Institutional theory. In C. L. Cooper & C. Argyris (Eds.), *Encyclopedia of management* (pp. 301–303). Oxford: Blackwell.

Priem, R. L., & Butler, J. E. (2001). Is the resource-based 'View' a useful perspective for strategic management research? *The Academy of Management Review, 26*, 22–40.

Reade, C., & Lee, H.-J. (2012). Organizational commitment in time of war: Assessing the impact and attenuation of employee sensitivity to ethnopolitical conflict. *Journal of International Management, 18*, 85–101.

Rees, C., Mamman, A., & Bin Braik, A. (2007). Emiratization as a strategic HRM change initiative: Case study evidence from a UAE petroleum company. *The International Journal of Human Resource Management, 18*, 33–53.

RES Forum. (2016). *The RES forum annual report: Beyond Uniformity – A world of opportunity*. Report authored by M. Dickmann, RES Forum, Harmony Relocation Network and Equus Software, 116 pages, London.

Richardson, J., & Mallon, M. (2005). Career interrupted? The case of the self-directed expatriate. *Journal of World Business, 40*, 409–420.

Rubin, B. R., & Rashid, A. (2008). From great game to grand bargain-ending chaos in Afghanistan and Pakistan. *Foreign Affairs, 87*, 30.

Scullion, H., & Collings, D. (Eds.). (2006). *Global staffing*. London: Routledge.

Scullion, H., & Collings, D. (2011). *Global talent management*. London: Routledge.
Seligson, M. A. (2002). The impact of corruption on regime legitimacy: A comparative study of four Latin American countries. *The Journal of Politics, 64*, 408–433.
Selmer, J. (2004a). Expatriates' hesitation and the localization of Western business operations in China. *The International Journal of Human Resource Management, 15*, 1094–1107.
Selmer, J. (2004b). Psychological barriers to adjustment of Western business expatriates in China: Newcomers vs long stayers. *The International Journal of Human Resource Management, 15*, 794–813.
Shenkar, O. (2001). Cultural distance revisited: Towards a more rigorous conceptualization and measurement of cultural differences. *Journal of International Business Studies, 32*, 519–535.
Slangen, A. H. (2006). National cultural distance and initial foreign acquisition performance: The moderating effect of integration. *Journal of World Business, 41*, 161–170.
Sullivan, S. E., & Arthur, M. B. (2006). The evolution of the boundaryless career concept: Examining physical and psychological mobility. *Journal of Vocational Behavior, 69*, 19–29.
Trompenaars, F., & Hampden-Turner, C. (2011). *Riding the waves of culture: Understanding diversity in global business*. London: Nicholas Brealey Publishing.
UNDP. (2013). *Afghanistan national development strategy*. Retrieved December 3, 2013, from http://www.undp.org.af/publications/KeyDocuments/ANDS_Full_Eng.pdf
Wang, C. L. (2007). Guanxi vs. relationship marketing: Exploring underlying differences. *Industrial Marketing Management, 36*, 81–86.
Wernerfelt, B. (1984). The resource-based view of the firm. *Strategic Management Journal, 5*, 171–180.
Williams, J., Bhanugopan, R., & Fish, A. (2011). Localization of human resources in the State of Qatar: Emerging issues and research agenda. *Education, Business and Society: Contemporary Middle Eastern Issues, 4*, 193–206.
Wong, C., & Law, K. S. (1999). Managing localization of human resources in the PRC: A practical model. *Journal of World Business, 34*, 26–40.
Wood, J., & Dupont, B. (Eds.). (2006). *Democracy, society, and the governance of security*. Cambridge: Cambridge University Press.
Wright, P., Dunford, B., & Snell, S. (2001). Human resources and the resource based view of the firm. *Journal of Management, 27*, 701–721.
Wright, P. M., McMahan, G. C., & McWilliams, A. (1994). Human resources and sustained competitive advantage: A resource based perspective. *The International Journal of Human Resource Management, 5*, 301–326.
Yin, R. K. (2003). *Case study research: Design and methods*. London: Sage.

Index

Note: Page numbers in **bold** refer to tables; page numbers in *italics* refer to figures.

For Product Safety Concerns and Information please contact our
EU representative GPSR@taylorandfrancis.com Taylor & Francis
Verlag GmbH, Kaufingerstraße 24, 80331 München, Germany